W9-COT-715

WITHDRAWN

Emerson in His Own Time

MONTGOMERY COLLEGE
ROCKVILLE CAMPUS LIBRARY
ROCKVILLE, MARYLAND

EMERSON

in His Own Time

A BIOGRAPHICAL
CHRONICLE OF HIS LIFE,
DRAWN FROM RECOLLECTIONS,
INTERVIEWS, AND
MEMOIRS BY FAMILY,
FRIENDS, AND
ASSOCIATES

EDITED BY

Ronald A. Bosco

AND Joel Myerson

University
of Iowa Press
Iowa City

NOV 1 0 2004

293268

University of Iowa Press, Iowa City 52242
Copyright © 2003 by the University of Iowa Press
All rights reserved
Printed in the United States of America
Design by Omega Clay
http://www.uiowa.edu/uiowapress

No part of this book may be reproduced or used in any form or by any means without permission in writing from the publisher. All reasonable steps have been taken to contact copyright holders of material used in this book. The publisher would be pleased to make suitable arrangements with any whom it has not been possible to reach.

Letters from Jane Welsh Carlyle to Harriet Baring, from Jane Welsh Carlyle to William Edward Foster, and from Thomas Carlyle to Harriet Baring are from vol. 22, pp. 139–44, of *The Collected Letters of Thomas and Jane Welsh Carlyle*, ed. Clyde de L. Ryals et al., copyright © 1995, Duke University Press. All rights reserved. Reproduced with permission.

[Emerson as Remembered by His Children] is taken from Edith Emerson Webster Gregg, "Emerson and His Children: Their Childhood Memories," *Harvard Library Bulletin* 28 (October 1980), copyright © 1980 by the President and Fellows of Harvard College.

[At Concord with the Emersons in 1842] is taken from Joel Myerson, "Margaret Fuller's 1842 Journal: At Concord with the Emersons," *Harvard Library Bulletin* 21 (July 1973), copyright © 1973 by the President and Fellows of Harvard College.

Quote from James Russell Lowell's 18 July 1867 letter to C. E. Norton is used by permission of the Houghton Library, Harvard University.

Herman Melville's letter to Evert A. Duyckinck is from *The Northwestern-Newberry Edition of the Writings of Herman Melville*, ed. Lynn Horth, copyright © 1993 by Northwestern University Press.

Unless otherwise noted, all illustrations are from the Joel Myerson Collection of Nineteenth-Century American Literature, University of South Carolina, and are reproduced here with permission.

The publication of this book was generously supported by the University of Iowa Foundation.

Printed on acid-free paper

Library of Congress Cataloging-in-Publication Data

Emerson in his own time: a biographical chronicle of his life, drawn from recollections, interviews, and memoirs by family, friends, and associates / edited by Ronald A. Bosco and Joel Myerson.
    p. cm.
Includes bibliographical references and index.
   ISBN 0-87745-841-3 (cloth), ISBN 0-87745-842-1 (pbk)
   1. Emerson, Ralph Waldo, 1803–1882. 2. Authors, American—19th century—Biography. 3. Transcendentalists (New England)—Biography. I. Bosco, Ronald A. II. Myerson, Joel.
PS1631 .E54 2003
814'.3—dc21
[B]   2002035379

03 04 05 06 07 C 5 4 3 2 1
03 04 05 06 07 P 5 4 3 2 1

Contents

Contents

Introduction

RALPH WALDO EMERSON enjoys an enduring reputation as a principal architect of American intellectual culture and as one of the most significant figures in all of American literary history. That reputation was made during his life, and it has solidified to the point of defying almost all challenges over the one hundred and twenty years since his death. For instance, writing in 1903 during the centenary celebration of Emerson's birth, Thomas Wentworth Higginson tells the story of a recent election for membership in an "American Hall of Fame" that was to be established in New York. One hundred men and women drawn from the ranks of national and state chief justices, college presidents, historians and scientists, magazine and newspaper editors, and authors were polled on fifty candidates proposed for the honor, and a majority of votes was required for election. In the end, twenty-nine persons were elected to the American Hall of Fame, the first seven of whom were presidents, statesmen, and jurists, and the eighth, Emerson.[1] When a similar poll was taken in New York City in 1928 to identify the "Ten Greatest Americans," and the rules were changed so that no one born before 1789 could be considered for the honor, Emerson fared even better. Abraham Lincoln came in first and, in an ironic twist, Emerson just barely edged out Henry David Thoreau for second place; William Lloyd Garrison, Theodore Parker, Walt Whitman, and Mark Twain, among others, followed. Emerson was praised as "our one clearest, purest and most exalted American mind. Not our greatest, but surely our serenest thinker. The friend pre-eminently of those who would live in the spirit."[2]

Such rankings close to his own time anticipate many of those we see today in which Emerson always places at or very close to the top of lists of America's most original native-born intellectuals and writers. His centrality to all accounts of American cultural history has been supported by the publication of a substantial body of his personal writings in recent decades, the scope of which surpasses that of the personal writings of any other American author. Comprehensive modern editions of Emerson's correspondence, journals, and notebooks, as well as of his sermons and lectures, are now available to amplify the range of reference in both biographical and critical studies of his life and thought.[3] The personal writings of those closest to him—his first wife, Ellen Louisa Tucker; his second wife, Lidian; his daughter Ellen; and his aunt Mary Moody Emerson—are now also available, and along with Emerson's personal writings form an extraordinary archaeology of his domestic sphere.[4] Complementing these Emerson family materials are authoritative editions of the personal and other writings of individuals with whom Emerson enjoyed the most long-lasting and, from the point of view of his intellectual and aesthetic development, influential relationships: Bronson Alcott, Louisa May Alcott, Thomas Carlyle, the poet William Ellery Channing, Margaret Fuller, Nathaniel Hawthorne, Elizabeth Hoar, Elizabeth Palmer Peabody, Henry David Thoreau, and Walt Whitman, to name just a few. Finally, recent primary and secondary bibliographies relating to Emerson's writings and writings about him and a chronology of his life provide reliable starting points for inquiry into his career and personal as well as professional relationships.[5]

But long before these remarkable resources became available for the study of Emerson, his friends and associates, reviewers of his lectures and publications, literary historians, social critics, and reporters of nineteenth-century American life writing for readers at home and abroad all had reason to comment on his life and, both before and after his death, speculate on his ultimate place in the pantheon of America's great writers and thinkers. In the accounts that follow, Emerson's contemporaries describe the essentials of his character, use personal observation to chart the development of his ideas and reputation, and detail significant transitions in his personal life across all the major phases of his career. William Henry Furness, Amos Bronson Alcott, Margaret Fuller, Frederic Henry Hedge, Edwin Percy Whipple, and Frank Bellew provide rare insights into Emerson's personality and his evolving friendships; Elizabeth Palmer Peabody and A. B. Muzzey into his life first in the pulpit and then on the lyceum circuit; Fredrika Bremer and Francis Espinasse into his emergence in the late 1840s and throughout the 1850s as an American with an international reputation; Julia Ward Howe, Ednah Dow Cheney, and Caroline Hazard into his commitment to social reforms of the 1850s and 1860s; Herman Melville, James Russell Lowell, and Franklin Benjamin Sanborn into multiple aspects of his career as a lecturer; Louisa

May Alcott, William James, Julian Hawthorne, and Kate Douglas Wiggin into his support of the ambitions and careers of the new generation of writers and thinkers that looked to him for inspiration; and Walt Whitman, Oliver Wendell Holmes, and Annie Adams Fields into his elevation as an important biographical subject. While Convers Francis, Octavius Brooks Frothingham, and others define Emerson's essential contributions to philosophic Transcendentalism as it was practiced in America, John Muir and W. J. Stillman provide otherwise undocumented glimpses of the philosopher of nature actually out in nature. And, finally, Edward Waldo Emerson, Edith Emerson Forbes, and Ellen Emerson candidly express their joy and occasional frustration at being children of a very famous father.

Collectively, then, the reminiscences, memoirs, interviews, and other writings printed in this volume portray both the public and the private Emerson, and as they do so, they create an image of a highly complex figure whose personal and intellectual reach was extraordinary for its time and place. At the same time, in a departure from the tendency of most biographers to either ignore or gloss over the last ten to fifteen years of his life, several pieces that appear here for the first time in over a century give first-hand evidence of Emerson's descent into old age and indicate how he was shown the greatest deference and respect by his contemporaries at that time.

Among the aspects of Emerson's biography and reputation that dominate the texts in this volume, one deserves particular notice. Virtually all the accounts confirm that, while among his friends and close acquaintances Emerson was most prized for his ability as a conversationalist who listened more often than he talked, for most of his contemporaries, the lecture platform served as their first introduction to the man and his thought, and they associated Emerson more with his service on the lyceum circuit for the greater part of his career between the mid-1830s and the 1870s than they appear to do with his writings or even with his involvement in momentous reforms of the era, such as abolitionism or the women's rights movement. In one respect this makes perfect sense: from the time Emerson returned to America in 1833 from his first European journey after the death of his first wife, Ellen Tucker Emerson, in 1831 and his resignation from Boston's Second Church in 1832, the lectern served as his new pulpit. Writing after Emerson's death in "Emerson as Preacher,"[6] lifelong friend Elizabeth Palmer Peabody confirms that he was always pre-eminently the preacher to his own generation and future ones, but as much—if not more—out of the pulpit as in it; faithful unto the end to his early chosen profession and the vows of his youth. Whether he spoke in the pulpit or lyceum chair, or to friends in his hospitable parlor, or *tête-à-tête* in his study, or in his favorite walks in the woods with chosen companions, or at the festive gatherings of scholars, or in the conventions of philanthropists, or in the popular assemblies of patriots in times and on occasions that try men's souls,—always and everywhere it was his conscious purpose to utter a "Thus saith the Lord."

An extension of his practice of keeping voluminous journals and notebooks, the lecture room served as the site where Emerson first tested his ideas aloud and, over the course of successive revisions, conveyed them to audiences in prose that was itself evolving into final form for publication. Journalists invariably found Emerson's ideas and his performance as a lecturer popular subjects for comment, and rarely were they subtle in expressing their opinions of them. For instance, when Walt Whitman attended Emerson's lecture on "The Poet" before the Society Library of New York on 5 March 1842, he used the occasion to poke fun at some of the types who were gathered in Emerson's audience and to lampoon Horace Greeley— Transcendentalist supporter and editor of the rival *New York Tribune*—in a report he wrote for the *New York Aurora*, but for Emerson, Whitman had only words of unqualified praise:

> The Transcendentalist had a very full house on Saturday evening. There were a few beautiful maids—but more ugly women, mostly blue stockings; several interesting young men with Byron collars, doctors, and parsons; Grahamites and abolitionists; sage editors, a few of whom were taking notes; and all the other species of literati. Greeley was in ecstasies whenever any thing particularly good was said, which seemed to be once in about five minutes—he would flounce about like a fish out of water, or a tickled girl—look around, to see those behind him and at his side; all of which very plainly told to those both far and near, that he knew a thing or two more about these matters than other men.
>
> This lecture was on the "Poetry of the Times." He said the first man who called another an ass was a poet. Because the business of the poet is expression— the giving utterance to the emotions and sentiments of the soul; and metaphors. But it would do the lecturer great injustice to attempt anything like a sketch of his ideas. Suffice it to say, the lecture was one of the richest and most beautiful compositions, both for its matter and style, we have ever heard anywhere, at any time.[7]

In contrast to Whitman's high regard for the "matter" of Emerson's lecture and the style of his delivery, other journalists found Emerson's ideas and performance on the speaker's platform subjects fit for criticism and even ridicule. In "Ralph Waldo Emerson,"† an unnamed reporter writing in 1865 for the New York periodical the *Knickerbocker* dubbed him "roaring Ralph" and mercilessly satirized his ideas, his language, and his overall style of delivery. According to this reporter, Emerson, "our flighty friend," "speaks vigorously, yet says nothing" through "metaphorical beauties" that are "bewildering, astounding and incomprehensible"; the reporter adds that just as "no thought can fathom his intentions," for "his finished sentences" are "bottomless," so too Emerson's "show business," "high-heeled, knock-kneed logic, [and] *au fait* dexterity in concocting flap-doodle mixtures" called lectures deliver unwary listeners into the lecturer's own strange realm of "gin and bitters, or opium discourses on—delirium tremens." Though harsh, such occasional criticism may well have been deserved, yet as Nathaniel Parker Willis recognized early on, reporters always had to be very careful about criticizing Emerson. In his "Second Look at Emerson," a review of Emerson's lecture on "The Spirit of the Times" before the Mercantile Library Association of New York City on 29 January 1850, Willis characterized Emerson as "our Prophet of the Intuitive" and praised his authority over his audience and topics. Emerson's audience, he wrote, comes "selectively out, like steel filings out of a handfull of sand to a magnet," and knows that he "has climbed above the atmosphere of this world and kicked away the ladder—holding no deferential communication . . . with any of the intermediate ladder-rounds. . . . If he descends at all, it is quite to the ground, otherwise he is out of reach—up with the Saviour or down with Lazarus and his sores." Alluding to Henry Wotton's classic dismissal of critics, Willis states, "That 'critics . . . are brushers of noblemen's clothes,' one feels very sensibly and reprovingly, in turning a pen to write any comment on Emerson. He says so many wonderful, and wonderfully true and good things, in one of his Delphic lectures, that, to find any fault with him, seems like measuring thunder by its echo down a back alley."8

There is a remarkable consistency among recorded responses to Emerson at the lectern. In England as in America, Emerson's style of delivery was invariably taken as a measure of his character as well as an extension of his literary and philosophical method. This is admirably shown in two detailed descriptions of Emerson lecturing at midcareer. The first account is by Alexander Ireland, who arranged the lecture tour in England and Scotland in 1847 and 1848 which made Emerson the best known American intellectual in the British Isles, and the second is by Rutherford B. Hayes—president of the United States—who as a young Ohio attorney attended a series of eight lectures that Emerson gave at the Universalist Church in Cincinnati in 1850. Ireland writes:

> The first impression one had in listening to [Emerson] in public was that his manner was so singularly quiet and unimpassioned that you began to fear the beauty and force of his thoughts were about to be marred by what might almost be described as monotony of expression. But very soon was this apprehension dispelled. The mingled dignity, sweetness, and strength of his features, the earnestness of his manner and voice, and the evident depth and sincerity of his convictions gradually extorted your deepest attention, and made you feel that you were within the grip of no ordinary man, but of one "sprung of earth's first blood," with "titles manifold"; and as he went on with serene self-possession and an air of conscious power, reading sentence after sentence, charged with well-weighed meaning, and set in words of faultless aptitude, you could no longer withstand his "so potent spell," but were forthwith compelled to surrender yourself to the fascination of his eloquence. He used little or no action, save occasionally a slight vibration of the body, as though rocking beneath the hand of some unseen power. The precious words dropped from his mouth in quick succession, and noiselessly sank into the hearts of his hearers, there to abide forever, and, like the famed carbuncle in Eastern cave, shed a mild radiance on all things therein. Perhaps no orator ever succeeded with so little exertion in éntrancing his audience, stealing away each faculty, and leading the listeners captive at his will. He abjured all force and excitement—dispensing his regal sentences in all mildness, goodness, and truth; but stealthily and surely he grew upon you, from the smallest proportions, as it were; steadily increasing, until he became a Titan, a commanding power—
>
> > To whom, as to the mountains and the stars,
> > The soul seems passive and submissive.
>
> The moment he finished, he took up his MS. and quietly glided away,—disappearing before his audience could give vent to their applause.[9]

Ireland's extended characterization of Emerson "stealthily and surely" growing upon him "until he became a Titan" accords precisely with Hayes's later characterization of how Emerson wore away at his "preconceived notions of him." Just as Ireland eventually finds the "mingled dignity, sweetness, and strength of [Emerson's] features," "the earnestness of his manner and voice," "the evident depth and sincerity of his convictions," and his "serene self-possession" and "air of conscious power" so remarkable and praiseworthy, Hayes comes to feel that the person who stands before him, "modest but self-possessed, of a good-humored, honest strain," naturally "gives one a favorable impression of his heart and character." As Hayes states in a letter to his sister Fanny Platt on 12 June 1850, speaking from the lectern, Emerson appears to have thoroughly externalized in his style of delivery not only his finer qualities of character, but also the subtleties of his intellectual method in lectures that are "a bead-string of suggestions, fancies, ideas, anecdotes, and illustrations . . . delivered in a subdued, earnest tone which is in perfect keeping with [his] . . . thought."

> . . . I have gossiped so much about [Emerson] lately that I am almost ashamed to open my lips about him. His qualifications and peculiarities as a lecturer or essayist on miscellaneous subjects stand quite differently in my estimation from his opinions—not opinions either, but impressions or "inspirations.". . . [He] is a charming, but not in an equal degree, an instructive lecturer. He strikes me, contrary to my preconceived notions of him, as a close, keen observer rather than a profound thinker. There is no logic or method in his essays or lectures. A syllogism he despises. The force of a connected chain of reasoning, his mind seems incapable of appreciating. There is no such thing as one of his thoughts following from another. The natural result of this lack of logic is that one finds it next to impossible to grasp and hold fast what he says. When you leave the lecture-room you remember that he said many witty, sensible, pretty, and some deep things, but you feel at a loss where to begin in attempting to recall them. The whole lecture seems but a bead-string of suggestions, fancies, ideas, anecdotes, and illustrations, having no connection with each other except that they are upon the same subject. They are all either quaint, paradoxical, sensible, humorous, or have some other element which gives them interest if not positive value. They are expressed in a terse, singular style—Saxon but not at all Carlylish, and delivered in a subdued, earnest tone which is in perfect keeping with the style and thought.
>
> Mr. Emerson is middle-aged, modest but self-possessed, of a good-humored, honest strain, which gives one a favorable impression of his heart and character. . . . I never knew one who could hold more undivided attention of his audience.
>
> The matter of his lectures—the substance of them—is contained in a few leading ideas which pervade all his productions. The filling up—the seasoning—is, of course, new and different in different lectures, and his lectures are remarkable for being stuffed with thoughts; but still the great stratum which underlies and sup-

ports all he writes and says consists of a very few notions which are repeated and reappear over and over again.[10]

The statements by Ireland and Hayes echo those of many writers who, like William Cullen Bryant, William Michael Rossetti, and Herman Melville, admit their pleasant surprise at finally seeing Emerson perform in person. After attending the same delivery of "The Poet" before the Society Library of New York that Whitman reviewed in March 1842, Bryant, who was then a reporter for the *New York Evening Post*, wrote:

> One thing has particularly struck us, in listening to [Emerson's] addresses, . . . and that is, they are perpetually growing upon your admiration. A great many passages, which at first, owing to peculiarities of phraseology and style, are obscure and aimless, after a while, become pregnant with important meanings. He convinces you that he is a man accustomed to profound and original thought, and not disposed, as you are at the outset inclined to suspect, to play with and baffle the intellects of his readers. He is eminently sincere and direct, strongly convinced of his own views, and anxious to present them in an earnest and striking manner. His style discovers a quick perception of analogies and the power of graceful as well as forcible expression.[11]

And even though Emerson's public performances sometimes provoked contradictory responses among individuals who otherwise tended to see things the same way, Emerson's defenders never gave ground to the opposite view. Writing to Moncure D. Conway on 9 June 1882 shortly after Emerson's death, Rossetti recalled the responses he and his friend Stauros Dilberoglue had to seeing Emerson deliver his lecture on "Napoleon" during his tour in England in 1847–1848. Rossetti remembered "Emerson's upright figure, clear-cut physiognomy," "clear elocution (Americans generally strike English people as clear and *chiselled* in this respect)," and "resolved self-possession" that generated warmth and general approval from the audience as he lectured. By contrast, when they discussed the same event years later, Dilberoglue, after critiquing Emerson's "impersonal demeanour," "impassivity," and "total want of sympathetic vital relation towards his audience," told Rossetti that he went out of the lecture-room "chilled to the bone." Dismissing his friend's assessment out of hand, Rossetti reported to Conway, "No such impression was produced on myself."[12] Similarly, when Melville attended his first Emerson lecture—on "Natural Aristocracy" in 1849—he wrote to Evert A. Duyckinck† to say that he "was very agreeably disappointed in Mr Emerson. I had heard of him as full of transcendental-isms, myths & oracular gibberish; . . . that was all I knew of him, till I heard him lecture.— To my surprise, I found him quite intelligible. . . . [There] is a something about every man elevated above mediocrity, which is . . . instinc-tively perceptible. This I see in Mr Emerson. And, frankly, for the sake of the argument, let us call him a fool;—then had I rather be a fool than a wise man.—"

Complementing their detailed descriptions of Emerson's performance as a lecturer, writers of many of the accounts that follow betray an almost uni-form preoccupation with his physical appearance both at the lectern and away from it. Not only is their preoccupation with his physical appearance uniform, but their descriptions of it, and of how it too reveals something of his character, are relatively uniform as well. Most notice Emerson's "New England figure," his prominent nose, and especially his eyes. For readers whose sense of Emerson's appearance was of the vague, second-hand vari-ety garnered from newspaper reports and illustrations, George Willis Cooke's candid description of it in *Ralph Waldo Emerson* brought Emerson to life:

> Emerson has a pronounced and an emphatic face, not at all remarkable at the first glance, but striking for its reserved power of expression. His head is high and well-formed, his nose very large, his chin strong. . . . He is of slender figure, more than medium height, head small, shoulders remarkably sloping. . . . In manner he is reticent, in general conversation he is not brilliant, and in ordinary intercourse with men he does not appear as a genius. Yet there is a reserved personality, that is commanding, powerful, and charming. It is a personality that carries immense force, that molds and sways others, less by a dazzling brilliancy and the tremen-dousness of intellect, than by the persuasive might of a pure, unadulterated, and perfectly loyal nature, which never swerves, which goes steadily on to the goal it seeks.[13]

Like Cooke, in *The Last Leaf* James Kendall Hosmer also portrayed for readers Emerson's "sloping rather narrow shoulders," his "slender frame erect and sinewy but [not] robust," and his "keen, firm face." Writing in 1912, Hosmer remembered that Emerson's "nose was markedly expressive, sharp, and well to the fore," that his lips showed "geniality as well as firm-ness," that his "smooth hair concealed a head and brow not large but well rounded," and that though slight, he projected a "vigorous" and "erect figure." But it was his eyes that Hosmer felt best revealed Emerson and his character: "In his glance," he wrote, "was complete kindliness and also profound penetration."[14]

Hosmer's assessment of Emerson's "glance" succinctly represents the thoughts of others who also remark on it. As early as the 1850s, writers had begun to take notice of Emerson's eyes and comment on how they bore an intimate relation to some other feature of his person or disclosed the secret of his character. Writing primarily for European readers, Fredrika Bremer stated in *The Homes of the New World*† that Emerson's "eyes cast a light upon" upon his "beautiful smile," while in *Transatlantic Tracings*, John Ross Dix found those same eyes "dreamy in their expression" and the perfect complement to Emerson's face, which was of "a thoughtful cast," and in *Emerson: His Life and Writings*, "January Searle" (George Searle Phillips) remarked that he thought Emerson's "eyes flashed as with the Delphic fire" at times, but at other times they seemed to possess a "singular expression . . . like the gleaming of the mystic spirit" of a "strong souled man."[15] As he reports in *Talks with Ralph Waldo Emerson*,† years after their first meeting at Williams College in the 1860s Charles J. Woodbury still recalled that Emerson's eyes were "divining rods" that complemented his voice, which carried his "soul" in it; similarly, in *My Own Story with Recollections of Noted Persons*, John Townsend Trowbridge detected in Emerson's "fine" eyes "a peculiar peering, penetrating expression" that drew attention to his "pure baritone voice" from which emanated "tones [that] cannot be taught," for, Trowbridge said, quoting another master speaker, " 'it is the soul that creates that voice.' "[16] By contrast, in his "Personal Glimpses of Emerson,"† Julian Hawthorne associated Emerson's eyes with an unexpected degree of earthly tenacity when he likened his presence on the speaker's platform to an eagle holding fast to its perch—"with the same piercing look from the eyes." In Emerson's eyes several observers found an expression of warm welcome which put them at ease and others an expression of fond farewell which they never forgot. For instance, writing for the *Ladies' Home Journal* more than twenty years after the fact, Edward Bok remembered exactly how he felt when, at the conclusion of a visit to Emerson only a few months before his death, he was rewarded with a warm handshake and a glance from Emerson's eyes, which "twinkled and smiled back at me."[17] Finally, Emerson's eyes could pose a question and, as Elizabeth Oakes Smith learned, they could also express his silent dismissal of a question or view that he did not wish to address. In her "Recollections of Emerson, His Household and Friends,"† she reports that as a way of drawing Emerson into conversation she once commented, "Perhaps in the great evolution of thought, old dogmas of vicarious suffering, and the remission of sin by the shedding of blood, may resolve themselves into this transmission of blood by heredity which is to be the ultimate Redeemer." Emerson, Oakes Smith says, gave her "a silent reply with his calm, mystic eyes—nothing more."

A master at assessing how an individual's physical presence could manifest interior qualities such as the individual's character, Daniel Chester French remarked in "A Sculptor's Reminiscences of Emerson"† that his "presence was a benediction." Trying to account for Emerson's "presence," which he termed an "indefinable atmosphere," French attributed it variously to "the soul that shone out upon you from his face," "the deep, full, beautiful voice with its matchless enunciation and perfect diction," "the clear, piercing eyes," and the perfect "courtesy towards man or child, high or lowly, which was unfailing." For persons such as Hayes, Bryant, and Melville, whose first sighting of Emerson in person occurred as he performed on the speaker's platform, and of course for French himself, there was a continual struggle to define his "presence" which, as French conceded, was indefinable. Emerson's presence, or his "aura" as it has been sometimes described, lessened the initial shock these persons experienced at the absence of logic, order, and philosophical method or system in his lectures, and it somehow transformed what they heard Emerson say into poetry. For Annie Adams Fields, who admits at the opening of her "Glimpses of Emerson"† that he was her model for the "perfect consistency of a truly great life, where inconsistencies . . . appear at once harmonized by the beauty of the whole," Emerson stands among those rare individuals who "warm and cheer us with something of their own beloved and human presences." After hearing Emerson deliver an academic lecture on the laws of the mind in his Natural History of the Intellect course at Harvard in 1870 during which he completely lost control of his subject, Fields, who attended the lecture with Henry Wadsworth Longfellow, wrote the following description of the setting and her reaction to Emerson's plight:

> There are laws of the mind, there are powers and analogies which we shall consider. First among them stands . . . Identity, then follow Metamorphosis, Flux

---

Here the papers became inextricably tangled and we were left in a kind of mist. I walked away with Mr. Longfellow, who could not resist a kindly smile of sympathy with me over something in this lecture which reminded us of "little wanton boys who swim on bladders." But no one could fail to be stimulated by [Emerson's] suggestion which was various and endless. It was indeed poetic seed-grain.[18]

Writing about the same scene almost half a century later, Francis Greenwood Peabody lightly transformed Emerson's mishap into an illustration of the very concepts he was attempting to explain. Commenting also that he thought the "academic harness seemed to gall [Emerson's] Pegassus," Peabody said, "[It] was not lectures to which we were listening, but poetry; not the teaching of the class-room, but the music of the spheres."[19]

Throughout Emerson's career, an aura seemed to gather about him wherever and whenever he spoke. His very presence encouraged individuals from all walks to forgive whatever lapses they may have encountered in his performance and transform them into one or another aspect of his genius. Recalling their personal experiences with Emerson as a teacher or a lecturer, John Holmes, Richard Henry Dana, and Daniel Ricketson suggest that at a fundamental level his character and powerful presence and his auditors' responses to them were apparent as early as the 1820s and 1830s. Both Holmes and Dana were Emerson's students in the 1820s. Holmes recalls Emerson as "a king in his dominion," but also "rather like a captive philosopher set to tending his flocks; resigned to his destiny, but not amused with its incongruities"; he adds that although Emerson was always calm, he was "[not] inclined to win boys by surface amiability, but [through] kindly . . . explanation or advice."[20] Dana, who in the 1840s revisited his experience of Emerson as a teacher in light of the famous "writer and lecturer upon what is called the transcendental philosophy" that he had become, remembers him as a "very pleasant instructor . . . although he had not system or discipline enough to insure regular and vigorous study"; he adds that he always considered it fortunate that he and his classmates "fell into the hands of more systematic and strict teachers, though not so popular with us, nor perhaps so elevated in their habits of thought as Mr. E."[21] Ricketson, on the other hand, first knew Emerson from his service in the pulpit and early forays onto the lecture platform in the 1830s; however, like Holmes and Dana, Ricketson, who wrote about his experience after Emerson's death, states that the Emerson he first saw was the completely formed person he knew for the next forty years: "His personal appearance was that of a delicate, scholarly youth, tall and slight, with sloping shoulders, a marked feature in his physique. His manner of address was as ever after, calm and dignified, meditative, as though he were improvising rather than reading or delivering matter previously prepared."[22]

Even though they clearly appreciated his character and influence, John Holmes, Dana, and Ricketson are nevertheless rather sedate in their depictions of Emerson's impact on them. In this respect, they anticipate the reserve of individuals such as Oliver Wendell Holmes, A. B. Muzzey, or Charles J. Woodbury, whose personal recollections of Emerson follow. By contrast, in some of the other selections that follow one will find individuals deploying a relatively uniform set of hyperbolic expressions to represent Emerson's powerful impact on them. In one of the more extreme examples of this, an unnamed reporter for the *Boston Post* † finally ran out of elaborate descriptors as he attempted to re-create for readers the aura that appeared around Emerson as he discoursed in anything but the then-traditional style of lecturing:

> [It] is quite out of character to say Mr. Emerson lectures—he does no such thing. He drops nectar—he chips out sparks—he exhales odors—he lets off mental skyrockets and fireworks—he spouts fire, and conjurer like, draws ribbons out of his mouth. He smokes, he sparkles, he improvises, he shouts, he sings, he explodes like a bundle of crackers, he goes off in fiery eruptions like a volcano, but he does not *lecture*.
>
> . . . He comes and goes like a spirit of whom one just hears the rustle of his wings. He is a vitalized speculation—a talking essence—a sort of celestial emanation—a bit of transparency broken from the spheres—a spiritual prism through which we see all beautiful rays of immaterial existences. His leaping fancy mounts upward like an India rubber ball, and drifts and falls like a snowflake or a feather. He moves in the regions of similitudes. He comes through the air like a cherubim with a golden trumpet in his mouth, out of which he blows tropes and figures and gossamer transparencies of suggestive fancies. He takes high flights, and sustains himself without ruffling a feather. He inverts the rainbow and uses it for a swing—now sweeping the earth, and now clapping his hands among the stars.

The account in the *Boston Post*, which anticipates the satirical review of Emerson's performance as a lecturer quoted above from the *Knickerbocker*,† is hardly unique, and in fact, together they demonstrate that a fine line often separated one writer's exuberant praise of Emerson's presence and performance from another writer's damning ridicule of them. As in the case of these two newspaper reports, sometimes one has to consider the overall tone of a writer's assessment of Emerson in order to determine whether he was being treated with praise or with censure; at other times, a writer's attitude toward Emerson is disclosed by something as subtle as that writer's use of a phrase or two or even a single word. For instance, after hearing Emerson's opening lecture in his *Mind and Manners of the Nineteenth Century* series in London in June 1848, Henry Crabb Robinson favorably described its effect on him as "one of those *rhapsodical* exercises of mind . . . which leave a dreamy sense of pleasure, not easy to analyze, or render an account of."[23] Writing in 1849, Abby Alcott, the wife of Emerson's lifelong friend Bronson Alcott, reported that she found Emerson's pithy though disconnected sentences, lofty sentiments, and presence more than satisfactory compensation for any inadequacies that she or anyone else occasionally detected in his delivery: "He is abrupt—disjointed[,] fragmentary[,] but you are arrested by a truth which like a cut diamond sparkles and radiates—you forget the rubbishy stuff which covered it in its normal state—the transition from Scenes of Misery to the Banquet of Beauty was too much—my brain reeled with it."[24] And George William Curtis, who while writing from the "Editor's Easy Chair"† served as an arbiter of aesthetic taste in nineteenth-century America, remarked after hearing Emerson speak on "Table-Talk" late in his career that "[it] was not a sermon, nor an oration, nor an argument; it was the perfection of talk; the talk of a poet, of a philosopher, of a scholar"; indeed, for Curtis, Emerson's capacity for delivering lectures that contained "maxims as full of glittering truth as a winter night sky of stars" and "an incessant spray of fine fancies like the November shower of meteors" never diminished, even with his advancing age.

Whether they were engaged primarily in constructing Emerson's biography, or in reviewing his lectures or writings, or in attempting to interpret his ideas for readers who were more often than not mystified by what he had to say or write, writers invariably used anecdotes to tell their story. This is, of course, a very Emersonian gesture, since Emerson himself repeatedly developed anecdotes as a means of organizing and conveying his thoughts. The interplay evident in many texts printed in this volume between a writer's assessment of Emerson's character or interpretation of his thoughts and anecdotes developed for the purpose of illustrating one or the other is true to

Emerson's own method. Emerson was not a systematic thinker, as most of his contemporaries, his literary executor and first editor, James Elliot Cabot, and his son and editor, Edward Waldo Emerson, frequently remarked. He was rather, as he characterized himself late in life, primarily a historian of culture and ideas and an analogical thinker. Describing his philosophical method in a lecture on the intellect that Cabot eventually mined for the essay "Powers and Laws of Thought," Emerson stated:

> I write anecdotes of the intellect; a sort of *Farmer's Almanac* of mental moods. I confine my ambition to true reporting of its play in natural action, though I should get only one new fact a year.
>
> I cannot myself use that systematic form which is reckoned essential in treating the science of the mind. But if one can say so without arrogance, I might suggest that he who contents himself with dotting a fragmentary curve, recording only what facts he has observed, without attempting to arrange them in one outline, follows a system also,—a system as grand as any other, though he does not inter-fere with its vast curves by prematurely forcing them into a circle or ellipse, but only draws that arc which he clearly sees, or perhaps at a later observation a re-mote curve of the same orbit, and waits for a new opportunity. . . .
>
> I confess to a little distrust of that completeness of system which metaphy-sicians are apt to affect.[25]

In her compilation of John Greenleaf Whittier's reminiscences, Mary B. Clafin records several conversations between Emerson and Whittier during their visits together that advantageously portray both figures. Clafin's report is instructive, for it demonstrates one of the ways in which writers regularly used anecdotes to humanize Emerson and, almost as often, to humanize the person featured with him in the anecdote. In the following report, Clafin first shows Emerson's capacity for humorous understatement and then shows Whittier catching Emerson short in what sounds like one of his rou-tine invocations of the ideal.

> Mr. Whittier had great pleasure in conversing with Mr. Emerson. . . . In driving, one day, Mr. Emerson pointed out a small, unpainted house by the roadside, and said, "There lives an old Calvinist in that house, and she says she prays for me every day. I am glad she does. I pray for myself."
>
> "Does thee?" said Mr. Whittier. "What does thee pray for, friend Emerson?"
>
> "Well," replied Mr. Emerson, "when I first open my eyes upon the morning meadows, and look out upon the beautiful world, I thank God that I am alive, and that I live so near Boston."

In one of their conversations, Mr. Emerson remarked that the world had not yet seen the highest development of manhood.

"Does thee think so?" said Mr. Whittier. "I suppose thee would admit that Jesus Christ is the highest development our world has seen?"

"Yes, yes; but not the highest it will see."

"Does thee think the world has yet reached the ideals the Christ has set for mankind?"

"No, no," said Mr. Emerson; "I think not."

"Then is it not the part of wisdom to be content with what has been given us, till we have lived up to that ideal? And when we need something higher, Infinite Wisdom will supply our needs."[26]

In addition to their being used to humanize Emerson, throughout his career and in the long history of reminiscences and recollections of him published after his death, anecdotes served to expose a subtle interplay among various aspects of Emerson's personality, reputation, and personal relationships. The typical form of this interplay is shown in this brief but comprehensive tale by Ernest Wadsworth Longfellow that describes Emerson's relationship with Longfellow's father, his manner and quick wit while lecturing, and his curious interactions with Bronson Alcott:

Ralph Waldo Emerson came seldom to my father's house, but I saw him occasionally at the Saturday Club, where my father sometimes took me, and also at lectures given by Mr. Emerson in Boston, where he invariably got his manuscript mixed and would fill in the space with his beaming smile, as if to take his audience into his confidence, and say, "You see how it is with philosophers, they can't be expected to do things like other people." That wonderful, benignant smile is the chief thing I remember about him. There is a story told about him and Alcott. . . . It seems that Alcott used to visit Emerson in the mornings and Emerson would get off some of his Orphic sayings, and in the afternoon Emerson would visit Alcott, when the latter would repeat some of the things Emerson had said in the morning. Emerson, quite forgetting that he had said them, would say, "What a remarkable mind Alcott has!"[27]

Not all the anecdotes reported in the memoirs, interviews, or reminiscences included in this volume are as elaborately developed as those by Clafin and Longfellow. Yet like them, almost all writers eventually turn to a telling anecdote or two as a way to define Emerson's otherwise elusive personality, to demonstrate that he was capable of great sympathy and emotion, to show that he possessed a sense of humor, or to establish his capacity for

meaningful interpersonal relationships. For example, although his friend Ellery Channing once accused Emerson of having "no heart,"[28] Louisa May
Alcott, in her "Reminiscences of Ralph Waldo Emerson,"† goes back to the
time she was eight years old and remembers how, as Emerson reported to
her the death of his little son Waldo, all she saw was his heart. In his account
of their first meeting,† Edwin Percy Whipple goes to great length to describe
Emerson's cordiality, generosity with his time, and willingness to engage
him in conversation as his equal. Some of the most unexpected but hu-
manizing anecdotes come from those who knew Emerson best: his children
Ellen, Edith, and Edward. Ellen, for instance, remembers one of the great
pleasures of her childhood was walking to a nearby brook with her father
and watching him throw in stones so that she could enjoy the splash, and
another was sauntering through Concord's meadows and woods, learning
the names of plants and trees and experiencing their scent for the first time,
under her father's patient instruction. Ellen also recalls that one of the ways
her father kept strict control over his composure while on the speaker's platform was to recite humorous stories and anecdotes over and over again at
home so that he would be past laughing when he told them again in public.
Edith recalls the special care her father took to always solicit and then follow
his wife's views on anything relating to the running of the household.
"Queenie" and "Asia" were Emerson's pet names for his wife and, according
to Edith, Lidian's answer to his question, "What do *you* think, O Queen?"
always settled a household matter once and for all. Edith also remembers
that although her father disliked pets, he greatly admired the beauty and
grace of cats. Finally, Edward, whose filial devotion to his father's reputation
and legacy certainly marked his own career as the editor of his essays and
journals, echoed his sister Edith's claim that their father delighted in children and possessed a knack for humorous understatement. Edward also respectfully recalls how his father never commanded or forbade his children
to do anything, but rather laid out principles and options before them and
then left them to decide on a course of action for themselves.

   Many writers of the reminiscences and recollections that follow repeated
almost verbatim in the texts printed here an anecdote that they also used in
some other printed material or that they extensively rewrote for publication
in the works reprinted here in order to romanticize Emerson and heighten
the importance of their personal relationship with him. One of the most extreme examples of the latter practice is disclosed by a comparison between

Moncure D. Conway's depiction of an incident in "Emerson: The Teacher and the Man"† (1903) and his depiction of the same incident in *Emerson at Home and Abroad*, which he published in 1882 immediately after Emerson's death. Conway's respective treatments of his relationship with Emerson are worth reading carefully because on more than one occasion Emerson himself expressed doubts about Conway's reliability as a reporter of their relationship. Like Franklin B. Sanborn, Conway, in Emerson's estimation, had an unfortunate tendency to rewrite personal history—always to his own advantage. Emerson acknowledged as much to his daughter Ellen when, following the burning of his house in 1872, he expressed his dread that either Sanborn or Conway should inherit his manuscripts;[29] Emerson also expressed his doubts about Conway to Pendleton King when, as King reports in his "Notes of Conversations with Emerson,"† he characterized Conway as "a quite worthy man, but unable to tell anything as he hears it."

In "Emerson: The Teacher and the Man,"† published during the centenary celebration of Emerson's birth, Conway quotes liberally from his correspondence with Emerson as well as from his own journals in order to reconstruct their relationship between their first meeting in 1853 and Emerson's death in 1882. For most of the essay he is concerned with recounting his first meeting with Emerson, treating it as an early predictor of the intimacy he would have the reader assume characterized their relationship. The relationship between Emerson and Conway was, in fact, close, but it was never as close or intimate as Conway implies in the essay. Is he lying in the essay? No. He is merely re-creating the nature of his relationship with Emerson out of an inflated, self-serving narrative of that same meeting which he had published twenty years earlier. In the first essay, Conway gives only passing notice to the time he and Emerson spent at Walden Pond on the first day they met. By contrast, in the following passage from *Emerson at Home and Abroad*, Conway thoroughly romanticizes their time at Walden; blurring the chronology of actual events such as his own first acquaintance with Carlyle, Conway uses the excursion to the pond as an occasion to portray the early, intimate character of his relationship with Emerson, to discourse authoritatively on the relative merits of Emerson and Carlyle as conversationalists and thinkers, to discuss Emerson's (and indirectly his own) admiration of Thoreau and Theodore Parker, and to elevate Emerson to the rank of Bunyan's Interpreter—all against the idyllic background of "woods [made] melodious with the faith and the flute of Thoreau":

On this first walk Emerson took me to Walden Water. A crystal was the lakelet that day, in setting of emerald, clear and calm, the fit haunt of a poet. In its transparent depths were seen the fishes, and around it sang many birds. . . .

Having bathed, we sat down on the shore, near the site of Thoreau's vanished hermitage; then Walden and its woods began to utter their soft spells through the lips of my poet. Emerson's conversation was different from that of any other I have met. The contrast between his talk and that of Carlyle was remarkable. Carlyle was, in a sense, the more striking figure, but his manner and tone revived dreams of historic characters. . . . But Emerson suggested none other; he was strictly incomparable, and he never appeared to speak what had been thought or said before that moment. One always felt that there was a line around Carlyle's vehemence and wrathful eloquence; there was something that stood for authority; but every word of Emerson began where authority ended. Emerson was an instinctive artist, and never brought out cannon to slay sparrows. Every one who has witnessed the imperial dignity . . . which characterised Carlyle's conversation to such an extent that his slight utterances seemed to stand out like pillars of Hercules, must also have felt the earth tremble, as if under "the hammer of Thor"[;] . . . but though the same falsehood might be fatally smitten by our American, it was by the invisible, inaudible sun-stroke, which left the sky as bright and blue as before. . . .

I remember him on that day at Walden as Bunyan's pilgrim might remember the Interpreter. He listened to some rough fishermen in boats, . . . remarking how their voices were intoned by the distance and the water to music. He pointed out some of the Walden flora, and observing the suggestiveness of some shapes . . . showed that he had already an original plant-lore. He spoke only as occasion arose. . . . There was no need that he should talk; simply to be with him was to me joy enough. . . . We were having heated debates in theology at the Divinity College, and to leave them for this presence was like a plunge from sultry air into Walden. "I am not much interested in such discussions," he said; "it does seem deplorable that there should be a tendency in some people to creeds which would take man back to the chimpanzee." "I have very good grounds for being a Unitarian and a Trinitarian too. I need not nibble for ever at one loaf, but eat it and thank God for it, and earn another." He told me about Theodore Parker, . . . and I think he compared him with Socrates. He also had once thought of building himself a study out there beside Walden. But Thoreau was "not in awe of early tea." He found in Thoreau that deeper piety vulgarly regarded as impiety, like George Herbert's sweet intimacy with his deity, "with whom he sometimes cracks jokes." What Emerson once called the "wailing sound" coming from the young world struggling to free itself from dogmas, was but faintly heard in woods melodious with the faith and the flute of Thoreau; but whenever that sound reached him, Emerson felt grateful to Theodore Parker. "It is a comfort to remember that there is one sane voice amid the religious and political confusions of the country."[30]

In the preserved remnants of a lecture called "Imagination" that he delivered at Harvard in 1870 and 1871, Emerson wrote: "Every speaker speaks to his best listener."[31] Reading the accounts that follow, one will be impressed by the acuteness and sympathy with which Emerson's listeners typically heard and took in his words, and the sense of excitement and urgency with which they preserved his words and thoughts first for themselves, then for their contemporaries, then for future readers such as ourselves. Because these accounts all date from Emerson's own time or are based on firsthand impressions of Emerson remembered and later published by individuals after his death, they reveal how the extraordinary reputation he enjoys today was carefully crafted and established during his life by his admirers and, indeed, by Emerson himself. Collectively, then, the reminiscences, memoirs, interviews, and other writings printed in this volume provide us with a very rich portrayal of the public and the private Emerson, and as they do so, they re-create the process of "the canonization of Ralph Waldo Emerson" as, arguably, America's foremost intellectual and writer.

. . .

Texts printed in this volume generally have been drawn from their earliest printed version. In all instances, texts drawn from modern editions that print genetic versions of manuscript texts have been silently regularized here to exclude the editorial apparatus used in genetic editions to show authorial emendations in the manuscript. Silent emendations have been employed by the editors to present readers of this volume with as clear and straightforward texts as possible, including, for instance, the insertion of terminal punctuation when missing in the source, the spelling out of abbreviations when necessary for clarity, and the correction of obvious typographical errors in sources. Throughout, the names of authors and the titles of essays and other works have been enclosed in brackets when they have been supplied by the editors, rather than by the authors; complete bibliographic information on the source for each text printed here is provided in an unnumbered footnote immediately following the text.

. . .

We should like to acknowledge our respective research assistants for their considerable help during our preparation of this volume: Susan H. Kayorie, University at Albany, State University of New York, and Todd Richardson, University of South Carolina at Columbia. In addition, Mr. Bosco wishes to express his gratitude to Dean V. Mark Durand, Provost Carlos Santiago, and President Karen R. Hitchcock of the University at Albany for providing him with the intellectual space to work on this volume; to Bradley P. Dean, media director of The Thoreau Institute at Walden Woods and editor of the *Thoreau Society Bulletin*, for his good counsel; and to Joseph C. Wheeler for sharing his wealth of Concord lore. Mr. Myerson wishes to thank Steve Lynn, chair of the Department of English at the University of South Carolina. We are both grateful to Holly Carver and Ed Folsom for the opportunity to publish this book.

Notes

1. Thomas Wentworth Higginson, "The Personality of Emerson," *Outlook*, 74 (23 May 1903): 223. According to Higginson, George Washington received every one of the 97 votes cast, Abraham Lincoln and Daniel Webster received 96 each, Benjamin Franklin 94, Ulysses S. Grant 93, John Marshall and Thomas Jefferson 91 each, and Emerson 87.

2. As reported in the *Concord Journal* (Massachusetts), 16 February 1928, p. 3. According to the report, Thoreau was judged "our most original native genius, a simon-pure American if there ever was one.... Above and beyond this he was a great literary artist, and an abler, if not braver, thinker than Emerson himself."

3. *The Letters of Ralph Waldo Emerson*, ed. Ralph L. Rusk (vols. 1–6) and Eleanor M. Tilton (vols. 7–10) (New York: Columbia University Press, 1939, 1990–1995); *The Correspondence of Emerson and Carlyle*, ed. Joseph Slater (New York: Columbia University Press, 1964); *The Journals and Miscellaneous Notebooks of Ralph Waldo Emerson*, ed. William H. Gilman, Ralph H. Orth, et al., 16 vols. (Cambridge: Harvard University Press, 1960–1982); *The Topical Notebooks of Ralph Waldo Emerson*, ed. Ralph H. Orth et al., 3 vols. (Columbia: University of Missouri Press, 1990–1994); *The Complete Sermons of Ralph Waldo Emerson*, ed. Albert J. von Frank et al., 4 vols. (Columbia: University of Missouri Press, 1989–1992); *The Early Lectures of Ralph Waldo Emerson*, ed. Stephen E. Whicher, Robert E. Spiller, and Wallace E. Williams, 3 vols. (Cambridge: Harvard University Press, 1959–1972); *The Later Lectures of Ralph Waldo Emerson, 1843–1871*, ed. Ronald A. Bosco and Joel Myerson, 2 vols. (Athens: University of Georgia Press, 2001).

4. *One First Love: The Letters of Ellen Louisa Tucker to Ralph Waldo Emerson*, ed. Edith W. Gregg (Cambridge: Harvard University Press, 1962); *The Selected Letters of Lidian Jackson Emerson*, ed. Delores Bird Carpenter (Columbia: University of Missouri Press, 1987); *The Letters of Ellen Tucker Emerson*, ed. Edith E. W. Gregg, 2 vols. (Kent, Ohio: Kent State

University Press, 1982); *The Selected Letters of Mary Moody Emerson*, ed. Nancy Craig Simmons (Athens: University of Georgia Press, 1993). Ronald A. Bosco and Joel Myerson are currently editing the unpublished lifelong correspondence among Emerson's brothers—Edward Bliss, Charles Chauncy, and William Emerson—for electronic and print publication by Oxford University Press.

5. See Joel Myerson, *Ralph Waldo Emerson: A Descriptive Bibliography* (Pittsburgh: University of Pittsburgh Press, 1982); Robert E. Burkholder and Joel Myerson, *Emerson: An Annotated Secondary Bibliography* (Pittsburgh: University of Pittsburgh Press, 1985); Robert E. Burkholder and Joel Myerson, *Ralph Waldo Emerson: An Annotated Bibliography of Criticism, 1980–1991* (Westport, Conn., and London: Greenwood Press, 1994); and Albert J. von Frank, *An Emerson Chronology* (New York: G. K. Hall, 1994). Joel Myerson, *Supplement to Ralph Waldo Emerson: A Descriptive Bibliography*, is forthcoming from the University of Pittsburgh Press.

6. Henceforth, a superscript dagger (†) following the title of a work indicates that the work is printed in this volume.

7. [Walt Whitman], "Mr. Emerson's Lecture," *New York Aurora*, 7 March 1842.

8. "Second Look at Emerson" (1850), reprinted in N. Parker Willis, *Hurry-Graphs; or, Sketches of Scenery, Celebrities and Society, Taken from Life* (New York: Charles Scribner, 1851), pp. 175, 177, 178.

9. Alexander Ireland, *Ralph Waldo Emerson: His Life, Genius, and Writings, A Biographical Sketch, to Which Are Added Personal Recollections of His Visits to England, Extracts from Unpublished Letters, and Miscellaneous Characteristic Records* (London: Simpkin, Marshall, 1882), pp. 53–55.

10. Charles Richard Williams, *The Life of Rutherford Birchard Hayes*, 2 vols. (Boston: Houghton Mifflin, 1914), 1:64.

11. [William Cullen Bryant], *New York Evening Post*, 7 March 1842; reprinted in Charles I. Glicksberg, "Bryant on Emerson the Lecturer," *New England Quarterly*, 12 (September 1939): 532.

12. *Selected Letters of William Michael Rossetti*, ed. Roger W. Pattie (University Park: Pennsylvania State University Press, 1990), p. 422.

13. George Willis Cooke, *Ralph Waldo Emerson: His Life, Writings, and Philosophy* (Boston: James R. Osgood, 1881), p. 193.

14. James Kendall Hosmer, *The Last Leaf: Observations, during Seventy-five Years, of Men and Events in America and Europe* (New York: Putnams, 1912), p. 247.

15. John Ross Dix, *Transatlantic Tracings; or, Sketches of Persons and Scenes in America* (London: W. Tweedie, [1853]), p. 126; January Searle [George Searle Phillips], *Emerson: His Life and Writings* (London: Holyoake, 1855), pp. 39–40.

16. John Townsend Trowbridge, *My Own Story with Recollections of Noted Persons* (Boston: Houghton, Mifflin, 1903), pp. 347–49.

17. [Edward Bok], "A Boy among Famous Folks. Part 2," *Ladies' Home Journal*, 22 (March 1905): 8.

18. Ronald A. Bosco, "His Lectures were Poetry, His Teaching the Music of the Spheres:

Annie Adams Fields and Francis Greenwood Peabody on Emerson's *Natural History of the Intellect* Lectures at Harvard in 1870," *Harvard Library Bulletin*, n.s. 8 (Summer 1997): 42.

19. Francis Greenwood Peabody, "The Germ of the Graduate School," *The Harvard Graduates' Magazine*, 27 (1918): 180–81.

20. John Holmes, as quoted in Oliver Wendell Holmes, *Ralph Waldo Emerson* (Boston: Houghton, Mifflin, 1884), p. 50.

21. Charles Francis Adams, *Richard Henry Dana: A Biography*, 2 vols. (Boston: Houghton, Mifflin, 1891), 1:5.

22. *Daniel Ricketson: Autobiographic and Miscellaneous*, ed. Anna and Walton Ricketson (New Bedford, Mass.: E. Anthony & Sons, 1910), p. 39.

23. *Diary, Reminiscences, and Correspondence of Henry Crabb Robinson, Barrister-at-Law, F.S.A.*, ed. Thomas Sadler, 3 vols. (London: Macmillan, 1869), 3:372; emphasis added.

24. In the Houghton Library, Harvard University; see *A 59 M-311 (2), folder 4.

25. "Powers and Laws of Thought," *The Complete Works of Ralph Waldo Emerson*, ed. Edward Waldo Emerson, 12 vols. (Boston: Houghton, Mifflin, 1903–1904), 12:11–12.

26. Mary B. Clafin, *Personal Recollections of John G. Whittier* (New York: Thomas Y. Crowell, 1893), pp. 25–27.

27. Ernest Wadsworth Longfellow, *Random Memories* (Boston: Houghton Mifflin, 1922), pp. 32–33.

28. Francis B. Dedmond, "The Selected Letters of William Ellery Channing the Younger (Part Two)," in *Studies in the American Renaissance 1990*, ed. Joel Myerson (Charlottesville: University Press of Virginia, 1990), pp. 236–37.

29. Ellen Tucker Emerson to Edith Emerson Forbes, 22 August 1872, *Letters of Ellen Tucker Emerson*, 1:690.

30. Moncure Daniel Conway, *Emerson at Home and Abroad* (Boston: James R. Osgood, 1882), pp. 287–89. Combining elements of the account quoted here and "Emerson: The Teacher and the Man,"† Conway composed yet another version of his first meeting with Emerson for use in his autobiography; see *Autobiography, Memoirs and Experiences of Moncure Daniel Conway*, 2 vols. (Boston: Houghton, Mifflin, 1904), 1:134–39.

31. In the Houghton Library, Harvard University; see bMS Am 1280.212, ms. p. 7.

Chronology

1796
25 October   Reverend William Emerson marries Ruth Haskins

1798
9 February   A sister, Phebe Ripley Emerson, born

1799
28 November   A brother, John Clarke Emerson, born

1800
28 September   Phebe Ripley Emerson dies

1801
31 July   A brother, William Emerson, born

1802
20 September   Lydia Jackson born

1803
25 May   Ralph Waldo Emerson born

1805
17 April   A brother, Edward Bliss Emerson, born

1807
11 April   A brother, Robert Bulkeley Emerson, born
26 April   John Clarke Emerson dies

1808
27 November   A brother, Charles Chauncy Emerson, born

1811
26 February   A sister, Mary Caroline Emerson, born
12 May   Reverend William Emerson dies

1812
Spring?   Enters Boston Latin School

1814
14 April   Mary Caroline Emerson dies

1817
October   Enters Harvard College

1818
January   Begins teaching school on occasion at Waltham

1821
29 August   Graduates from Harvard College
October   Assists brother William in a school for young ladies

1822
November   "Thoughts on the Religion of the Middle Ages," RWE's first
                 publication, appears in the *Christian Disciple and Theo-
                 logical Review*

1823
5 December   Takes over William's school when he leaves for study in
                 Germany
1824
April   Begins formally studying religion
31 December   Closes school

1825
11 February   Registers as a student of divinity at Harvard
12 September   Opens school at Chelmsford; closes it at end of the year

1826
3 January   Takes over Edward's school in Roxbury when he leaves for
                 Europe; closes it on 28 March
1 April   Opens school in Cambridge; closes it on 23 October
10 October   Approbated by American Unitarian Association to preach
25 November   Sails to Charleston, South Carolina, and St. Augustine,
                 Florida, to improve health

1827
3 June   Returns to Boston
25 December   Meets Ellen Louisa Tucker in Concord, New Hampshire

1828
2 July   Edward is committed to McLean Asylum; released in the fall
17 December   Engaged to Ellen Tucker

1829
30 January   Becomes colleague pastor at Second Church, Boston

11 March	Ordained at Second Church
1 July	Promoted to pastor
30 September	Marries Ellen Tucker

1830

12 December	Edward goes to Puerto Rico for his health; returns briefly to Boston in August 1832

1831

8 February	Ellen Louisa Tucker Emerson dies of tuberculosis
7 December	Charles goes to Puerto Rico for his health; returns 1 May 1832

1832

6 October	Edward returns to Puerto Rico for his health
22 December	Sends farewell letter to Second Church, resigning his position
25 December	Sails for Europe

1833

26 August	Meets Thomas and Jane Welsh Carlyle
7 October	Returns to America
5 November	Delivers first public lecture, "The Uses of Natural History," in Boston
3 December	William Emerson marries Susan Woodward Haven

1834

March	Meets Lydia Jackson of Plymouth
13 May	Receives partial inheritance ($11,600) from Ellen Emerson's estate
1 October	Edward dies of tuberculosis in Puerto Rico
9 October	Moves to Concord

1835

24 January	Proposes to Lydia Jackson; announces engagement at end of the month
29 January	Begins first lecture series—on *Biography*—in Boston
12 September	Delivers discourse on Concord's history, which is published in November
14 September	Marries Lydia Jackson, whom he calls "Lidian"

1836

9 May	Charles dies in New York City an hour before Elizabeth Sherman Hoar, to whom he was engaged, and RWE arrive
9 September	*Nature* published
19 September	First meeting of the Transcendental Club

| 30 October | Waldo Emerson born |
| 8 December | Begins lecture series on *Philosophy of History* in Boston |

1837

late July	Receives remainder of inheritance ($11,675) from Ellen Emerson's estate
31 August	Delivers address on the "American Scholar" at Harvard; published 23 September
6 December	Begins lecture series on *Human Culture* in Boston

1838

14 July	Carlyle's *Critical and Miscellaneous Essays* published, edited by RWE
15 July	Delivers address at the Harvard Divinity School; published 21 August
24 July	Delivers address on "Literary Ethics" at Dartmouth College; published 8 September

1839

24 February	Ellen Tucker Emerson born
7 September	Jones Very's *Essays and Poems* published, edited by RWE
4 December	Begins lecture series on *The Present Age* in Boston

1840

20 March	Begins lecture series on *Human Life* in Providence
1 July	First issue of *Dial* appears
2 September	Attends the last meeting of the Transcendental Club

1841

19 March	*Essays* [*First Series*] published (and in England on 25 August)
11 August	Delivers "The Method of Nature" at Waterville College, Maine; published 21 October
22 November	Edith Emerson born

1842

| 27 January | Waldo Emerson dies suddenly of scarlatina |
| March | Margaret Fuller resigns as editor of *Dial*; RWE becomes editor |

1843

| 10 January | Begins lecture series on *New England* in Baltimore |
| May | Carlyle's *Past and Present* published, edited by RWE |

1844

| 8 April | Last issue of *Dial* appears |
| 10 July | Edward Waldo Emerson born |

1 August	Delivers address on "Emancipation of the Negroes in the British West Indies" at Concord Court House; published 9 September (and in England in October)
19 October	*Essays: Second Series* published (and in England on 9 November)

1845

2 December	Purchases forty-one acres at Walden Pond
31 December	Begins lecture series on *Representative Men* in Concord

1846

12 December	*Poems* published in England (and in America on 25 December)

1847

5 October	Sails for England to begin lecture tour of the British Isles

1848

7 May	Arrives in Paris
2 June	Returns to England
6 June	Begins lecture series on *Mind and Manners of the Nineteenth Century* in London
27 July	Returns to America

1849

1 February	Begins lecture series on *English Traits* in Chelmsford, Massachusetts
20 March	First meeting of Town and Country Club
11 September	*Nature; Addresses, and Lectures* published

1850

1 January	*Representative Men* published (and in England on 5 January)
13 May	Begins midwestern lecture tour; returns 28 June
19 July	Margaret Fuller dies

1851

22 December	Begins lecture series on *Conduct of Life* in Boston

1852

14 February	*Memoirs of Margaret Fuller Ossoli* published, co-edited by RWE
April	Lectures in Montreal
24 November	Begins midwestern lecture tour; returns mid-February 1853

1853

16 November	Ruth Haskins Emerson dies

1854

2 January	Begins midwestern lecture tour; returns 20 February
3 January	Begins lecture series on *Topics of Modern Times* in Philadelphia
16 December	First meeting of the Saturday Club

1855

20 September	Delivers address at the Women's Rights Convention in Boston
29 September	Delivers address at the consecration of Sleepy Hollow Cemetery in Concord
ca. 27 Dec.	Begins midwestern lecture tour; returns late January 1856

1856

6 August	*English Traits* published (and in England on 6 September)

1857

8 January	Begins midwestern lecture tour; returns 10 February

1858

3 March	Begins lecture series on *The Natural Method of Mental Philosophy* in Boston

1859

27 May	Robert Bulkeley Emerson dies
4 December	Oversees memorial services for John Brown in Boston during which he delivers a lecture on "Morals"

1860

16 January	Begins midwestern lecture tour; returns 25 February
8 December	*The Conduct of Life* published (and in England on 8 December)

1861

2 April	Begins lecture series on *Life and Literature* in Boston
16 July	Edward Waldo Emerson admitted to Harvard

1862

6 May	Henry David Thoreau dies
August	"Thoreau" appears in *Atlantic Monthly*

1863

2 January	Begins midwestern lecture tour; returns 7 February
1 May	Mary Moody Emerson dies
10 October	Thoreau's *Excursions* published, edited by RWE
27 November	Begins lecture series on *American Life* in Boston

1865

11 January	Begins midwestern lecture tour; returns 10 February

22 July	Thoreau's *Letters to Various Persons* published, edited by RWE
3 October	Edith Emerson marries William Hathaway Forbes

1866

9 January	Begins midwestern lecture tour; returns 20 February
14 April	Begins lecture series on *Philosophy for the People* in Boston
23 June	*Complete Works* published in two volumes in England
10 July	Ralph Emerson Forbes, RWE's first grandchild, born
18 July	Awarded LL.D. degree by Harvard University

1867

8 January	Begins midwestern lecture tour; returns 22 or 23 March
29 April	*May-Day and Other Pieces* published (and in England on 8 June)
17 July	Appointed overseer of Harvard University
2 December	Begins midwestern lecture tour; returns 2 January 1868

1868

13 September	William Emerson dies

1869

27 October	*Prose Works* published in two volumes in America

1870

5 March	*Society and Solitude* published (and in England on 5 March)
26 April	Begins a course of lectures on *Natural History of the Intellect* at Harvard

1871

14 February	Begins a second course of lectures on *Natural History of the Intellect* at Harvard
11 April	Begins trip to California; returns 30 May
25 November	Begins midwestern lecture tour; returns 14 December

1872

15 April	Begins a series of "Conversations" on literature in Boston
24 July	RWE's house substantially damaged by fire
23 October	Travels to Europe with Ellen
25 December	Arrives in Egypt

1873

19 February	Returns to Europe
27 April	Sees Carlyle for the last time
26 May	Returns to America
1 October	Delivers address at opening of the Concord Free Public Library

1874

19 September   Edward Waldo Emerson marries Annie Shepard Keyes

19 December   *Parnassus* published, a poetry collection edited by RWE

1875

15 December   *Letters and Social Aims* published (and in England on 8 January 1876)

1876

24 June   The "Little Classic Edition" of RWE's works is published in nine volumes

1878

25 February   Delivers address on "Fortune of the Republic" in Boston; published 10 August

7 April   Elizabeth Sherman Hoar dies

1880

4 February   Delivers one hundredth lecture before the Concord Lyceum

1882

20 April   Catches a cold, which develops into pneumonia

27 April   Ralph Waldo Emerson dies in Concord

30 April   Buried in Sleepy Hollow Cemetery, Concord

Emerson in His Own Time

[A Visit to Emerson at Concord in 1837]

AMOS BRONSON ALCOTT

> Amos Bronson Alcott and Emerson became lifelong friends after their first
> meetings in the 1830s. Following unsuccessful stints as a teacher in Philadel-
> phia, Alcott, who had lived in Boston between 1828 and 1830, returned there in
> 1834 to operate the Temple School with the assistance of Elizabeth Palmer Pea-
> body. He was an original member of the Transcendental Club founded in 1836,
> and as the following passage from his journal indicates, an early defender of
> Emerson and his particular brand of idealism. Alcott's delight in the conver-
> sation he enjoyed with Emerson during this visit in 1837 anticipates the nature
> of their relationship for the next forty-five years, and especially so after 1857,
> when Alcott moved his family permanently to Concord. Alcott's admiration of
> Emerson was returned in kind; writing in his journal in 1848, Emerson stated,
> "Alcott is a . . . fluid in which men of a certain spirit can easily expand them-
> selves & swim at large, they who elsewhere found themselves confined. He
> gives them nothing but themselves. . . . Me he has served . . . in that way; he
> was the reasonable creature to speak to, that I wanted" (*Journals and Miscella-
> neous Notebooks*, 11:19).

I spent a few days with Mr. Emerson at his own house in Concord. I left
home on Monday morning [15 May 1837], and returned on Friday afternoon [19 May]; having seen Mr. E. at Concord, and Mr. [Convers] Francis
at Watertown. With the latter I spent a night, taking his house on my way
home. During my visits to these gentlemen, various topics of interest were
discussed. Little difference of *opinion* seemed to exist between us: the
means and method of communicating with the age were the chief points of
difference. *Emerson*, true to his genius, favors written works. He holds men
and things at a distance; pleases himself with using them for his own benefit,
and as means of gathering material for his works. He does not believe in the
actual. His sympathies are all intellectual. He persuades me to leave the actual, devote myself to the speculative, and embody my thoughts in written
works.—*Francis*, on the other hand, inclines more to the actual; sympa-
thises in the wants and pursuits of men. Emerson idealizes all things. This

idealized picture is the true and real one to him; all else is nought.... Beauty, beauty, this it is that charms him. But beauty has pure and delicate tastes, and hence all that mars or displeases this sense, with however much of truth or of goodness it may be associated, is of no interest to the mind. Emerson seeks the beauty of truth: it is not so much a quest of truth in itself, as the beauty thereof: not so much the desire of being holy and true, as of setting forth in fit and graceful terms, the beauty of truth and holiness. With him all men and things have a beauty; but this is the result of his point of vision, and often falls wide of the actual truth.... What is beautiful in man, nature, or art, this he apprehends, and with the poets power sets forth.

His genius is high and commanding. He will do honour to his age. As a man, however, this visit has somewhat modified my former notions of him. He seems not to be fully in earnest. He writes and speaks for effect. Fame stands before him as a dazzling award, and he holds himself somewhat too proudly, nor seeks the humble and sincere regard of his race. His life has been one of opportunity, and he has sought to realize in it, more of the accomplished scholar, than the perfect man.—A great intellect, refined by elegant study, rather than a divine life, radiant with the beauty of truth and holiness. He is an *eye*, more than a *heart*—an *intellect*, more than a *soul*.

Larry A. Carlson, "Bronson Alcott's 'Journal for 1837' (Part 2)," in *Studies in the American Renaissance 1982*, ed. Joel Myerson (Boston: Twayne Publishers, 1982), pp. 75–76.

[Remarks on Emerson in 1838, 1855, and 1858]

CONVERS FRANCIS

The Unitarian minister and historian, and Parkman Professor of Pulpit Eloquence at Harvard, Convers Francis first met Emerson in the 1830s. Francis was an original member of the Transcendental Club and a close friend of most of its members, but because he stopped short of Emerson's intellectual radicalism and Bronson Alcott's and Theodore Parker's social radicalism, he stands out as one of the more moderate voices of Transcendentalism. Of the selections that follow, Francis's letters to Frederic Henry Hedge describing Emerson's address at the Harvard Divinity School in 1838 are important as eyewitness accounts of Emerson's calm amid the firestorm his address had created at Harvard, while his journal entries on his relationship with Emerson between 1838 and 1858 suggest that, although Francis never wavered in his admiration of Emerson's character and conversation, he was increasingly critical of his friend who, he says, "never gets or has got beyond the old thought, however good that may be." Reflecting on "Self-possession," the last lecture in Emerson's lecture series on the *Natural Method of Mental Philosophy* in 1858, Francis found only the "old topics, subjectiveness and individuality."

Convers Francis to Frederic Henry Hedge, 10 August 1838

My good friend,

. . . Have you heard that Waldo Emerson delivered the sermon this summer to the class at the Divinity School, on their leaving the seminary? I went to hear it, & found it crowded with stirring, honest, lofty thoughts. I don't know that anything of his has excited me more. He dwelt much on the downfallen state of the church, i.e., the want of a living, real interest in the present Christianity (where I think he rather exaggerated, but not much), on the tendency to make only a historical Christ, separated from actual humanity,—& on the want of reference to the great laws of man's moral nature in preaching. These were his principal points, & were put forth with great power, & sometimes (under the first head especially) with unique humor. The discourse was full of divine life,—and was a true word from a true soul. I did not agree with him in some of his positions, & think perhaps he did not make the peculiar significance of Jesus so prominent as he ought,—though I am inclined to believe not that he thinks less of Jesus than others do, but more of man, every man as a divine being.—The discourse gave dire offence to the rulers at Cambridge. The dean & Mr. Norton have pronounced sentences of fearful condemnation, & their whole *clique* in Boston & Cambridge are in commotion. The harshest words are not spared, & "infidel" & "atheist" are the best terms poor E. gets. I have sometimes thought that to Mr. E. & his numerous detractors might be applied what Plato says of the winged soul, that has risen to the sight of the absolute, essential, & true, & therefore is said by the many to be stark mad . . .

Convers Francis to Frederic Henry Hedge, 12 November 1838

My good friend,

. . . You know of course what a hubbub there has been here about Emerson's Discourse,—an excitement which, whether right or wrong, has been, it seems to me, wholly disproportionate to the occasion. But the truth was, the fluid of malignity had been collecting a good while,—& needed but a slight point of attraction to draw it down on E's head. His popularity, especially among the brightest young people, had become very annoying to the *dii majores* of the pulpits & the Divinity School;—& no sooner was the overt act of printing something, that would not lie peaceably in the topic-holes of their minds, committed, then as if by general consent among them there was an outbreak of wrath, the hotter for having been smothered. The Discourse itself did not seem to me adapted to excite any such turmoil, except from certain expressions rather than thoughts, which seem almost as if chosen for offense. On the whole I liked it very well; but there are quite debateable things in it,—& as usual with him, a want of an adequate appreciation on the *Christian* element in the world's culture.—E., you know, is not a man, who can very well justify his own processes of thought to another person, i.e. is not at all a man of logic: he is a seer, who looks into the infinite, & reports what he sees;—if you like the report & agree with him, all the better;—if not, 'tis a pity,—& there's an end of it,—there's no more to be said. This is a high class of minds,—a class, with which I have much, but by no means an entire, sympathy.—E. is about to commence another course of lectures in Boston,—to make the experiment whether he can get an audience, or is henceforth to be shut out of the lecture-rooms:—if so,—he says, he still has his pen & study,—& can give the world the written, if not the spoken, word.— . . .

From Convers Francis's Journal

10 January 1838. Went to Boston—left the party to attend Mr. Emerson's lecture, which was on the *heart* as signifying *intellectual integrity,*—i.e. that we must do things *from the heart,* we must *be,* and not *seem.* It was full of his rich moral eloquence, striking down deep into the truth which underlies all outside things. But after the lecture, I had some debate with him for saying that Walter Scott sometimes was not *real,* but acted the fine gentleman. The *spiritual* men, I find, are not disposed to do justice to Scott, because he lived so in the phenomenal, the outward; they will not allow him to be a *true man,* because he was not what they require. But why was not his development as true, hearty and real, as if he had been a spiritualist? It had as much reality, though it was different. I hold Scott to have been as true a *man* as Coleridge.

6 February 1838. Went to Boston to attend Mr. Emerson's lecture. It was the last in the course, and was a most delightful survey or recapitulation of some of the principles of Human Culture. I suppose every one present was sad to think it was the last: it was like a beautiful strain of music which one would fain have continued indefinitely. I could not but think of Milton's exquisite description, for I felt as his Adam felt:

> "The angel ended, and in Adam's ear
> [quoted from this line down to]
> "With glory attributed to the high Creator."
> (Par[adise]. Lost. Bk. VIII. 1-13.)

Mr. Emerson in this course of lectures has spoken of high things, and spoken of them as one filled with the pure inspiration of truth.

14 February 1838. Went to Cambridge to hear Mr. E., who is to repeat his lectures there. Heard the lecture on the "doctrine of the hands," man's double-speeders, as he called them,—the culture arising from labor. We had heard it before in Boston; but it was as fresh and beautiful as ever.

22 February 1838. To Cambridge to hear Mr. Emerson's lecture. It was on the culture of the *intellect,*—what the intellect is, how it grows and what *we can do* for it. The lecture, on the whole, I think superior to any I have heard from Mr. E., more methodical, and coherent,—at the same time full of lofty and far reaching views. The two practical directions to the student, have a room to yourself, and keep a journal?

8 March 1838. To Cambridge to hear Mr. Emerson's lecture;—it was on

[5]

the heart, or the affections, the social nature,—full to overflowing of beauty and truth; he closed with a description of a family of young, intelligent boys, struggling for education, and acquiring culture, amidst the rough training of poverty and hardship; nothing could exceed it for power of truth, and for felicitous sketching.

15 March 1838. To Cambridge to hear Mr. Emerson's lecture; it was the second part on the Affections, a noble and beautiful thing. . . .

22 March 1838. Went to Cambridge and heard Mr. Emerson's lecture on the heroic: it was grand in accordance with the subject. . . .

28 March 1838. Went to hear Mr. Emerson's lecture on the culture of the moral sentiment, *the holy* in man. This is the lecture, which, when delivered in Boston, alarmed some people not a little, as certain parts of it were supposed to deny the personality of the Deity and to border close upon atheism. Strange what interpretations are sometimes put upon the words of a man, who is unique and original in thought and expression! So far from this lecture containing anything like atheism, it seemed to me a noble strain of fervent, lofty, philosophical piety. It was, like its topic, *holy.* The only idea of personality in the Deity, which he impugned, was, I think, the vulgar idea, which considers God as occupying space:—the personality which consists in a *will* and *consciousness* (and what other personality can there be?) he seemed to me to express or take for granted, though, it is true, some of his incidental expressions might look differently. I thought that in one passage of the lecture he seemed to take away the distinct, individual existence of man, as a conscious being, after death, and resolve him into the All, the Divine Soul: but my impression is probably erroneous. I wish exceedingly to see Mr. E. in private and hear him expound these matters more with all the sweet charm of his delightful conversation. After return from Cambridge, read and wrote, but not much; my head and heart were too full of Mr. E.'s lecture for that.

29 March 1838. Went to C[ambridge]. . . . to hear Mr. Emerson. It was the last lecture of the course, and that was the only sad thing about it: it gave a view of the obstacles to culture, the excitements to it, a noble conclusion to a noble course of wisdom and philosophical eloquence.

10 September 1838. Took tea at ____, a family belonging to the straitest sect of Boston conservatism. I found they had been taught by ____ to abhor and abominate R. W. Emerson as a sort of mad dog: and when I defended

that pure and angelic spirit and told them he was full of piety and truthfulness (as he is, no man more so), they laughed at me with amazement,—for no such sounds had penetrated their *clique* before.

22 September 1838. Returned to Mr. Emerson's, and spent the night. There was abundance of good talk, which I hardly know how to report. What a pure, noble, loving, far-reaching spirit is Mr. E.! When we were alone, he talked of his Discourse at the Divinity School, and of the obloquy it had brought upon him: he is perfectly quiet amidst the storm; to my objections and remarks he gave the most candid replies, though we could not agree upon some points: the more I see of this beautiful spirit, the more I revere and love him; such a calm, steady, simple soul, always looking for truth and living in wisdom, and in love for man, and goodness, I have never met. Mr. E. is not a philosopher, so called, not a logic-man, not one whose vocation it is to state processes of argument; he is a *seer* who reports in sweet and significant words what he sees; he looks into the infinite of truth, and records what there passes before his vision: if you see it as he does, you will recognise him for a gifted teacher; if not, there is little or nothing to be said about it and you will go elsewhere for truth: but do not brand him with the names of *visionary*, or *fanatic*, or *pretender*: he is no such thing,—he is a true, godful man, though in his love of the ideal he disregards too much the actual.

23 September 1838. In the morning at Mr. E.'s, we talked chiefly on matters of natural science, where Mr. [John Lewis] Russell was continually giving us information and excellent remarks. I laughed heartily at a quotation made by Mr. E. in his arch, quiet way; Mr. R. had told us of a naturalist, who spent much time and pains in investigating the habits and nature of the *louse* on *the cod-fish*; "O star eyed science" said Mr. E. "hast thou wandered there?"

9 January 1839. [Wife] and I rode to Boston, to hear Mr. Emerson's lecture. It was on Genius. Never before have I been so much delighted and excited even by this most delightful and exciting of all lecturers. It was a strain of inspiration, at once lofty and sweet, throughout. It was a burst of that power, of which it treated. I was reminded of the oft quoted line about Longinus,—"And is himself the great sublime he draws." Mr. E. gives one such a succession of the best things in condensed sentences, that we can scarcely *remember* any of them. He has not, like common writers, any of those dry,

sandy spots, indifferent passages,—where we can rest for a few moments, and think of and remember the good things. Hence it is so difficult to give an account to others of what he says. . . .

27 January 1855. Thursday evening, heard R. W. Emerson's lecture in the course on Slavery: it was characteristic of him, of course,—for all he writes is so admirable in parts, wise and true in all,—yet not well adapted on the whole for popular impression, though there was some hearty applause:—what a deep power sometimes wells out from his face!

28 July 1855. Went . . . to R. W. Emerson's and had an altogether charming time of it. His brother, Wm. Emerson from N. York, was there. R. W. E. talked a good deal of Thomas Carlyle with whom he corresponds, and of Miss [Delia] Bacon of New Haven. He read a letter from the former, most characteristic and amusing, in which C. complains, in his own quaint way, of his disappointment about Frederick the Great, of whom he is making a book, and who turns out, he says, to be no hero to him.

10 April 1858. Wednesday went with my wife to hear R. W. Emerson's lecture in Boston. Many years ago that strain of the poet-philosopher fell upon my ear often, and it always brought a charm with it. Now, after a long interval, heard again, it seemed just the same thing. The subject was "Self-possession," and I think there was no idea which I had not found in his lectures from 15 to 20 years ago, and the very words were about the same. The old topics, subjectiveness and individuality,—we create all that we see,—we are lords of all that is. I had hoped to find by this time something else; but, I doubt, Mr. E. never gets or has got beyond the old thought, however good that may be. The fault of his manner of discussing a subject seems to be that he never makes any progress in the subject itself: he empties before you a box or bag of jewels as he goes on, which you may take and make the most you can of; but you find no progress in the subject, no opening out, expanding, motion outwards,— but instead thereof standing still and giving the utterance that comes at the moment. He might as well begin anywhere else and end anywhere else, as where he does begin and end. The mind of the hearer has not the satisfaction of moving steadily on till the consummation is effected,—sweeping forward till the march of thought is brought to its natural close.

2 October 1858. Cattle-fairs and Agricultural shows are now the order of the day all over our Commonwealth. There was one at Concord, at which

Mr. Emerson delivered the address, marked with his usual felicity of thought and expression:—it is quite noticeable what a *practical* man he is,—just what people generally think he is *not*. I wish I had the privilege of seeing him more than I am ever likely to do in a world where every man has his own peculiar work, which drives him to the wall.

Guy R. Woodall, "The Record of a Friendship: The Letters of Convers Francis to Frederic Henry Hedge in Bangor and Providence, 1835–1850," in *Studies in the American Renaissance 1991*, ed. Joel Myerson (Charlottesville: University Press of Virginia, 1991), pp. 34–36.

Joel Myerson, "Convers Francis and Emerson," *American Literature*, 50 (March 1978): 26–29, 34–35.

[A Visit from Emerson in 1838]

ELLIS GRAY LORING

Boston lawyer and abolitionist Ellis Gray Loring had known Emerson from their days together at the Boston Latin School and, later, at Harvard College. A co-founder of the New England Anti-Slavery Society, Loring had argued an important case before the state supreme court establishing the legal precedent that every slave brought on Massachusetts soil by the owner was legally free, and he also defended Abner Kneeland in a precedent-setting case involving freedom of speech. When Emerson was preparing his address on emancipation in the British West Indies, it was Loring who assisted him with the research and writing. His interview with Emerson in 1838 displays the concerns that both Emerson and his auditors would have for half a century to follow. Emerson clearly states his preference for the ideal world, one in which the mind creates the external landscape, as well as for the unity of all things. For his part, Loring questions Emerson's religious beliefs and his connection to traditional Christianity.

[29 March 1838]

R. W. Emerson spent an hour at my office. I asked him whether he did not conceive the Deity as personal in the sense of his being a will. He said he called him impersonal, because "person" did not express enough for God.— I said I could say that God was perfect benevolence, justice, truth; but that in speaking thus I used a figure of speech. I meant that he was a personal *being* in whom these perfections resided. For instance, Benevolence is a *personal* attribute; is not itself a subject. It means well wishing and this implies a well wisher. The universe is full of the marks of *design*;—but design supposes a will.

After considerable conversation, I discovered that our point of divergence was this. He does not believe, or rather he positively *dis*believes in any thing out of himself. He carries idealism to the Extreme. Consequently if there is a God, he is God. God and he are one—and . . . the external universe is only a form of him; a manifestation which only exists from and for him.

In illustrating his view of man's being or becoming God, he said the time was when your cradle, your spoon, your nurse, were you. These things have ceased to be you. One after another all things which are individual or pecul-iar will fall off from you,—you will be universal, absolute—you will be pure love, perfect justice and truth. Then you will be infinite and God. Even now, people say *I* in very different senses. There is the *I* that is selfish, false, im-pure, atheistic;—but the *I* that says "I shall never die" is the God within us. It is the love, justice, truth.

He remarked that Jesus claimed to be God, and had this view.

He said his own tendency was to unify. It was quite conceivable to him that all minds might so beat with one pulsation, as to be one, and lose all sep-arate consciousness.

He spoke of a higher revelation than that by Jesus Christ.—On my ex-pressing some doubt, he asked if I did not think it was to come. I said I thought there might be more knowledge given than is contained in the Gos-pel,—that . . . there might be merely intellectually considered a higher rev-elation, but I doubted as to this—but that I felt . . . there could never be a higher revelation of duty, that the character of Jesus seemed to me to be of absolute perfection. . . .

I thought he differed. He only remarked that Jesus said, "*I, I,*"—if *he* were to come now, he would say "*You.*"

Len Gougeon, "1838: Ellis Gray Loring and a Journal for the Times," in *Studies in the American Renaissance 1990*, ed. Joel Myerson (Charlottesville: University Press of Virginia, 1990), p. 42.

[Reminiscences of a Childhood in Concord in the 1840s]

[ANNIE SAWYER DOWNS]

Annie Sawyer Downs (ca. 1836–1901) was born in Manchester, New Hampshire, and moved to Concord with her family in the early 1840s, where she lived for about ten years. Because she did not write it until 1891, Downs's reminiscence interweaves childhood memories with anecdotes of the relations among the Alcotts, the Hawthornes, the Hoars, Thoreau, and Emerson at midcentury and later. Like most Concord writers, Downs acknowledges that the very atmosphere of the town encouraged the "heroic examples" that the everyday lives of these figures represented, but at times she assumes the role of small-town gossip as when she reports that Emerson, who "read very few of the books written by his contemporaries," never read one of Louisa May Alcott's writings and that his endorsement of Bronson Alcott puzzled everyone in Concord, so that she was "pleased to hear [him] say in later years that he deplored the uncertainty of Mr. Alcott's inspiration in public conversation, and that the man he knew and prized could not be found in any of his writings" (pp. 98, 101). Similarly, though Downs reports the now-legendary anecdote about the meeting between Emerson and Thoreau after the latter's night in jail, she says that popular sympathy was not with either of them but with Sam Staples, "the irate sheriff who declared in season and out . . . that 'he'd a let [Thoreau] stay until he got enough of it'" (p. 100).

Hawthorne, Channing, Alcott, Margaret Fuller . . . and Thoreau are all names which bear for me a conjuror's spell, but I have as yet mentioned only incidentally the one for whose sake far more than for all the attractions of Concord they gathered themselves together. I have not yet said what was Mr. Emerson's influence on the childhood and youth of Concord.

We knew that he was a great writer, that he corresponded with Carlyle, that Mrs. Tennyson had sent him beautiful crayon portraits of herself and husband, that he entertained poets, philosophers, and nobles, that Daniel Webster visited him every summer, that he had books by the hundreds, as well as many very rare and ancient things from the Tiber and the Nile. I cannot say just how much our knowledge of these facts influenced our opinion, but I do not think very much, for his personality, unlike that of Thoreau or Hawthorne, possessed even for the youngest a unique charm. He was perfectly simple, but if he smiled, you appeared to feel the sunshine, and if he said, "Good morning," you thought of it as a blessing. He walked several hours daily arranging his thoughts as he walked, and his habits being well known, we frequently stood in little groups on the chance of a passing word. We sometimes sought him in Sleepy Hollow, not then a cemetery, simply a green amphitheatre where poets sauntered, children frolicked, and wild birds warbled. . . .

We were immensely entertained by the odd people who came from all parts of the world to see him. Not only men with beards which hung below their waists, but men who chose to go without shoes and stockings and who if they condescended to wear hats at all, insisted on keeping them on in the house as well as in the street. We felt a curious kind of personal pride as we were told how Mr. Emerson's unfailing courtesy and personal dignity managed one of these pseudo-reformers. Mr. Emerson on seeing him about to seat himself still wearing his hat offered to relieve him of it, but was met by a flat refusal. Mr. Emerson then took his own hat and saying, "Well, then, if you prefer it, we will talk in the yard," led the way out!

He visited only one or two houses and those infrequently. He regarded Miss Elizabeth Hoar as his sister, she having been on the eve of marriage with his brother Charles . . . when his health suddenly failed and death snatched him away. He always called Miss Hoar "Elizabeth the Wise," declaring that she knew everything, and what was of so much more importance to his ignorance that her generosity equalled her wisdom.

Miss Hoar lived with her father, Mr. Samuel Hoar, and sometimes when Mrs. Emerson went away, the children stayed with her. Probably to entertain them she invited their school friends and read aloud to us Lamb's *Tales from Shakespeare*. Portia for many years looked like Miss Elizabeth Hoar to the eyes of my mind and even now I associate queer little flat cakes and sewing for the Negroes in Liberia with *The Merchant of Venice*. Judge Rockwood Hoar, [her] brother, was Mr. Emerson's closest friend and one of the very few persons who called him by his Christian name. . . .

He sometimes came to the private school kept by Miss Jane Whiting, which his own children attended, and heard us read. We did not do much

studying at this delightful school, but we were given many exercises in dicta-
tion and read several hours daily, principally *Marmion, Lady of the Lake*,
and *Lay of the Last Minstrel*. One auspicious morning Mr. Emerson told us
of the aged Wordsworth whom he had seen upon both his visits to England.
He described his little home nestled under Rydal Mount and by the side of
Rydal Water, how they walked together on the high ridge behind the house,
and the poet pointed out the trees he had planted and the walk in which he
had composed thousands of his verses. He hoped when we were older we
should enjoy reading this aged poet as we then enjoyed *Marmion* and he
was not sure but he knew some of his verses we might like, young though we
were. Then throwing back his head in a manner I afterwards learned to associate with any occasions where he felt great pleasure, he began:

> Three years she grew in sun and shower
> Then nature said, 'A lovelier flower
> On earth was never sown;
> This child I to myself will take
> She shall be mine, and I will make a lady of my own.'

Anyone who has heard Mr. Emerson read poetry he liked will know how
these lines fell upon our impressionable ears. I formed then the opinion . . .
that considered as an instrument Mr. Emerson's voice was as nearly perfect
as human limitations allow. In such reading it was not so much voice as
rhythmical pulsations of ordered thought. I . . . cannot be definite as to the
number of verses he read, but after . . . he stopped [, no] sound excepting
long breath-like sighs broke the silence until one of the children piped up,
"Is that all, Mr. Emerson?"

And now that they are all gone into the world of light, Hawthorne, Thoreau, Louisa and Bronson Alcott . . . and Mr. Emerson himself, what can I
say but hail and farewell! For while this light and trifling resume of a child's
recollections presents only the familiar domestic side of their natures, you
must not forget that there is another point of view! You must not forget that
whimsical, self-centered Henry Thoreau held the hand of old John Brown
when a whole nation shrieked and howled and that dreaming half-awake
Bronson Alcott walked through the blinding snows of many a winter night
to set the shivering bondman safe on his northward way.

And you must try to imagine, too, what it was for sensitive intelligent children to hear that courtly, gentle and charming Mr. Emerson had stood un-

moved amid the hisses and insults of Harvard College and said of their idol Daniel Webster after his 7th of March speech, "Every drop of his blood has eyes that look downward. He knows the heroes of 1776 but cannot see the heroes of 1851 when he meets them in the street. It is not a question of ability, expediency, or even legality. It is a question of sides. How come Daniel Webster on that side?"

And even more powerful in the formation of character than these heroic examples was the daily environment. . . . Concord was perhaps the only town in New England at that time when the house you lived in, the clothes you wore, the servants you did or did not keep were matters of absolutely no importance. It was . . . inconceivable that you should subjugate your life to such trifles . . . when those whom you were taught to respect walked before you in such straight and narrow paths. Realizing this, is it any wonder that the memory of those days is tenderly cherished [by] . . . some who were once children on the green banks of the Concord?

Annie Sawyer Downs, "Mr. Hawthorne, Mr. Thoreau, Miss Alcott, Mr. Emerson, and Me," ed. Walter Harding, *American Heritage*, 30 (December 1978): 103–105.

"The Younger Generation in 1840 from the Diary of a New England Boy"

RICHARD FREDERICK FULLER

> Richard Frederick Fuller, Margaret Fuller's younger brother, was born in Cambridge, Massachusetts, in 1824. After the death of his father, Timothy Fuller, Richard gave up his ambition of entering Harvard and took a job in a dry goods store in Boston. But on his sister's advice, and armed with a letter of introduction from her, he visited Emerson in 1840 to seek his counsel on preparing for his entrance exams to Harvard. Emerson offered to take him under his wing and Richard moved to Concord, where for five months he studied for fourteen hours a day except on those occasions when he walked with Henry Thoreau or Barzillai Frost or recited the classics under Elizabeth Hoar's instruction. The effort paid off, for he was admitted to Harvard by President Josiah Quincy and graduated in 1844. Fuller's account of his stay in Concord provides a rare outside glimpse into Emerson's household of the early 1840s, which at that time included young Waldo, his infant sister Ellen, and Emerson's mother Ruth Haskins Emerson.

I resolved to go to college, and . . . if any efforts of mine could accomplish it, to do this at a very small cost. Margaret gave me a letter to Ralph Waldo Emerson, of Concord, that I might talk my affairs over with him.

This interview is fresh in my mind.

I had small expectations from it; I regarded him as a great man and myself as a little one; I did not expect him to be willing to take a microscope to look at me or my affairs. I was thoroughly astonished when he came in and took me by the hand and with words soft and sweet as music talked with me like a brother. I saw that his gentleness made him great. There was no condescension. He believed in the innate greatness of men and had a prescience to forecast unfolded powers while they yet lay in the unconscious germ. Every sincere person, therefore, interested him, and he, in regard to the capacities common to every human being, already gave them credit for attainments which were far distant in the future.

My dread of the presence of a great man was at once taken away when I saw he almost seemed bashful himself. This was, however, only the demeanor of a perfect sincerity and simplicity, for he had the same confidence in himself which he generously extended to others.

He at once entered into my feeling about mercantile life and my desire for a sphere of activity not only more elevated, but better conformed to conscience. He told me such feelings as mine were shared by many.

One sentence particularly impressed me, as he said of the favored classes in society, with rhythmic sweetness: 'Their bread no longer gives them comfort; their cake is no longer sweet to them.'

I was delighted with my interview and encouraged to prosecute my studies in Concord. Margaret had always liked Concord: not only on account of the deep thinker who had there lighted his 'golden lamp,' but also for other friends, and for the natural beauties of ... that town.

I hired a room in an old unpainted house, and here I lived and studied for five months. . . . I studied fourteen hours a day and only occasionally exercised, when invited to walk by Henry Thoreau or Reverend Mr. Frost. I sometimes felt as if I must give out, but I would then call to mind my object and renew my resolutions. My condition was greatly amended by the sincere kindness of several persons in Concord.

I hesitated to go much to Mr. Emerson's for fear of being burdensome. I felt I had nothing to impart to him and ought not to take up his time. I disdained to make amends for my commons by his good table. But he complained of my not coming to see him; so I feared he might think me not to appreciate his kindness, and when he invited me to come every night to tea I concluded he must like to see me and I would feel free to come often. I did not, however, go to the extent of his invitation.

Mrs. Emerson was in the habit once a week of sending round pies to a good many objects of her benevolence. It was winter and some dozen pies she sent to various quarters were drawn by a boy on a large sled. This regularly stopped at my door with a pie for me. I am sure I was as grateful as any of the pensioners of her bounty and I think it did me as much good as any. It helped the brown bread wonderfully. Mrs. Samuel Hoar also was very mindful of me. . . .

In five months I reviewed my preparatory studies. . . . I did not really expect to get admitted, for it did not seem possible. But I meant to spare no possible effort and leave the event with Providence.

Mr. Emerson's family was quite as much a magnet for me as Mr. [Samuel] Hoar's. If I had been a distinguished person whose hospitality he was returning, Mr. Emerson and his family could not have treated me with more consideration. Though I have often met persons of celebrity at his home or his own personal friends, he never allowed them to cast me into the shade. Nor was his conduct singular toward me in this respect. Such was his admirable courtesy that there seemed to be 'no great and no small' in his presence. His politeness was perfect. No, it was not politeness; for that never could or did attain such entire consideration for all others that persons of different degree in the same society felt perfectly satisfied. This was no labor with Mr. Emerson, but sprang spontaneously from his almost feminine delicacy and refinement. Besides, he not only served his guests, but made them serve him. Men were his books. I could see that clearly, and it often pleased me to notice these books read unconsciously to themselves. Indeed he made them their own enumerators, and as they talked it was a feast to me to watch the interest in his eyes. I could read too by what I saw reflected in his vision.

I was rejoiced when I could sit, as perhaps the disembodied do, an unnoticed observer. I gained much culture in this way.

Emerson did not like old or stale books, dictionaries, or spelling-books. Each of these human books had something piquant and peculiar about it. Generally it was quickly read—often a glance at the title-page and table of contents was enough; and then he wished it closed and needed not to open it again. Too often, however, the book would continue to read and reread itself after it was emeritus. . . .

A delightful remembrance is the fireside-reading by Emerson of his lectures. Elizabeth Hoar used to be there and she acted as chorus; so I had to say nothing, and indeed I had nothing to say. I admired the coruscations of his style. I knew he would teach us to be self-reliant and brave. But beyond a spirit of exhilaration from his intellectual fireworks, shooting like stars from the spheres, what could a boy of my years apprehend of such profound idealism? It did, however, stimulate me to think. He once carried me to a neighboring town to hear him lecture. How different he seemed to me from the men who gathered to listen, but not to understand him! He was like Orion, stalking among the stars of that wintry night, stepping far above their heads.

Although among Emerson admirers, and with gratitude mingling with admiration, I do not claim to be of his school. Indeed I believe he is misjudged by those who fancy he has fitted a system of philosophy to square men's

[18]

minds withal. I find his writing stimulating to thought, but his system no-where.

He was as truly a scholar as any person I have ever known. For he was al-ways learning. You never could tell and you cannot to-day what he will ac-quire next. You think he does not love music, you think there is a music of soul as well as sound, a devotional sphere of which he has no cognizance. But in his development he is protean, and this may be his next shape. Emer-son is an iconoclast; that is his mission.

The idolatry of dead antiquity, the turning back to fall at great men's feet, instead of pressing forward to realize ourselves great lives—with all this he has waged an exterminating war. And who can compute what he has done in this respect as the vanguard of American literature. . . .

I think these considerations are necessary to do justice to Emerson. A sweeter and a truer gentleman never graced our American circles. He is to be thanked for stimulating thought. He is to be followed—by me at least—no further than I find my own convictions agree with his statements.

I must speak yet further of the household of Mr. Emerson. I have already paid a tribute of gratitude to Mrs. Emerson. Her devotional spirit has found much quickening in the thoughts of Swedenborg; but she was not alone and merely an æsthetic Christian, for the warm fountain of charity welled gener-ously in her bosom and flowed abroad in rills of beneficence.

Well I remember, too, the dignified and matronly Madame Emerson, Mr. Emerson's mother. No gift of her son could make her gentle graces for-gotten; and none more than he kept them in thoughtful remembrance. Two children of his household attracted my frequent observation. Waldo, a lovely boy of six or eight years, made an impression on me which time has not ef-faced. He was singularly grave and dignified in his bearing and like an angel in his thoughts—a child angel, to be sure, inquiring with a child's eye into the things of life. Henry Thoreau . . . especially interested him by little feats of mechanic invention.

Waldo had a pure unconsciousness of the sins and sorrows of earth. He made once inquiries as to death and the grave which it seemed hard to an-swer to such unsullied thought as his. His gentle brow, pure as that of a ser-aph, we were not willing to trouble with the realities of this lower world. But his intelligence in its germ was grave and inquisitive, and the endeavor to present things in a suitable light to him disclosed our own need. This gentle boy was tenderly loved, but his singular childish dignity rather restrained affection from the usual caresses. His fair form was seen among us a little while and 'he was not, for God took him.'

I hardly dared enter their home after this unexpected stroke. What could I say to relieve, and dared I intrude upon such sorrow? I, however, received a note from Elizabeth Hoar, mentioning the time when 'they would lay the little statue away,' and I attended. . . .

I underwent my examinations with small expectations of success. But the way appeared to have been smoothed for me and I suspected my Concord friends of having spoken a good word. . . . At any rate, my . . . labors were brought to a close by success and to my astonishment, when I went to the President's to learn the result, the only fault found with me was that I did not pronounce Latin correctly!

Richard Frederick Fuller, "The Younger Generation in 1840 from the Diary of a New England Boy," ed. Margaret Fuller Marquand, *Atlantic Monthly Magazine*, 36 (August 1925): 218–22.

[At Concord with the Emersons in 1842]

[MARGARET FULLER]

Margaret Fuller was one of the most important women in Emerson's life. They had heard about each other through mutual friends, and they shared a desire to meet. This was fulfilled when she spent three weeks visiting him in Concord in the summer of 1836. Although Emerson was at first put off by Fuller's physical mannerisms, he soon praised her intelligence, though he was (and always remained) bothered by what he considered her egotism. Fuller became a regular attendant at the meetings of the Transcendental Club, the closest thing the movement had to a social center, and she served as the first editor of the *Dial* from 1840 to 1842, which also brought her into regular contact with Emerson, one of the magazine's major contributors. Their relationship soon became an awkward one, for Fuller had expected a lowering of Emerson's traditional reserve as they saw each other more often and worked together on the *Dial* more closely, and he did not comply. For his part, Emerson was both fascinated and repelled by Fuller, an intellectually stimulating companion who also wanted an emotional as well as a mental relationship.

Although Fuller began to accept Emerson's position by 1840 (as in the famous scene at the dining table in this selection demonstrates), she joined with two other young women, Caroline Sturgis Tappan and Anna Hazard Barker Ward, in continuing to try to draw Emerson out about issues such as marriage and friendship over the next few years, and some of the group's correspondence was incorporated into Emerson's writings. She moved to New York in 1844, published a narrative of her trip to the Midwest as *Summer on the Lakes in 1843*, served as a literary and cultural critic for the *New-York Daily Tribune*, wrote her feminist masterpiece *Woman in the Nineteenth Century* (1845), collected her reviews as *Papers on Literature and Art* (1846), and left for Europe in 1846. While there, Fuller served in the Roman Revolution of 1848 as a nurse, where she met and later probably married Giovanni Ossoli, by whom she had a son. The family perished by drowning when their ship went down off Fire Island, New York, in 1850 as they were returning from Europe. After her death, Emerson joined William Henry Channing and James Freeman Clarke in editing *Memoirs of Margaret Fuller Ossoli* (1852), in which they created a "Margaret Fuller" more consistent with their views of what constituted a traditional nine-

(*continued*)

teenth-century woman. The excerpts from Fuller's journal, describing a stay with the Emerson family in Concord for five weeks in the summer of 1842, is perhaps the finest depiction of the Emerson household written by an outsider we have for this period.

Waldo & I went to walk to Walden pond, as usual, & staid till near sunset on the water's brink beneath the pines. It was a very lovely afternoon, great happy clouds floating, a light breeze rippling the water to our feet: it was altogether sweet, and not out of memory, as is too often the case between us, but from the present moment & to be remembered. We go but very little way on our topics, just touch & taste and leave the cup not visibly shallower. Waldo said once his were short flights from bough to bough, & so it is not up into the blue. I feel more at home with him constantly, but we do not act powerfully on one another. He is a much better companion than formerly, for once he would talk obstinately through the walk, but now we can be silent and see things together. We talked on the subject of his late letter, the threatenings of the time which come to so little, and of some individual cases where Sorrow is still the word, of those who began with such high resolve. Too high I said, & W. agreed. We spoke of the prayer of a friend Lord use me only for high purposes, no mean ones.—We must not dictate to the spirit. . . .

Friday [19 August 1842]. In the evening I took a walk with W. Looking at the moon in the river he said the same thing as in his letter, how each twinkling light breaking there summons to demand the whole secret, and how "promising, promising nature never fulfils what she thus gives us a right to expect." I said I never could meet him here, the beauty does not stimulate me to ask *why?*, and press to the centre, I was satisfied for the moment, full as if my existence was filled out, for nature had said the very word that was lying in my heart. Then we had an excellent talk: We agreed that my god was love, his truth. W. said that these statements alternate, of course, in every mind, the only difference was in which you were most at home, that he liked the pure mathematics of the thing. . . .

[1 September.] This golden afternoon I walked with Waldo to the hemlocks. There we sat down and staid till near sunset. He read me verses.—

[22]

Dichtung und Wahrheit is certainly the name for his life, for he does not care for facts, except so far as the immortal essence can be distilled from them. He has little sympathy with mere life: does not seem to see the plants grow, merely that he may rejoice in their energy.

We got to talking, as we almost always do, on Man and Woman, and Marriage.—W. took his usual ground. Love is only phenomenal, a contrivance of nature, in her circular motion. Man, in proportion as he is completely unfolded is man and woman by turns. The soul knows nothing of marriage, in the sense of a permanent union between two personal existences. The soul is married to each new thought as it enters into it. If this thought puts on the form of man or woman, if it last you seventy years, what then? There is but one love, that for the Soul of all Souls, let it put on what cunning disguises it will, still at last you find yourself lonely,—*the Soul.*

There seems to be no end to these conversations: they always leave us both where they found us, but we enjoy them, for we often get a good expression.

Waldo said "Ask any woman whether her aim in this union is to further the genius of her husband; and she will say yes, but her conduct will always be to claim a devotion day by day that will be injurious to him, if he yields." "Those who hold their heads highest," quoth he, with a satirical side glance, "would do no better, if they were tried." I made no reply, for it is not worthwhile to, in such cases, by *words.*

[2 September.] It is a most brilliant day, & I stole the morning from my writing to take Lidian and then Mamma to ride. L. has had a slow fever which has confined her to her chamber almost ever since I came, & I have not been attentive to her as I should have been, if I had thought she cared about it. I did not go into her room at all for a day or two, simply because I was engaged all the time and kept expecting to see her down stairs. When I *did* go in, she burst into tears, at sight of me, but laid the blame on her nerves, having taken opium &c. I felt embarrassed, & did not know whether I ought to stay or go. Presently she said something which made me suppose she thought W. passed the evenings in talking with me, & a painful feeling flashed across me, such as I have not had, all has seemed so perfectly understood between us. I said that I was with Ellery [Channing] or H[enry]. T[horeau]. both of the evenings & that W. was writing in the study.

I thought it all over a little, whether I was considerate enough. As to W. I never keep him from any such duties, any more than a book would.—He lives in his own way, & he dont soothe the illness, or morbid feelings of a friend, because he would not wish any one to do it *for him*. It is useless to expect it; what does it signify whether he is with me or at his writing. L. knows perfectly well, that he has no regard for me or any one that would make him wish to be with me, a minute longer than I could fill up the time with thoughts.

As to my being more his companion that cannot be helped, his life is in the intellect not the affections. He has affection for me, but it is because I quicken his intellect.—I dismissed it all, as a mere sick moment of L's.

Yesterday she said to me, at dinner, I have not yet been out, will you be my guide for a little walk this afternoon. I said "I am engaged to walk with Mr E. but"—(I was going to say, I will walk with you first,) when L. burst into tears. The family were all present, they looked at their plates. Waldo looked on the ground, but soft & serene as ever. I said "My dear Lidian, certainly I will go with you." "No!" she said "I do not want you to make any sacrifice, but I do feel perfectly desolate, and forlorn, and I thought if I once got out, the fresh air would do me good, and that with you, I should have courage, but go with Mr E. I will not go."

I hardly knew what to say, but I insisted on going with her, & then she insisted on going so that I might return in time for my other walk. Waldo said not a word: he retained his sweetness of look, but never offered to do the least thing. I can never admire him enough at such times; he is so true to himself. In our walk and during our ride this morning L. talked so fully that I felt reassured except that I think she will always have these pains, because she has always a lurking hope that Waldo's character will alter, and that he will be capable of an intimate union; now I feel convinced that it will never be more perfect between them two. I do not believe it will be less: for he is sorely troubled by imperfections in the tie, because he dont believe in any thing better.—And where he loved her first, he loves her always. Then the influence of any one with him would be just in proportion to independence of him, combined with pure love of him for his own sake. Yet in reply to all L. said, I would not but own that though I thought it was the only way, to take him for what he is, as he wishes to be taken, and though my experience of him has been, for that very reason, so precious to me, I dont know that I could have fortitude for it in a more intimate relation. Yet nothing could be nobler, nor more consoling than to be his wife, if one's mind were only thoroughly made up to the truth.—As for myself, if I have not done as much as I ought for L. it is that her magnanimity has led her to deceive me. I have really thought that she was happy to have me in the house solely for Waldo's sake, and my own, and she is, I know, in the long account, but there are pains of every day which I am apt to neglect for others as for myself.—But Truth, spotless Truth, and Prayer and Love shall yield a talisman to teach me how to steer.

I suppose the whole amount of the feeling is that women cant bear to be left out of the question. And they dont see the whole truth about one like me, if they did they would understand why the brow of Muse or Priestess must wear a shade of sadness. On my side I dont remember them enough. They have so much that I have not, I cant conceive of their wishing for what I have. (*enjoying* is not the word: these I know are too generous for that) But when Waldo's wife, & the mother of that child that is gone thinks me the most privileged of women, & that E[lizabeth]. H[oar]. was happy because her love was snatched away for a life long separation, & thus she can know none but ideal love: it does seem a little too insulting at first blush.—And yet they are not altogether wrong. . . .

Aft[ernoon]. Waldo came into my room to read me what he has written in his journal about marriage, & we had a long talk. He listens with a soft wistful look to what I say, but is nowise convinced. It was late in a dark afternoon, the fine light in that red room always so rich, cast a beautiful light upon him, as he read and talked. *Since* I have found in his journal two sentences that represent the two sides of his thought.

In time, "Marriage should be a covenant to secure to either party the sweetness and the handsomeness of being a calm continuing inevitable benefactor to the other."

In eternity, "Is it not enough that souls should meet in a law, in a thought, obey the same love, demonstrate the same idea. These alone are the nuptials of minds. I marry you for better, not for worse, I marry impersonally."

I shall write to him about it. . . .

Waldo had got through with his tedious prose, & to day he got into the mood to finish his poem. Just at night he came into the red room to read the passage he had inserted. This is to me the loveliest way to live that we have. I wish it would be so always that I could live in the red room, & Waldo be stimulated by the fine days to write poems & come the rainy days to read them to me. My time to go to him is late in the evening. Then I go knock at the library door, & we have our long word walk through the growths of things with glimmers of light from the causes of things. Afterward, W. goes out & walks beneath the stars to compose himself for his pillow, & I open the window, & sit in the great red chair to watch them. . . .

He has put more of himself into Saadi and the other poem Masque than in any thing he has written before. On

> "yet it doth not seem to rue
> That the high gods love tragedy"

His voice was beautiful.

He seems indeed to have entirely dismissed the other province. Whenever in his journal he speaks of his peculiar character & limitations he has written in the margin "*Accept*," and Saadi is one acceptance throughout.

Late in the evening, he came in again, to read me some lines he had been adding. When he had done he asked me how I got such a cold. I could not but laugh then to see that grief was the *last* thing Saadi ever thought of, and I told him Lidian had been making me cry. "What" said he "my boy"? I told him afterward how I was affected for I did not wish him to think it was all for the child's sake, but I dont know that I did well for Saadi the joygiver walked in deep shadow for one or two days after. . . .

Saturday [24 September]. . . . In the evening, Waldo & I . . . took a long moonlight walk. I cant think about what passed all the time. I have only an indefinite recollection of the moonlight & the river. We were more truly together than usual.

Sunday [25 September]. All this morning I spent in reading W's journals for the last year, or rather in finishing them, for I have had them by me for weeks. This afternoon I meant to have gone into the woods . . . but I went into the library after dinner & staid till night: it was our last talk and my best. We talked over many things in the journal, especially a good lead was given by "Sickness is generally the coat in which genius is drest," an unusual remark for W.—We talked too of Bulwer & the people of talent,—W grows more merciful day by day. I ought to go away now these last days I have been fairly intoxicated with his mind. I am not in full possession of my own. I feel faint in the presence of too strong a fragrance. I think, too, he will be glad to get rid of me. . . . Farewell, dearest friend, there has been dissonance between us, & may be again, for we do not fully meet, and to me you are too much & too little by turns, yet thanks be to the Parent of Souls, that gave us to be born into the same age and the same country and to meet with so much nobleness and sweetness as we do, & I think constantly with more and more.

Joel Myerson, "Margaret Fuller's 1842 Journal: At Concord with the Emersons," *Harvard Library Bulletin*, 21(July 1973): 323–24, 330–32, 335, 338–39, 340.

[A Visit from Emerson in 1847]

Jane Welsh Carlyle and Thomas Carlyle

After reading several seminal essays on German idealism and history published in the *Edinburgh Review* in the late 1820s and early 1830s, Emerson instinctively knew that their author was appealing to a generation, in America and abroad, bristling under the confinement of tradition and rationalist thought. When he finally met Thomas Carlyle and his wife Jane Welsh Carlyle and spent an entire night talking with them at Craigenputtoch, their farm near Glasgow, Scotland, in 1833, Emerson believed that he had found a kindred spirit in Carlyle and a sympathetic listener in his wife. On returning to America, he began what would be a lifelong correspondence with Carlyle, and he arranged for the American publication of many of Carlyle's books at terms advantageous to his friend. When Alexander Ireland arranged for him to make an extended lecture tour of the British Isles in 1847 and 1848, Emerson looked forward to the occasion the tour would provide to renew his contact with Carlyle and reconcile in person some of their diverging ideas and opinions.

For much of the 1840s, while Emerson continued to promote his distinctive brand of idealism in lectures and essays, Carlyle had moved progressively away from the idealism of his early years to espouse rationalism, an appreciation of factual history, and an increasingly conservative political bias with respect to democracy and social reform. The two met several times in London, but as Jane Welsh Carlyle's letters to Lady Harriet Baring and William Edward Foster and Carlyle's own letter to Lady Baring printed here suggest, Emerson and the Carlyles had grown far apart. Whereas in 1833 Carlyle could write, "The visit of Emerson from Concord, and our quiet night of clear fine talk, was . . . very pretty to both of us" (*Reminiscences*, ed. James Anthony Froude [New York: Harpers, 1881], p. 245), in 1847 his characterization of Emerson as "proud," intellectually "*elevated* but without *breadth*," and possessing a "delicate, but thin pinched triangular face, no jaws nor lips, lean hook-nose," and the "face of a *cock*" was nothing short of nasty. Although Carlyle and Emerson continued to correspond and support each other's reputations in their respective countries after these visits, the fervor of their earlier relations was gone. And as for his wife, by the late 1840s Jane Welsh Carlyle had become so contemptuous of Emerson that she could not stand to be in the same room with him. In his *Lit-*

(*continued*)

erary Recollections and Sketches (1893),[†] Francis Espinasse explains she disliked Emerson's ethics and what she took as his gross sensuality. He gives as an example one of Emerson's lectures in which he is reported to have said, "in his high-flown optimistic way on the ultimate triumph of good over evil," that even "when in a certain haunt of sensual vice, unmentionable to ears polite (though Emerson called it by its plain English name), man is still tending upwards." While Espinasse comments that "Mrs. Carlyle's moral indignation at this statement knew no bounds," he suspected her real disagreement with Emerson originated in a "certain wife-like jealousy [of him], as a sort of rival of her husband."

Jane Welsh Carlyle to Lady Harriet Baring, 28 October 1847

"Dearest" Lady

. . . . He is come then,—is here this Yankee-Seraph! We have seen him "face to face and (over-) soul to (over-) soul"! for two days I have lived on the *manna* of his speech, and now I have escaped to my bedroom to *bathe my head* in *cold* water, and report progress to *you*.

So far, all has gone better than . . . predicted; they do not *hate* one another *yet*; C still calls Emerson "a most polite and gentle creature! a man of really quite *Seraphic* nature! tho' on certain sides of him overlaid with mad rubbish"—and Emerson still (in confidence, to me) calls C "a good Child(!) in spite of all his deification of *the Positive, the Practical*—most astonishing for those who had first made acquaintance with him in his *Books*"!

Polite and *Gentle*, this Emerson certainly *is*; he avoids with a laudable tact, all occasions of dispute, and when dragged into it, by the hair of his head, (morally speaking) he *gives*, under the most provoking contradictions, with the softness of a feather-bed.

For the rest; I hardly know what to think of him, or whether I like him or not. The man has *two* faces to begin with which are continually changing into one another like '*dissolving views*,' the one young, refined, almost beautiful, radiant with—what shall I say?—"*virtue its own reward*"! the other decidedly old, hatchet-like, crotchety, inconclusive—like an incarnation of one of his own *poems*! In his speech he is not dogmatical the least in the world, nor anything like so *fantastical* as his letters give one to suppose; in fact; ex-

[29]

cept for a few phrases consisting chiefly of odd applications, of the words *'beauty'* and *'child'*; he speaks simply and clearly, but without any eloquence or warmth—What I should say he failed in is what the Yorkshire wool-cleaner called 'natur'—He is *genial*, but it seems to be with his *head* rather than his *heart*—a sort of theoretic geniality that (as Mazzini would say) "leaves me *cold*." He is perhaps the most *elevated* man I ever saw—but it is the elevation of a *reed*—run all to hight without taking breadth along with it. You will not I think dislike him as you expected, but neither will you like him—He is to breakfast with Rogers tomorrow morning under the escort of *Mrs* Bancroft, and goes to Liverpool I believe tomorrow night, to lecture "*all about*"—When he returns to London, as a Lecturer, I fancy he will go into Lodgings—

I am sure C. is *disappointed*, thinks him, if he would "tell the truth, and shame the Devil" a man of no sort of significance—but he is still under the restraining grace of Hospitality, and of a *certain* regard to consistency: besides he has had no opportunity of unbosoming himself to me on the subject, as we have literally not been *five minutes* alone together since Emerson arrived: he (Emerson) sits up after me at nights and is down before me in the mornings, till I begin to feel as if I had got the measles or some such thing.
. . .

Jane Welsh Carlyle to William Edward Foster, 28 October 1847

Dear William
. . . Emerson is here has been here since Monday night I have seen him "face to face & (over-) soul to (over-) soul" & (I may just as well "speak the truth & chance the Devil) I do *not* like him the least bit! C. says he is a "most polite & gentle creature—a man really of a quite *seraphic* nature"; & all that may be true, at all rates C has good cause to say it; for Emerson with a tact as laudable as prudent avoids all occasions of dispute, & when dragged into it, by the hair of his head, so to speak he receives the most provoking contradictions with the softness of a feather-bed—*gives* under them for the moment & so, no "dreadful collision" takes place, such as I was looking for. But with his *politeness* & tolerance, *my* approbation ends. The man has no "*natur*" about him, his geniality is of the *head* not the *heart*—a theoretic systematic geniality that (as Mazzini would say) "leaves me *cold*" In fact you can get no *hold* of him—nor yet feel *held* by him—his is neither *impressive* nor *impressionable* a sort of man I cannot get on with, *that*! His very face is *two* or

[30]

rather ½ a dozen faces! that change into one another like *"dissolving views,"* he has one face—young refined almost beautiful, radiant with *"virtue its own reward"* and another that is old hatchet-like; A crotchety, inclusive, like an incarnation of one of his own poems. Whever way you take him he slips thro' your fingers, "like water that cannot be gathered["]—fine pure spring water, but water all the same C. & he will end I predict in disliking one another pretty well tho' C. under the first restraining grace of hospitality & *a certain* regard to consistency makes the best of him as yet, altho' the other (in confidence with me) calls C. "a good child(!) in spite of his love of *the positive*, the *practical*, wh must be very astonishing to all who have learnt to know him thro' his Books." very astonishing indeed thou Americain *Seraph*! & you will find many things to astonish you on this side the atlantic "I guess"!—I never saw better come of men who wait upon what is called *elevation. y*r *elevated* man *par excellence* is always, as far as my experience goes a sort of moral *reed*—has run all to hight without taking breadth along with him—Oh give me *Naetur Natur*! nobody is loveable without *that*; however he may "strike the stars with his sublime head"—nor turns to any good practical acct—I am rather satisfied that he is going away tomorrow night to commence his orations in the north—He will return to London when the town fills, to lecture here—but *then* I fancy he will go into *lodgings*—I hope you will decide for London; if it can be done without hurt to yourself, what a blessing you would be to *me*! Verily I feel quite SCHWESTERLICH [sisterly] towards you. That journey into Yorkshire was a modern version of Saul going out to meet his Father's asses & finding a Kingdom. I went to seek the *picturesque* & found *you*—& catch me losing you again!—Dear W*m* Edw*d* you are worth a cartload of Emersons & so God bless you with *calm & * all good things. . . .

Thomas Carlyle to Lady Harriet Baring, 3 November 1847

. . . Emerson went on Friday night last; I was torn to pieces talking with him; for his sad Yankee rule seemed to be, That talk should go on incessantly except when sleep interrupted it: a frightful rule. The man, as you have heard, is not above bargain;—nor, if one will be candid, is he fairly much below it. A pure-minded elevated man; *elevated* but without *breadth*, as a willow is, as a reed is; no fruit at all to be gathered from him. A delicate, but thin pinched triangular face, no jaws nor lips, lean hook-nose; face of a *cock*: by none such was the Thames ever burnt! A proud man too; a certain sensitive fastidious *stickishness,* which reminded me of a miniature Washington's; very exotic, tho' Anglosaxon enough; rather curious to think of. No getting into any intimacy with him, talk as you will. You have my leave to fall in love with him if you can!—And so he plays his part: gone to lecture in Lancashire; to return hither he knows not when:—it is privately hoped he may go to Rome! I wish him honestly well, do as I am bound respect him honestly; but *Friends,* it is clear, we can never in this world, to any real purpose, be. . . .

The Collected Letters of Thomas and Jane Welsh Carlyle, Duke-Edinburgh Edition, ed. Clyde de L. Ryals, Kenneth J. Fielding, et al. (Durham, N.C., and London: Duke University Press, 1995), 22:139–44.

"Emerson as a Lecturer" (1849)

ANONYMOUS

This anonymous account in the *Boston Post* is of Emerson's lecture on "The Re-lation of Intellect to Natural Science," part of his *Mind and Manners of the Nine-teenth Century* series. While the *Post*'s reporter had problems with the lecture's content, he was pleased with the lecturer's performance. Other papers were not as impressed: the *Boston Daily Evening Transcript* reprinted the *Post*'s ac-count, stating that "the brilliant description is itself an exemplification of thing described," and the *New-York Tribune* published a satirical account of Emerson depicting him swinging in an inverted rainbow (see *Later Lectures*, 1:153).

We listened to Mr. Ralph Waldo Emerson's second lecture on Monday eve-ning, as we always listen to him, with admiration and delight. Yet it is quite out of character to say Mr. Emerson lectures—he does no such thing. He drops nectar—he chips out sparks—he exhales odors—he lets off mental skyrockets and fireworks—he spouts fire, and conjurer like, draws ribbons out of his mouth. He smokes, he sparkles, he improvises, he shouts, he sings, he explodes like a bundle of crackers, he goes off in fiery eruptions like a volcano, but he does not *lecture*.

No mere description can do Mr. Emerson justice. We think he is improv-ing *in his line*, and every body knows, or ought to know, what that line is, for he is, doubtless, one of the most remarkable men of the day. He is the tallest kind of "corn." He exhibited on Monday evening a wealth of imagination, an opulence of imagery, and of original and peculiar thought which amounted to a surfeit. He went swiftly over the ground of knowledge with a Damascus blade, severing every thing from its bottom, leaving one in doubt whether any thing would ever grow again. Yet he seems as innocent as a little child who goes into a garden and pulls up a whole bed of violets, laughs over their beauty, and throws them down again. So that, after all, we are inclined to think no great harm has been done. He comes and goes like a spirit of whom one just hears the rustle of his wings. He is a vitalized speculation—a talking essence—a sort of celestial emanation—a bit of transparency broken from the spheres—a spiritual prism through which we see all beautiful rays of immaterial existences. His leaping fancy mounts upward like an India rubber ball, and drifts and falls like a snow-flake or a feather. He moves in the regions of similitudes. He comes through the air like a cherubim with a golden trumpet in his mouth, out of which he blows tropes and figures and gossamer transparencies of suggestive fancies. He takes high flights, and sustains himself without ruffling a feather. He inverts the rainbow and uses it for a swing—now sweeping the earth, and now clapping his hands among the stars.

We wonder if he will ever die like other men? It seems to us he will find some way of slipping out of the world and shutting the door behind him before any body knows he is going. We cannot believe he will be *translated*, for this would be too gross a method of exit. He is more likely to be evaporated some sunshiny day, or to be exhaled like a perfume. He will certainly not be seen to go—he will only *vanish*.

Boston Post, 25 January 1849, p. 2.

[Letter to Evert A. Duyckinck about Emerson as a Lecturer] (1849)

HERMAN MELVILLE

Herman Melville first heard Emerson lecture in 1849 and read many of his works. While he appreciated Emerson's Platonism and sense of the correspondences that existed among things, he eventually became disturbed by the optimistic strain that Emerson had toward the natural world, which Melville did not share, believing that nature was at best indifferent toward humankind's activities and strivings. In later years Melville became even more exasperated by Emerson, feeling that his overly positive view of the world resulted from a lack of experience in it, and he satirized him as Mark Winsome in *The Confidence-Man* (1857). Melville's comment that "I do not oscillate in Emerson's rainbow" refers to a satirical account published in the *New-York Tribune* depicting Emerson swinging in an inverted rainbow (see *Later Lectures*, 1:153). Melville must have been accused of following Emerson by his correspondent, Evert A. Duyckinck, a literary anthologist and editor of the *Literary World*.

Herman Melville to Evert A. Duyckinck, 3 March 1849

Nay, I do not oscillate in Emerson's rainbow, but prefer rather to hang myself in mine own halter than swing in any other man's swing. Yet I think Emerson is more than a brilliant fellow. Be his stuff begged, borrowed, or stolen, or of his own domestic manufacture he is an uncommon man. Swear he is a humbug—then is he no common humbug. Lay it down that had not Sir Thomas Browne lived, Emerson would not have mystified—I will answer, that had not Old Zack's [Zachary Taylor] father begot him, Old Zack would never have been the hero of Palo Alto. The truth is that we are all sons, grandsons, or nephews or great-nephews of those who go before us. No one is his own sire.—I was very agreeably disappointed in Mr Emerson. I had heard of him as full of transcendentalisms, myths & oracular gibberish; I had only glanced at a book of his once in Putnam's store—that was all I knew of him, till I heard him lecture.—To my surprise, I found him quite intelligi-

ble, tho' to say truth, they told me that that night he was unusually plain.—
Now, there is a something about every man elevated above mediocrity,
which is, for the most part, instinctively perceptible. This I see in Mr Emerson. And, frankly, for the sake of the argument, let us call him a fool;—then
had I rather be a fool than a wise man.—I love all men who *dive*. Any fish can
swim near the surface, but it takes a great whale to go down stairs five miles
or more; & if he dont attain the bottom, why, all the lead in Galena can't
fashion the plummet that will. I'm not talking of Mr Emerson now—but of
the whole corps of thought-divers, that have been diving & coming up again
with blood-shot eyes since the world began.

I could readily see in Emerson, notwithstanding his merit, a gaping flaw. It
was, the insinuation, that had he lived in those days when the world was
made, he might have offered some valuable suggestions. These men are all
cracked right across the brow. And never will the pullers-down be able to
cope with the builders-up. And this pulling down is easy enough—a keg of
powder blew up Brock's Monument—but the man who applied the match,
could not, alone, build such a pile to save his soul from the shark-maw of the
Devil. But enough of this Plato who talks thro' his nose. To one of your habits of thought, I confess that in my last, I seemed, but only *seemed* irreverent.
And do not think, my boy, that because I, impulsively broke forth in jubilla-
tions over Shakspeare, that, therefore, I am of the number of the *snobs* who
burn their tuns of rancid fat at his shrine. No, I would stand afar off & alone,
& burn some pure Palm oil, the product of some overtopping trunk.

—I would to God Shakspeare had lived later, & promenaded in Broad-
way. Not that I might have had the pleasure of leaving my card for him at the
Astor, or made merry with him over a bowl of the fine Duyckinck punch; but
that the muzzle which all men wore on their souls in the Elizebethan day,
might not have intercepted Shakspeare's full articulations. For I hold it a ver-
ity, that even Shakspeare, was not a frank man to the uttermost. And, indeed,
who in this intolerant Universe is, or can be? But the Declaration of Independence makes a difference.—There, I have driven my horse so hard that I
have made my inn before sundown. I was going to say something more—It
was this.—You complain that Emerson tho' a denizen of the land of ginger-
bread, is above munching a plain cake in company of jolly fellows, & swiging
off his ale like you & me. Ah, my dear sir, that's his misfortune, not his fault.
His belly, sir, is in his chest, & his brains descend down into his neck, &

offer an obstacle to a draught of ale or a mouthful of cake. But here I am. Good bye—

Letter of 3 March 1849 to Evert A. Duyckinck, *The Correspondence of Herman Melville*, ed. Lynn Horth (Evanston, Ill.: Northwestern University Press, 1993), pp. 121–22.

From *The Homes of the New World;*
Impressions of America (1853)

FREDRIKA BREMER

Born in Finland, novelist Fredrika Bremer spent most of her life in Sweden. She visited America in the late 1840s and early 1850s, and her very popular book, *The Homes of the New World; Impressions of America*, in which she mingled common gossip and "Old World" prejudices with extended commentary on American culture at midcentury, is among the best produced in the genre during this period. Like John Ross Dix's *Transatlantic Tracings; or, Sketches of Persons and Scenes in America* (1853), Bremer's treatment of America was appealing to both European and American readers, and especially so given her access to all the major literary and intellectual figures of the day. In the selections that follow, Bremer humanizes Emerson for her international audience, providing glimpses into his home life, the "griefs" he sustained in the loss of his brothers Edward and Charles and young son Waldo, his relationships with the leading lights of Boston and New York, and the sources of his immense popularity as a writer and lecturer. Bremer's admiration of Emerson is measured at times; however, she openly grants to his credit an unusual consistency between his public and private lives, as when, for instance, after hearing him lecture on "The Spirit of the Times," she remarks, "I do not . . . think him more remarkable as [a lecturer in public] than during a private conversation on some subject of deep interest. There is the same deep, strong, and at the same time melodious . . . tone; the same . . . happy phraseology, naturally brilliant; the same calm and reposing strength" (p. 224).

Since most passages in *The Homes of the New World* are undated, in the excerpts that follow, dates have been editorially supplied from *America of the Fifties: Letters of Fredrika Bremer*, ed. Adolph B. Benson (New York: American-Scandinavian Foundation, 1924).

[4 December 1849.] Just returned from my little journey . . . to Concord, the oldest town in Massachusetts, and the residence of Ralph Waldo Emerson. We drove there, and arrived in the midst of a regular snow-storm. But the rail-way carriages are well warmed, and one sits there in beautiful ease and comfort, excepting that one gets well shook, for the rail-roads here are much more uneven than those on which I have traveled in Europe.

Emerson came to meet us, walking down the little avenue of spruce firs which leads from his house bare-headed amid the falling snow. He is a quiet, nobly grave figure, his complexion pale, with strongly marked features, and dark hair. He seemed to me a younger man, but not so handsome as I had imagined him; his exterior less fascinating, but more significant. He occupied himself with us, however, and with me in particular, as a lady and a foreigner, kindly and agreeably. He is a very peculiar character, but too cold and hypercritical to please me entirely; a strong, clear eye, always looking out for an ideal, which he never finds realized on earth; discovering wants, shortcomings, imperfections; and too strong and healthy himself to understand other people's weaknesses and sufferings, for he even despises suffering as a weakness unworthy of higher natures. This singularity of character leads one to suppose that he has never been ill: sorrows, however, he has had, and has felt them deeply, as some of his most beautiful poems prove; nevertheless, he has only allowed himself to be bowed for a short time by these griefs—the deaths of two beautiful and beloved brothers, as well as that of a beautiful little boy, his eldest son. He has also lost his first wife, after having been married scarcely a year.

Emerson is now married for the second time, and has three children. His pretty little boy, the youngest of his children, seems to be, in particular, dear to him. Mrs. Emerson has beautiful eyes, full of feeling, but she appears delicate, and is in character very different to her husband. He interested me without warming me. That critical, crystalline, and cold nature may be very estimable, quite healthy, and, in its way, beneficial for those who possess it, and also for others who allow themselves to be measured and criticised by it; but—for me—David's heart with David's songs!

I shall return to this home in consequence of a very kind invitation to do so from Emerson and his wife, and in order that I may see more of this sphinx-like individual....

...I am not sure that I have judged rightly of Emerson. I confess that I was a little staggered by the deprecating manner in which he expressed himself about things and persons whom I admired. I am not certain whether a steadfastness and pride so little akin to my own did not tempt me to act the fox and the grapes. Certain it is that Emerson's behavior and manner made upon me an impression unlike that which other haughty natures produce, and which it is easy for me to condemn as such, or as such to despise. Not so with Emerson; he ought not to be acquitted so easily. He may be unjust or unreasonable, but it certainly is not from selfish motives: there is a higher nature in this man; and I must see more of him, and understand him better. For the rest, this acquaintance may end as it will; I shall be calm. "If we are kindred, we shall meet!" and if not—the time is long since past when I wished very much to please men. . . .

[22 January 1850.] I must now tell you about Concord, and the sphinx in Concord, Waldo Emerson, because I went to Concord five days ago, attended by—"himself." . . .

. . . [During] the four days that I remained in Emerson's house, I had a real enjoyment in the study of this strong, noble, eagle-like nature. Any near approximation was, as it were, imperfect, because our characters and views are fundamentally dissimilar, and that secret antagonism which exists in me toward him, spite of my admiration, would at times awake, and this easily called forth his icy alp nature, repulsive and chilling. But this is not the original nature of the man; he does not rightly thrive in it, and he gladly throws it off, if he can, and is much happier, as one can see, in a mild and sunny atmosphere, where the natural beauty of his being may breathe freely and expand into blossom, touched by that of others as by a living breeze. I enjoyed the contemplation of him, in his demeanor, his expression, his mode of talking, and his every-day life, as I enjoy contemplating the calm flow of a river bearing along, and between flowery shores, large and small vessels—as I love to see the eagle circling in the clouds, resting upon them and its pinions. In this calm elevation Emerson allows nothing to reach him, neither great nor small; neither prosperity nor adversity.

Pantheistic as Emerson is in his philosophy, in the moral view with which he regards the world and life, he is in a high degree pure, noble, and severe, demanding as much from himself as he demands from others. His words are severe, his judgment often keen and merciless, but his demeanor is alike noble and pleasing, and his voice beautiful. One may quarrel with Emerson's thoughts, with his judgment, but not with himself. That which struck me most, as distinguishing him from most other human beings, is *nobility*. He is a born nobleman. . . .

. . . In proportion as the critical bent of Emerson's mind is strong, and as he finds a great want in human beings, and in things generally—measuring them by his ideal standard, is his faith strong in the power of good, and its ultimate triumph in the arrangement of the world. And he understands perfectly what constitutes noble republicanism and Americanism, and what a nobly-framed community and social intercourse. But the principle, the vitalizing, the strengthening source—yes, that Emerson sees merely in the pure consciousness of man himself! He believes in the original purity and glory of this source, and will cleanse away every thing which impedes or sullies it—all conventionality, untruth, and paltriness.

I said to an amiable woman, a sincere friend of Emerson's, and one who, at the same time, is possessed of a deeply religious mind, "How can you love him so deeply when he does not love nor put faith in the Highest, which we love?" "He is so faultless," replied she; "and then he is lovely!"

Lovable he is, also, as one sees him in his home and amid his domestic relations. But you shall hear more about him when we meet, and you shall see his strong, beautiful head in my album, among many American acquaintance. I feel that my intercourse with him will leave a deep trace in my soul. I could desire in him warmer sympathies, larger interest in such social questions as touch upon the well-being of mankind, and more feeling for the suffering and the sorrow of earth. . . .

[19 February 1850.] Emerson came and remained a good hour with me. He is iron, . . . [yet] his world floats in an element of disintegration, and has no firm, unwavering shapes. Wonderful is it how so powerful and concrete a nature as his can be satisfied with such disintegrated views. I can find fault with Emerson's mode of thought, but I must bow before his spirit and his nature. He was now on his way to New York, where he was invited to give a course of lectures. He has promised, when he returns again, to visit me. I must sometime have a more thorough conversation with him, as well on religious subjects as on the future prospects of America. I feel also a little desire for combat with him; for I never see a lion in human form without feeling my lion-heart beat. And a combat with a spirit like that is always a pleasure even if one wins no victory.

From *The Homes of the New World; Impressions of America*, trans. Mary Howitt, 2 vols. (New York: Harper & Brothers, 1853), 1:117–18, 121–22, 153–56, 175–76.

"Mr. Emerson's Lectures" (1864)

[Franklin Benjamin Sanborn]

Over his long and varied career as a teacher, journalist, social reformer, prolific reporter of Transcendentalism in New England, and biographer of Emerson, Thoreau, Alcott, and others, Franklin Benjamin Sanborn earned immense respect from his contemporaries. Today, however, Sanborn's reputation is mixed at best. For although as a second-generation Transcendentalist he—probably more than anyone else—transmitted the intellectual fervor of the founders of the movement to twentieth-century readers, Sanborn, like Moncure D. Conway, had an unfortunate tendency to rewrite history, and did so always to his own advantage. Emerson acknowledged as much to his daughter Ellen when, following the burning of his house in 1872, he expressed his dread that either Sanborn or Conway should inherit his manuscripts (see Ellen Tucker Emerson to Edith Emerson Forbes, 22 August 1872, *Letters of Ellen Tucker Emerson*, 1:690).

Thus, under most circumstances one has to review at least two or three reports by Sanborn of a particular event in order to construct an account of what actually occurred. In the present case, however, Sanborn's review of Emerson as a lecturer stands on its own. His entire focus is on Emerson, whose lecture series on *American Life* he praises for disrupting the dull routine that lecture series had become in Boston by the mid-1860s. Like many in Emerson's audience, Sanborn is fascinated by and genuinely admires "the quality of what he says, not its volume, or its manner of expression." Treating Emerson as the pride of Boston, he argues that Emerson's substance—his "moral certitude"— re-creates in New England the tradition of Socrates's "Athenian *liturgy*."

The course of lectures on "American Life" which Mr. Emerson is now reading in this city deserves a notice more adequate than we have yet given. We have become so acclimated and inured to lectures and courses of lectures, here in Boston, that we are in some danger of losing our interest in everything called by that name. Do we read the report of a lecture in the *Advertiser* with any more zest than wait upon the daily doings of the "State Valuation Committee," or the unctuous chronicle of "Whalers" on the fourth page?

This indifference ought to be dispelled by the announcement of a new lecture by Mr. Emerson, and so it always is in the minds of the earnest and the thoughtful. On the evening announced, the benches are filled by an audience which in itself is a pleasure and a study. There sit the gray-haired couple, who have listened to every one of his lectures since the music of the young scholar's voice first enchanted them thirty years ago. There, too, are their children and their grandchildren, ... who can scarcely remember when they first heard what is yet constantly new to them, and nevertheless recalls to mind some gracious memory of earlier lessons from the same lips. There is the saintly woman, the adored beauty, the polished gentleman, and beside them the brown-faced farmer, the rustic maiden, and the shy stripling from the Maine woods, to whom a single evening at one of these lectures is the event of the year, perhaps impossible to be repeated. There are always just so many students from Cambridge, and so many fair-faced girls from Boston parlors. And scattered among the audience are always a few strangers, a foreigner or two, a great many clergymen, and reformers.

Of this audience, so various, yet so select and so appreciative, about one-third disappears every two years, ... and their places are filled by new hearers. And so, while they meet like old friends from one course of lectures to another, there is constantly a band of novices, in whom the elders of the company see with joy their own emotions of years ago reproduced and perpetuated. So much that is exalted in character and ardent in aspiration,—so much serene gravity and so much rosy enthusiasm,—assembles nowhere else and on no other occasion in Boston.

If this were a tribute to the lecturer, ... it could not be better deserved. This grave and melodious voice, which has now been heard in Boston for more than a generation ... never uttered an ignoble word, or failed to appeal to high sentiments. It has advocated opinions which were for the moment unpopular, and others about which men will always contend, but all who listened to it were forced to recognize the lofty key which it struck, and to which the moral sentiment in the hearer was sure to respond. Amid a people slow to appreciate what is purely ideal, Mr. Emerson has made the most ideal themes familiar and admired. He, better than any American, verifies his own definition of the Scholar, who "is to resist the vulgar prosperity that retrogrades ever to barbarism, by preserving and communicating heroic sentiments, noble biographies, melodious verse, and the conclusions of history."
. . .

[43]

The charm and the power of Mr. Emerson's lectures is not merely that they "preserve and communicate" the words and thoughts of other men, though for this they are remarkable. His quotations are numerous and apt, and they seem to adorn not only his own subject, but the name of his authority. To be quoted by him is a stamp of renown, and though he will not transmit to memory so many forgotten sayings as Montaigne, they will be sweeter and more enduring. But the secret of his profound influence on the minds of his hearers and the literature of his time, lies in his creative and inspiring genius, combined as it is with a rectitude and simplicity of the moral sense which makes his criticism as decisive as it is searching. "If you are to live near Mr. Emerson," said one of his neighbors, "you might as well be made of glass as any other way." His piercing eye detects every sham and makes disguise useless, whether he is dealing with a person or a form of thought or of society. In many men this would be a dangerous quality; but here it is lodged where it is scarcely susceptible of misuse.

It may seem strange to some of our readers that we speak of the "creative" genius of a man who has produced no great work of the imagination or of the philosophic intellect,—who has founded no system of thought, and organized no institution or association of men. It is true that Mr. Emerson has done none of these things, but none the less is he to be styled original and creative. He has directed his attention to Life rather than to Art, and has presented to his own age with irresistible force and persuasion the problems which it must meet, and the method to be pursued. He has thus acted directly upon the hearts of his hearers and readers, not as the artist works, by representation, or as the man of science by observation and deduction; but rather as Love or Conscience dart their suggestions into the soul. We are not conscious how we were convinced or inspired; it seems, rather, as if we had always cherished the sentiment which glows so warm at the kindling breath of the speaker.

Nothing less than this will account for Mr. Emerson's power over his hearers. Except the tones of his voice, (nor are these greatly varied,) he has few of the graces of an orator. He is neither fluent nor passionate, nor excellent in action. It is the quality of what he says, not its volume, or its manner of expression, which fascinates and is remembered. His style is admirable, to be sure, but no more so than that of many men of far inferior powers. The purity of his English, the salt of his wit, the simple grandeur of his periods, are agreeable accidents of his oratory; but they are only accidents. Its substance is the moral certitude which it expresses, and the immediate flight which it makes to the listener's spirit, like an unseen arrow cleaving the white of the target.

It should be the pride of Boston that she gave this wise poet a birthplace, and for so many years a hearing. She has not always known how to receive what he delivered, and has pouted, or chattered, or shuddered, at some of his winged words. . . .

But now the city is happily more in accord with the words of the speaker. The *Advertiser* and the *Post* vie in their reports of his lectures, and the voice of censure seems to be hushed at last. We are almost sorry to find it so, for as Socrates called himself the gadfly of the Athenians, so has Mr. Emerson performed the same office for his native town. With all the virtues of Boston, she cherishes such vices and prejudices as call for the stern reprehension of the philosopher whose theme is American life. Without bitterness and without complaisance he will surely speak of these things, and we shall not believe the city hears him if she does not give some sign of dissent.

We have heard it intimated that these may be the last lectures which Mr. Emerson will read in Boston. He has long cherished the hope of withdrawing from the active duties of an American scholar, and exchanging the platform for the study. It will be hard to excuse him from the burden of public speaking, which, like the Athenian *liturgy*, is imposed on every man according to his ability. Few have done their part so well as Mr. Emerson. . . .

Boston Commonwealth, 10 December 1864, p. 2.

[Emerson as Seen from the "Editor's Easy Chair" in 1865]

[GEORGE WILLIAM CURTIS]

George William Curtis, author, travel writer, critic, and journalist, knew most of the people of the Transcendentalist period. He and his brother Burrill joined the Brook Farm community in West Roxbury, Massachusetts, in 1842, staying almost a year and a half. Following a brief stint in New York, Curtis joined his brother in Concord, where they spent most of 1844–1846 with a farmer's family. He became one of the editors of *Putnam's Monthly Magazine* when it began in 1852, and the following year he began a series of columns, "Editor's Easy Chair," in *Harper's New Monthly Magazine*, which he continued for many years. Curtis does not conceal his admiration for Emerson the man or his message in this report of "Table-Talk," and he appears unconcerned that Emerson's lectures typically lacked "argument," "description," or "appeal," since their purpose was to impart "wit and wisdom"—often leavened by humor—that "inspired."

Many years ago the Easy Chair—a mere foot-stool in those days—used to hear Ralph Waldo Emerson lecture. Perhaps it was in the small Sunday-school room under a country meeting-house, on sparkling winter nights, when all the neighborhood came stamping and chattering to the door in hood and muffler, or else ringing in from a few miles away, buried under buffalo skins. The little low room was dimly lighted with oil lamps, and the boys clumped about the stoves in their cowhide boots, and laughed and buzzed and ate apples and peanuts and giggled, and grew suddenly solemn when the grave men and women looked at them. In the desk stood the lecturer and read his manuscript, and all but the boys sat silent and enthralled by the musical spell. Some of the hearers remembered the speaker as a boy, as a young man. Some wondered what he was talking about. Some thought him very queer. All laughed at the delightful humor or the illustrative anecdote that beaded for a moment upon the surface of his talk; and some sat inspired with unknown resolves and soaring upon lofty hopes as they heard. A nobler life, a better manhood, a purer purpose, wooed every listening soul. It was not argument, nor description, nor appeal. It was wit and wisdom, and hard sense and poetry, and scholarship and music. And when the words were spoken and the lecturer sat down, the poor little foot-stool sat still and heard the rich cadences lingering in the air, as the young Priest's heart throbs with the long vibrations when the organist has risen.

The same speaker had been heard a few years previously in this Masonic Temple in Boston. It was the fashion among the gay to call him transcendental. When some one said that, he had the air of having said something he understood. It was uttered in the same tone with which certain lovely beings declare that they are not "strong-minded." And, dear lovely beings! was it ever suspected that you were? Grave parents were quoted as saying, "I don't go to hear Mr. Emerson; I don't understand him. But my daughters do." Extinction of the lecturer was supposed by many to have been achieved by that remark. Then came a volume containing the discourses. They were called "Essays." Has our literature produced any wiser or more influential book?

As the lyceum or lecture system extended the philosopher whom "my daughters understood" was called to speak. A simplicity of manner that could be called rustic if it were not of a shy, scholarly elegance; perfect composure, clear, clean, crisp sentences; maxims as full of glittering truth as a winter night sky of stars; an incessant spray of fine fancies like the November shower of meteors; and the same intellectual and moral lift, expansion, and aspiration, were the peculiarity of all his lectures.

He was never exactly popular, but always gave a tone and flavor to the whole course, as the lump of ambergris serves the Sultan for his year's cups of coffee. "We can have him once in three or four seasons," said the Committees. But really they had him all the time without knowing it. It was the philosopher Proteus who spoke through the more popular mouths. The speakers were acceptable because they were liberal, and he was the great liberalizer. They were, and they are, the middle-men between him and the public. They watered the nectar, and made it easy to drink.

The little foot-stool, gradually becoming an Easy Chair, heard from time to time of Proteus on the platform—how he was more and more eccentric—how he could not be understood—how abrupt his manner was; but the Chair did not believe that the flame which had once been so pure could ever be dimmer, especially as he recognized its soft lustre on every aspect of life around him.

And so, after many years, the opportunity to hear him came again; and although the experiment was dangerous the Chair did not hesitate to try it. The hall was pretty and not too large, and the audience was the best that the country could furnish. Every one came solely to hear the speaker, for it was one lecture in a course of his only. It was pleasant to look around and mark the famous men and the accomplished women gathering quietly in the same city where they used to gather to hear him a quarter of a century before. How much the man who was presently to speak had done for their lives, and their children's, and the country! The power of one man is not easily traced in its channels and details, but it is marked upon the whole. The word "Transcendentalism" had long passed by. It has not perhaps gone out of fashion to smile at wisdom as visionary, but this particular wise man had been acquitted of being "understood by my daughters," and there were rows of "hardheads," "practical people," curious and interesting to contemplate in the audience.

The tall figure entered at a side-door, and sat down upon a sofa behind the desk. Age seemed not to have touched him since the evenings in the country Sunday-school room. As he stood at the desk the posture, the figure, the movement, were all unchanged. There was the same rapt introverted glance as he began in a low voice, and for an hour the older tree shook off a ceaseless shower of riper, fairer fruit. The topic was Table-Talk, or Conversation; and the lecture was its own most perfect illustration. It was not a sermon, nor an oration, nor an argument; it was the perfection of talk; the talk of a poet, of a philosopher, of a scholar. Its wit was a rapier, smooth, sharp, incisive, delicate, exquisite. The blade was pure as an icicle. You would have sworn the hilt was diamond. The criticism was humane, lofty, wise, sparkling. The anecdote so choice and apt, and trickling from so many sources, that we seemed to be hearing the best things of the wittiest people. It was altogether delightful, and the audience sat suffused with a warm glow of satisfaction. There was no rhetoric, no oratory, no grimace, no dramatic familiarity and action; but the manner was self-respectful and courteous to the audience, and the tone supremely just and sincere. "He is easily King of us all," whispered one orator to another; and if the Easy Chair had been of the brotherhood how heartily it would have cried Amen!

"Editor's Easy Chair," *Harper's New Monthly Magazine*, 30 (February 1865): 395–96.

"Ralph Waldo Emerson" (1865)

ANONYMOUS

> Not all reviewers appreciated Emerson's performance or his ideas as a lecturer. The New York periodical the *Knickerbocker* had long been an opponent of Transcendentalism in general and Emerson in particular. It reviewed his books negatively, continually grouped him with Thomas Carlyle as examples of bad writing, and kept up a decades-long battle with what it considered the foggy notions originating in Boston. This critical and sarcastic view of "roaring Ralph" manages to say with a great deal of hyperbole and venom that its subject "says nothing."

Of all the public lecturers of our time, and place, none have attracted more attention from the press, and subsequently the people, than Ralph Waldo Emerson. Lecturing has become quite a fashionable science—and now, instead of using the old style phrases for illustrating facts, we call travelling preachers, perambulating show-men, and floating politicians lecturers. As a lecturer, Ralph Waldo Emerson is extensively known around these parts; but whether his lectures come under the head of law, logic, politics, Scripture, or the show business, is a matter of much speculation; for our own part, the more we read or hear of Ralph, the more we don't know what it is all about. Somebody has said that to his singularity of style or expression, Carlyle and his works owe their great notoriety or fame—and many compare Ralph Waldo to old Carlyle. They cannot trace exactly any great affinity between these two great geniuses of the flash literary school. Carlyle writes vigorously, quaintly enough, but almost always speaks when he says something; on the contrary, our flighty friend Ralph speaks vigorously, yet says nothing. Of all men that have ever stood and delivered in presence of a reporter, none surely ever led these indefatigable knights of the pen such a wild-goose chase over the verdant and flowery pastures of King's English as Ralph Waldo Emerson. In ordinary cases, a reporter, well versed in his art, catches a sentence of his speaker, and goes on to fill it out upon the most correct impression of what was intended, or what was implied. But no such license fol-

lows the out-pourings of Mr. Emerson; no thought can fathom his intentions, and quite as bottomless are even his finished sentences. We have
known "old stagers" in the newspaporial line, veteran reporters, so dumb-
founded and confounded by the first fire of Ralph, and his grand and lofty
acrobating in elocution, that they up, seized their hat and paper, and departed, horrified at the prospect of an attempt to "take down" Mr. Emerson.
If roaring Ralph touches a homely mullen weed, upon a donkey-heath,
straightway he makes it a full-blown rose, in the land of Ophir, shedding an
odor balmy as the gales of Arabia; while with a facility the wonderful London auctioneer Robbins might envy, Ralph imparts to a lime-box, or pig-sty,
a negro hovel, or an Irish shanty, all the romance, artistic elegance and finish
of a first-class manor-house, or Swiss cottage, inlaid with alabaster and
fresco, surrounded by elfin bowers, grand walks, bee-hives, and honey-suck-
les. Ralph don't group his metaphorical beauties, or dainties of Webster,
Walker, &c., but rushes them out in torrents—rattles them down in cataracts
and avalanches—bewildering, astounding and incomprehensible. He hits
you upon the left lug of your knowledge-box with a metaphor so unwieldy
and original, that your breath is soon gone—and before it is recovered, he
gives you another rhapsody on t'other side, and as you try to steady yourself,
bim! comes another, heavier than the first two, while a fourth batch of this
sort of elocution fetches you a bang over the eyes, giving you a vertigo in the
ribs of your bewildered senses, and before you can say: "God bless us!"
down he has you, presto!—with a deluge of high-heeled grammar and three
storied Anglo-Saxon settling your hash—and brings you to the ground by
the run, as though you were struck by lightning, or in the way of a thirty-six
pounder. Ralph Waldo is death, and an entire *stud* of pale horses on flowery
expressions and japonica-domish flubdubs. He revels in all those knock-
kneed, antique, or crooked and twisted words we used all of us to puzzle our
brains over in the days of our youth, and grammar lessons, and rhetoric exercises. He has a penchant as strong as cheap boarding-house butter, for
mystification, and a free delivery of hard words, perfectly and unequivocally
wonderful. We listened one long hour by the clock, one night, to an out-
pouring of *argumentum ad hominem* of Mr. Emerson's—at what? a boy
under an apple tree! If ten persons out of the five hundred present were put
to their oaths, they could no more have deciphered, or translated Mr.
Ralph's argumentation, than they could the hieroglyphics upon the walls of
Thebes, or the sarcophagus of old king Pharaoh! When Ralph Waldo opens

he may be as calm as a May morn—he may talk for five minutes, like a book—
we mean a common-sensed, understandable book; but all of a sudden the
fluid will strike him—up he goes, down he fetches them. He throws a double
summerset backwards over Asia Minor—flip-flaps in Greece—wings Tur-
key—and skeets over Iceland; here he slips up with a flower garden. A tor-
rent of gilt-edged metaphors, that would last a country parson's moderate
demand a long life-time, are whirled with the fury and fleetness of Jove's
thunderbolts. After exhausting his sweet-scented receiver of this floral elocution, he pauses four seconds; pointing to vacuum, over the heads of his
audience, he asks, in anxious tone, "Do you see that?" Of course the audience are not expected to be so unmannerly as to ask "what?" If they were,
Ralph would not give them time to "go in," for, after asking them if they see
that, he continues—"There! Mark! Note! It is a malaria prism! Now then;
there—here; see it! note it! watch it!" During this time, half of the audience,
especially the old women and children, look around, fearful of the ceiling
falling in, or big bugs lighting on them. But the pause is for a moment, and
anxiety ceases when they learn it was only a false alarm, only "Egotism! The
lame, the pestiferous exhalation or concrete malformation of society!" You
breathe freer, and Ralph goes in, gloves on. "Egotism! a metaphysical, cal-
careous, oleracerous amentum of—society!—the mental varioloid of this
sublunary hemisphere! One of its worst feelings or features is, the craving of
sympathy. It even loves sickness, because actual pain engenders signs of
sympathy. All cultivated men are infected more or less with this dropsy. But
they are still the leaders. The life of a few men is the life of every place. In
Boston you hear and see a few, so in New-York; then you may as well die.
Life is very narrow: bring a few men together, and under the spell of one
calm genius, what frank sad confessions will be made! Culture is the suggestion from a few best thoughts that a man should not be a charlatan, but
temper and subdue life. Culture redresses his balance, and puts him among
his equals. It is a poor compliment always to talk with a man upon his *specialty*, as if he were a cheese-mite, and were therefore strong on Cheshire
and Stilton. Culture takes the grocer out of his molasses and makes him genial. We pay a heavy price for those fancy goods, the fine arts and philosophy. No performance is worth loss of geniality. That unhappy man called of
genius, is an unfortunate man. Nature always carries her point despite the
means!" If that don't convince you of Ralph's high-heeled, knock-kneed
logic, or *au fait* dexterity in concocting flap-doodle mixtures, you're ahead

of ordinary intellect as far as this famed lecturer is in advance of gin and bitters, or opium discourses on—delirium tremens! In short, Ralph Waldo Emerson can wrap up a subject in more mystery and science of language than ever a defunct Egyptian received at the hands of the mummy manufacturers! In person, Mr. Ralph is rather a pleasing sort of man; in manners frank and agreeable. . . . As a lawyer he would have been the 'horror' of jurors and judges; as a lecturer, he is, as near as possible, what we have described him.

"Ralph Waldo Emerson," *Knickerbocker*, 65 (June 1865): 545-47.

From *My Study Windows* (1871)

JAMES RUSSELL LOWELL

As a poet, essayist, and editor of the *Atlantic Monthly* (1857–1861) and the *North American Review* (1863–1872), James Russell Lowell influenced American literary and aesthetic taste for the better part of the nineteenth century. Students of American Transcendentalism have recognized that, while Lowell rejected the mysticism associated with the movement and Emerson's championing of some of its more eccentric practitioners, including Bronson Alcott and Thoreau, he nevertheless respected Emerson as a person and a friend. Lowell was a very perceptive and sympathetic reader of Emerson's character and his works. In *A Fable for Critics* (1848), he captured the essential competing elements of Emerson's character when he wrote that he possessed a "Greek head on right Yankee shoulders, whose range / Has Olympus for one pole, for t' other the Exchange," and he aptly characterized what for many was the greatest limitation of Emerson's writings and thought: "though he builds glorious temples, 't is odd / He leaves never a doorway to get in."

Lowell drew most of his chapter on Emerson in *My Study Windows* directly from a previously published review, "Mr. Emerson's New Course of Lectures," *Nation*, 7 (12 November 1868): 389–90. The occasion for this review was a series of six private lectures that Emerson delivered in Boston between 12 October and 16 November 1868. Managed by his publishers Ticknor and Fields, the series included "Historical Notes of American Life and Letters," "Hospitality," and "Greatness," three of Emerson's most popular lectures at this time; however, in his highly favorable account of the series, Lowell is far less interested in the content or popularity of the lectures than he is in Emerson's enduring appeal as a lecturer. Taking the long view of his own familiarity with and appreciation of Emerson's platform manner and style of delivery, he offers this summary judgment: "I have heard some great speakers and some accomplished orators, but never any that so moved and persuaded men as he." As a public judgment, this assessment accords precisely with Lowell's private appraisal of Emerson's impact on his audience. Writing to Charles Eliot Norton on 18 July 1867, Lowell gave this report of Emerson's delivery of "The Progress of Culture" before the Phi Beta Kappa Society at Harvard University earlier that day:

(continued)

Emerson's oration was more disjointed than usual even for *him*. It began nowhere & ended everywhere, & yet, as always with that divine man, it left you feeling that something beautiful had passed that way—something more beautiful than anything else, like the rising & setting of stars. Every possible criticism might have been made but one—that it was not noble. There was a tone in it that awakened all elevating associations. He boggled, he lost his place, he had to put on his glasses, but it was as if a creature from some fairer world had lost his way in our fogs, & it was *our* fault, not his. It was chaotic, but it was all such stuff as stars are made of, & you couldn't help feeling that, if you waited a little, all that was nebulous would be whirled into planets & would assume the mathematical gravity of a system. All through it I felt something in me that cried "ha, ha, to the sound of the trumpets." (In the Houghton Library, Harvard University; see bMS Am 765 [98].)

It is a singular fact, that Mr. Emerson is the most steadily attractive lecturer in America.... A lecturer now for something like a third of a century, one of the pioneers of the lecturing system, the charm of his voice, his manner, and his matter has never lost its power over his earlier hearers, and continually winds new ones in its enchanting meshes. What they do not fully understand they take on trust....

We call it a singular fact, because we Yankees are thought to be fond of the spread-eagle style, and nothing can be more remote from that than his. We are reckoned a practical folk, who would rather hear about a new air-tight stove than about Plato; yet our favorite teacher's practicality is not in the least of the Poor Richard variety.... [I]f he were to make an almanac, his directions to farmers would be something like this: "OCTOBER: *Indian Summer*; now is the time to get in your early Vedas." What, then, is his secret? Is it not that he out-Yankees us all? that his range includes us all? that he is equally at home with the potato-disease and original sin, with pegging shoes and the Over-soul? that, as we try all trades, so has he tried all cultures? and above all, that his mysticism gives us a counterpoise to our super-practicality?

There is no man living to whom, as a writer, so many of us feel and thankfully acknowledge so great an indebtedness for ennobling impulses,—none whom so many cannot abide. What does he mean? ... Where is his system? What is the use of it all? ... I will only say that one may find grandeur and consolation in a starlit night without caring to ask what it means, save grandeur and consolation; one may like Montaigne, as some ten generations before us have done, without thinking him so systematic as some more eminently tedious (or shall we say tediously eminent?) authors. . . .

The bother with Mr. Emerson is, that, though he writes in prose, he is essentially a poet. . . . We look upon him as one of the few men of genius whom our age has produced, and there needs no better proof of it than his masculine faculty of fecundating other minds. Search for his eloquence in his books and you will perchance miss it, but meanwhile you will find that it has kindled all your thoughts. For choice and pith of language he belongs to a better age than ours, and might rub shoulders with Fuller and Browne. . . . His eye for a fine, telling phrase that will carry true is like that of a backwoodsman for a rifle; and he will dredge you up a choice word from the mud of Cotton Mather himself. . . . As in all original men, there is something for every palate. . . .

The announcement that such a pleasure as a new course of lectures by him is coming, to people as old as I am, is something like those forebodings of spring that prepare us every year for a familiar novelty, none the less novel, when it arrives, because it is familiar. We know perfectly well what we are to expect from Mr. Emerson, and yet what he says always penetrates and stirs us, as is apt to be the case with genius, in a very unlooked-for fashion. . . . At sixty-five . . . he has that privilege of soul which abolishes the calendar, and presents him to us always the unwasted contemporary of his own prime. I do not know if he seem old to his younger hearers, but we who have known him so long wonder at the tenacity with which he maintains himself even in the outposts of youth. I suppose it is not the Emerson of 1868 to whom we listen. For us the whole life of the man is distilled in the clear drop of every sentence, and behind each word we divine the force of a noble character, the weight of a large capital of thinking and being. We do not go to hear what Emerson says so much as to hear Emerson. Not that we perceive any falling-off in anything that ever was essential to the charm of Mr. Emerson's peculiar style of thought or phrase. The first lecture, to be sure, was more disjointed even than common. It was as if, after vainly trying to get his paragraphs into sequence and order, he had at last tried the desperate expedient of *shuffling* them. It was chaos come again, but it was a chaos full of shooting-stars, a jumble of creative forces. The second lecture, on "Criticism and Poetry," was quite up to the level of old times, full of that power of strangely-subtle association whose indirect approaches startle the mind into almost painful attention, of those flashes of mutual understanding between speaker and hearer that are gone ere one can say it lightens. The vice of Emerson's criticism seems to be, that while no man is so sensitive to what is poetical, few men are less sensible than he of what makes a poem. He values the solid meaning of thought above the subtler meaning of style. . . .

To be young is surely the best, if the most precarious, gift of life; yet there are some of us who would hardly consent to be young again, if it were at the cost of our recollection of Mr. Emerson's first lectures during the consulate of Van Buren. We used to walk in from the country to the Masonic Temple . . . through the crisp winter night, and listen to that thrilling voice of his, so charged with subtle meaning and subtle music, as shipwrecked men on a raft to the hail of a ship that came with unhoped-for food and rescue. Cynics might say what they liked. Did our own imaginations transfigure dry remainder-biscuit into ambrosia? At any rate, he brought us *life*, which, on the whole, is no bad thing. Was it all transcendentalism? magic-lantern pictures on mist? As you will. Those, then, were just what we wanted. But it was not so. The delight and the benefit were that he put us in communication with a larger style of thought, sharpened our wits with a more pungent phrase, gave us ravishing glimpses of an ideal under the dry husk of our New England; made us conscious of the supreme and everlasting originality of whatever bit of soul might be in any of us; freed us, in short, from the stocks of prose in which we had sat so long that we had grown well nigh contented in our cramps. And who that saw the audience will ever forget it, where every one still capable of fire, or longing to renew in them the half-forgotten sense of it, was gathered? Those faces, young and old, agleam with pale intellectual light, eager with pleased attention, flash upon me once more. . . . I hear again that rustle of sensation, as they turned to exchange glances over some pithier thought, some keener flash of that humor which always played about the horizon of his mind like heat-lightning. . . .

To some of us that long-past experience remains as the most marvellous and fruitful we have ever had. Emerson awakened us, saved us from the body of this death. It is the sound of the trumpet that the young soul longs for, careless what breath may fill it. . . . Did they say he was disconnected? So were the stars, that seemed larger to our eyes, still keen with that excitement, as we walked homeward with prouder stride over the creaking snow. And were *they* not knit together by a higher logic than our mere sense could master? Were we enthusiasts? I hope and believe we were, and am thankful to the man who made us worth something for once in our lives. . . .

. . . Few men have been so much to so many, and through so large a range of aptitudes and temperaments, and this simply because all of us value manhood beyond any or all other qualities of character. We may suspect in him, here and there, a certain thinness and vagueness of quality, but let the waters go over him as they list, this masculine fibre of his will keep its lively color and its toughness of texture. I have heard some great speakers and some accomplished orators, but never any that so moved and persuaded men as he. There is a kind of undertow in that rich baritone of his that sweeps our minds from their foothold into deeper waters with a drift we cannot and would not resist. . . . I can never help applying to him what Ben Jonson said of Bacon: "There happened in my time one noble speaker, who was full of gravity in his speaking. His language was nobly censorious. No man ever spake more neatly, more pressly, more weightily, or suffered less emptiness, less idleness, in what he uttered. No member of his speech but consisted of his own graces. His hearers could not cough, or look aside from him, without loss. He commanded where he spoke."

From *My Study Windows* (Boston: James R. Osgood, 1871), pp. 375–81, 383–84.

"Fuller, Thoreau, Emerson. . . . The Substance of a 'Conversation'" (1871)

BRONSON ALCOTT

In this estimate of the character of his friends Margaret Fuller, Henry David Thoreau, and Emerson, and his weighing of their relative merits as lecturers, conversationalists, and writers, Bronson Alcott praises Fuller as an "imperial" conversationalist who "carried her head as a goddess," and he credits Thoreau as "the most original mind the country has produced." By contrast, Alcott characterizes Emerson as a "simple man" with "graceful manners," "fine culture, and modesty becoming his eminent talents." In treating Emerson, Alcott reveals the "secret" of his method of composition and touches on his enduring popularity as a lecturer; he also argues for the cohesiveness of Emerson's thought and says that his thought and style defy imitation. Praising Emerson as "a university to our people," Alcott concludes that he possesses a "grand mind which is pretty nearly divinized."

Alcott's positive estimate of Emerson in this article printed in 1871 anticipates his glowing account of Emerson as a lecturer and writer in his *Concord Days* (Boston: Roberts Brothers, 1872), pp. 25–40. In the later piece, however, Alcott unexpectedly chides Emerson for the secretiveness of his thought process and the impersonal quality of his conversation. Likening him to Plutarch, Montaigne, Coleridge, Goethe, and others, he writes:

> We characterize and class [Emerson] with the moralists who surprise us with an accidental wisdom, strokes of wit, felicities of phrase, . . . with whose delightful essays, notwithstanding all the pleasure they give us, we still plead our disappointment at not having been admitted to the closer intimacy which these loyal leaves had with their owners' mind before torn from his note-books, jealous, even, at not having been taken into his confidence in the editing itself. . . .
>
> I know of but one subtraction from the pleasure the reading of his books—shall I say his conversation?—gives me,—his pains to be impersonal or discrete, as if he feared any the least intrusion of himself were an offence offered to self-respect, the courtesy due to intercourse and authorship; thus depriving his page, his company, of attractions the great masters of both knew how to insinuate into their text and talk without overstepping the bounds of social or literary decorum. (pp. 30, 35–36)

We come now to Mr. Emerson, . . . our central figure. I suppose the present company have all seen Mr. Emerson; perhaps not any of the others I have mentioned. He is a very plain, simple man, graceful manners, and fine culture, and modesty becoming his eminent talents. A scholar by genius, culture and habit, his books are more read, perhaps, by thoughtful persons all over the country than those of any other author; and it would not be an unfair test, in my judgment, if one were to go into any city and take the census of the readers of his books to find the number of thoughtful and earnest people.

I will tell you a secret about his method of composing books, since it will explain what a great many people have not comprehended, and will really show them how to read his books. It makes no difference, they say, whether you begin at the last paragraph and read backwards, or begin at what he meant for the beginning. There is some principle in that. There is, nevertheless, a thread running through all his writings; it takes a very subtle, fluent, and ingenious reader to find that thread; but be assured there is a thread on which he strings all his pearls; it is not accidental.

He is a man who lives for thought, and who is a thinker. He is a benevolent man, since, on all occasions when the town of Concord wishes his aid, Mr. Emerson is ready to perform any service for his fellow towns-people. On many great occasions, . . . he has given his voice to determine questions which arose in the history of our country, and if the speeches were collected which he made we should see how much he contributed in that way, perhaps more than any other person except Mr. [Theodore] Parker. He lives for thought, which means life, since those who do not think do not live in any high or real sense. Thinking makes the man.

How does he live, and what are his habits? Imagine a man who says: "Here is a day now before me; a day is a fortune and an estate; who loses a day loses life." Therefore he is alert, busy, awake. If he walks he sees what there is to see, and remembers it. He has a tablet in his pocket, and puts it down on the spot, not when he gets home. If he has visits to make, which is not often, any conversation that occurs goes into his commonplace book without order. If he dreams, and any thought occurs in his dreams, that goes down also. If he reads a book, and it suggests a thought, that goes down in his commonplace book. Whatever he hears, or sees, having all his senses awake, whatever product they give him, goes into his tablet; and any time he has an invitation to speak, or that he knows he is to speak, he sits down and reads what is in his commonplace book.

Perhaps some topic has been growing on his mind for some time. In every true man and woman things grow and get the ascendency, and all who are fruitful will give birth to their thought. How shall it be clothed? is the next question, since before the arrival we prepare the garments. The garments are already partially prepared; the material, at least, is there for dressing the thought. He finds what he has in his commonplace book; looks over it and sees what passages he has written, perhaps during the last twenty or forty years, touching the question. He copies them off; sees in what order they can be strung together; perhaps spreads them before him. I remember hearing of an instance when a neighbor went in to see him, and there was the philosopher and poet leaning over his papers spread out on the floor before him, singling out paragraphs, perhaps, or trying what would be best for the introduction.

After going over many times, he goes to the lecture-room and reads to see whether it has any connection or not. If the people think he is turning somersaults and cannot get from one paragraph to another without some explanation, he must continue to build a bridge, so that he may at least seem to get across; how he gets across is a miracle to most people. Sometimes it seems as if he had a bridge let down from above. He never falls or stumbles; there he is on the other side, and how he got there is a miracle. When you get acquainted with his style, however, you begin to feel confident he will pass over, and that there will not be a fearful plunge into the chasm between his paragraphs. I mention this for the information of those who read Emerson. They see no connection between one paragraph and another; but there certainly is, or he would not have classified them as he did.

Something has to be said about his style. That is entirely his own. It is Emersonian; it is not imitable. It is ridiculous for young men and women to try to imitate him; it cannot be done. The style is his, and entirely his, and we are happy that it is so. A good style fits like a good costume. His thought is deep and measures the intelligence of his readers. His suggestions are good. He helps us most who helps us to answer our own questions. . . . He gets us to do our work, does not do it for us. He does his work well, for he never produces any finished piece of work. That is his great excellence.

By so doing, consider what a lesson he teaches those young authors who rush into print with the first little essay they write, instead of keeping them for years, and letting them ripen and mellow, and looking at them. A thing that has not been slept upon and talked about is not worth printing. Sleep upon it, talk about it, sit upon it, drink it, digest it, corporate it in your flesh and blood, make it yours, and then it will do to print. Never show it to anybody. If you ever write anything tell scholars that it is good, but by no means show it to anybody; they will take all the charm out of it. The best of the great books are so simply natural and fine that we don't know that we wrote them; we didn't write them, they wrote themselves. Such are all his books. When he has thought a thing and committed it to paper he stops. It is a great thing to stop; it is as hard to stop as to begin.

Mr. Emerson has certainly been a university to our people. Think of his value as a lecturer. For thirty years every winter he has travelled from East to West, and been heard by select audiences. Now no lecture-course in any State of intelligence is thought to be perfect without at least one lecture from Mr. Emerson for those who wish it and can enjoy it; because the best things are not enjoyed by all. I think we may say he made the lecture. The lyceum is Emerson's work really, since he began lecturing earlier than any one and holds his place as no other lecturer has. A great many of the lecturers have fallen away, but Emerson is still a bright star, and sought after, though now beginning to be 70 years of age. I will not speak of his verses particularly. I suppose they are less poetical, as a whole, than his prose. A poet by genius, he always writes poetry, though it be in prose form. A good deal of verse is made in that mood, but I think we will find less in Emerson than in any other writer except Henry Thoreau, who has none at all. He is as wholesome as spring. With him it is all fair weather, all out of doors. . . . His is a grand mind which is pretty nearly divinized.

"Fuller, Thoreau, Emerson. Estimate by Bronson Alcott. The Substance of a 'Conversation,'" *Boston Commonwealth*, 6 May 1871, pp. 1–2.

["House burned, Wednesday, 24 July (1872)"]

Anna Alcott Pratt, Louisa May Alcott,
and Ellen Tucker Emerson

"House burned, Wednesday, 24 July" (*Journals and Miscellaneous Notebooks*, 16:278). With these few words entered into his journal, Emerson recorded the most traumatic experience of his later life. It was an experience from which neither his body nor his mind ever fully recovered. The fire, which may have been caused by a defective chimney flue or a kerosene lamp left burning in the attic, began in the early morning hours, and it was only due to the speed with which his Concord neighbors came to his aid that, as Ellen and others report, a goodly portion of Emerson's books and manuscripts and some of the family's clothes, furniture, and other household items were saved.

The house was valued at $5,000, but Emerson had insured it for only $2,500. Although he was hardly in need of money at this point in his life, Emerson was astonished by the generosity of his friends who came forward to assist in the rebuilding of the house. Within days of the fire, as Ellen writes to her brother Edward, Frank Lowell brought a check for $5,000 as a gift from friends, and Caroline Sturgis Tappan offered another $5,000. In August, Ebenezer Rockwood Hoar told Emerson that a company of friends, headed by LeBaron Russell, had deposited $10,000 in an account in Emerson's name at the Concord bank, which was to be drawn upon to rebuild and refurnish the house and to pay for a recuperative journey to Europe (see Ellen Tucker Emerson to Haven Emerson, 16 August 1872, *Letters of Ellen Tucker Emerson*, 1:685).

Between 17 and 23 August, Ellen accompanied her father on a short trip to New Hampshire and Maine, during which Emerson finally acknowledged the toll that the fire had taken on him. In a long letter to her sister Edith written from Waterford, Maine, which she captioned "Read to yourself," Ellen reported that their father had told her where all the family's money was—"in case I roll into the water"—and she shared with Edith his detailed instructions about the disposition of his manuscripts. According to Ellen, her father wanted all of his early manuscripts burned; she also said he dreaded that either Moncure D. Conway or Frank Sanborn should ever get their hands on his papers, and he regretted that his son Edward, to whom he would otherwise happily entrust his

(continued)

manuscripts, was not "a scholar by profession." At the close of her letter, Ellen remarked that their father had rejected her suggestion that James Elliot Cabot be asked to take over control of his papers (see Ellen Tucker Emerson to Edith Emerson Forbes, 22 August 1872, *Letters of Ellen Tucker Emerson*, 1:690–93).

Between 23 October 1872 and 27 May 1873, Emerson and Ellen traveled to England, the Continent, and Egypt. Ellen's personal diary of their travels and her detailed letters home at this time reveal that, while her father seemed to enjoy the opportunity for one last visit to old friends such as Thomas Carlyle and the chance to finally see Egypt, the journey was not the complete recuperative cure from the shock of the fire that friends and family had hoped it might be (see *Letters of Ellen Tucker Emerson*, 2:3–91). On their return home, the townspeople of Concord gathered to greet its most famous citizen, and in the months that followed Emerson settled into the pattern that would characterize his later years. He entrusted all his business affairs to his son-in-law William Hathaway Forbes. He accepted Edith's help in bringing his work on *Parnassus* to closure; the anthology of poems and poetic excerpts that Emerson had been collecting for nearly fifty years appeared on 19 December 1874, and it proved to be one of his best-selling books. Emerson finally agreed to Cabot's appointment as his literary executor, and with Ellen's assistance Cabot helped Emerson cull from his papers several lectures that he delivered between 1874 and 1881, arrange for the publication of a number of essays under his name, and complete his work on *Letters and Social Aims*, which appeared on 15 December 1875.

Fragment of a letter by Anna Alcott Pratt; addressee and date unknown

You ask about the fire. Well—they had a funny time in spite of the dreadfulness of it all. It is supposed to have caught or rather "growed" in a closet in the attic, a sort of a spontaneous combustion, as no one had been there, or any light or matches. Mr E. awoke early in the morning to find the garret all in fire. The alarm was given. All the neighbors flocked in, and before the roof fell, all the books, pictures & valuable furniture was removed.

I believe nothing was lost, but a few papers & manuscripts from the attic. Louisa & May found the Poet of America wandering forlornly about in an old muddy coat, & no stockings smiling serenely if any one spoke to him, & looking calmly on the wreck of his home as if it were a matter of no special consequence to him. His chief trouble seemed to be that he could not find his clothes, his bureau having disappeared. Mrs E. beautifully arrayed in her best bonnet & bearing carefully in her hand a large bundle of caps & blue ribbons, floated about saying cheerfully, "Oh well we shall have a better house now."

The lawn & street were filled with furniture among which the young Paddies disported joyfully, feasting on forgotten goodies, smashing open preserve cans, & drinking raw tomato with a relish.

Louy established herself as a sort of policeman & saved quantities of things, that seemed to be lying round loose, while May ordered every body right & left and soon got things in good shape.

The Emersons are for the present at the old Manse with Miss Ripley, but the house will be rebuilt immediately as the walls are standing unhurt, & the Insurance will cover the loss principally.

Louisa May Alcott to Louisa Wells, 27 July 1872

Dear Lu,

Your two notes were not as cheery as I could have wished, but I see that you are the right girl in the right place, & that's well.

We had a topsy turvy day at the fire. I saved some valuable papers for my Ralph, & most of their furniture, books & pictures were safe. The upper story is all gone & the lawn strewed with wrecks of beds, books & clothes.

They all take it very coolly & in a truly Emersonian way. Ellen says, she only regrets not selling the old papers & rags up garret. Mrs E. floats about trying to find her clothes, & Mr E. beams affably upon the world & remarks with his head cocked up like a sparrow—

"I now see my library under a new aspect."

He looked pathetically funny that morning wandering about in his night gown, pants, old coat & no hose. His dear bald head lightly covered with his best hat, & an old pair of rubbers wobbling on his Platonic feet.

Our entry is full of half burnt papers & books, & the neighbors are collecting the clothes of the family nicely mixed up with pots & pans, works of art, & cinders. Sad but funny. The house was insured & will be built right up at once. "Our turn next," Ma darkly predicts. . . .

Ellen Tucker Emerson to Edward Waldo Emerson, 30 July 1872

Dear Edward,

Who would believe I should have waited six days after a fire at Bush to write to you about it? But I had to write notes to anxious friends & relations here and I knew Annie had written to you. You know I was in Beverly. Ida told me afterwards that Maj. Higginson brought her the Transcript looking quite pale with fright and told her to show me the paragraph about our house. She came behind me, held the paper before me and said "Ellen, something has happened at your house, but your Father & Mother are safe." I tried to read and very slowly took it in, it was so surprising. It was neither pain nor fright but it took my breath away, and half an hour after when I walked out to bid goodbye I found my knees were shaky. When I was coming home in the cars all alone, I saw very clearly that this might be a stroke to Father or Mother, or both, that they would never get over, and no longer wondered that Ida urged me to fly to them without a minutes delay. Now after a week, I think it hasn't hurt either of them. Father seems & has all along, just the same, and very happy. If it doesn't impoverish him, and it looks to me as if it couldn't, I think it will not seriously affect him. There is no doubt it was a tragedy to him at the time, and that he suffered very much. I suppose we shall never hear a word about that. Nothing ever showed me so distinctly how faithful he is never to mention himself as this week has. I am full of curiosity, yea anxiety, about it and watch & listen & lead in vain, and I could not ask him you know. He is having better food & comfort and less care at the Manse than he ever does at home. . . . Why didn't the fire hurt? In a great measure because our house is to me associated with dirt, waste, bottomless abysses of expense to no profit, deceit, ill-temper & shirking. Margaret Lacy was just this . . . [and] all the rest have been worse. This is one side. The other side is much larger, I love the house. I entirely agree with every word of lament over it in the blessed pile of letters of condolence that we have received. It is "a historic homestead" and precious to us as all dear & happy homes must be to families and it is so handsome and convenient that when Mr Keyes told us we could have any little alterations & additions, with one accord we said "not one have we ever desired." So when I saw the house I had supposed forever lost, standing safely in its old shape among the healthy untouched trees, I was very thankful. All our things smell of the fire strong, and that smell that has hitherto seemed to me the abomination of desolation, is now sweet & dear to me. It smells of a great deliverance. Mother's state I haven't yet reported. Many people have expressed a doubt & anxiety as to how Mother would bear it. I never had the least. How little outside of her own family Mother is understood! Yet let me not forget that Judge Hoar found me in the barn Thursday afternoon and said "Have you then got home, my dear?" so affectionately I almost jumped for joy, and then asked after Mother. "She rose above the occasion, as she always does, but I didn't know but she might have caught cold, or suffered more than she thought she should." Judge Hoar gave her her due. Mrs Lombard is at the Manse & she says Mother acknowledged that her only trouble was thinking how badly we children should all feel, but that she was simply absorbed in thankfulness that Father was safe & well, because when he called her that morning she thought something had happened to him. She was sick two or three days in her bed, but now is getting better, and it looks as if she was getting that vacation now which we have always longed for for her, and with a freedom of mind never before possible. I can't help believing 'twill be good for her. When Father & I go up into her room now we have such blissful times we almost die of joy. . . . I must here insert something that has just happened. A letter from Naushon was brought me. I opened it. It contains a check for five hundred dollars from Mr Forbes & Mrs Forbes, a present to me to buy me some new clothes for all my dresses are burnt, except two muslins, my lavender delaine & 2 street dresses. All my winter clothes and my red dressing-gown are gone too. They have heard of it and sent me this monstrous present! Did you ever? And Mrs Tappan wrote yesterday offering Father five thousand to rebuild the house! Judge Hoar, during or immediately after the fire, told him he might draw freely on his account at the Concord Bank. Now let me attempt to chronicle the deeds of the town. Father, having seen that private efforts availed not, ran to the gate and called Fire! Whitcomb! Staples! Fire! and instantly saw a movement in both houses indicating that he was understood. I'm supposing that A[nnie]. has told you how it was; the fire was crackling inside the plastering when it waked Father, and he called Mother from redroom. He could see it through the crack it had caused between plastering & corner moulding inside closet he couldn't open till Mother came up & opened waste-paper cupboard door when it flashed out. It descended from above, garret was already on fire. He ran to garret-door. Dense smoke above. Messrs S. & W. on the ground immediately. Mr Staples

. . . sees the smoke, smells burnt carpets, shuts door, says it can't be stopped, plenty of time for down stairs, chambers must be cleared quick. Mr Whitcomb at gate sends first teams that pass for help and to give the alarm, stops the rest. . . . Mother's room & mine were first attacked. Mother says that as she took down the clothes from her entry closet her bureau was carried out and that Mr Staples was working in her room. The time they had must have been very short. There were ten men there in five or ten minutes. They couldn't take down the bedstead, the secretary or the corner bureau, they are all badly burned & the carpet is still on the floor. Mr George Heywood & Mr Staples stayed as long as possible throwing out the bureau drawers. At last Mr Staples called to Mr Heywood that he must go & shut the door. Mr Heywood saw several drawers still left, he wouldn't go, he saved two drawers, the ceiling fell. He was in the sec. corner & unhurt, he threw out the last drawer, the room was full of smoke & fire & he jumped for his life, right out of the West window. His trowsers caught on the parlour blind, tore from bottom to top & eased his fall. He was unhurt! One of the first wagons that passed was Mr Gray's and Arthur Gray was with him. Ar. ran straight to my room, even then the smoke was so bad he had to hold his breath, saw my pictures, thought how I must value them and took down all but Fisher boy & some you never saw. John meanwhile carried down my what-not, Aunt Susan's work-table, Charley's chair & all my chairs in plain sight & my bureau & small table were saved fresh & clean. Next Arthur saved Edith's room pictures, and Ned Bartlett arriving made straight for my room. The sight of the things Ned saved shows what he must have undergone to do it, they are black & blistered, it was at real risk of his life. He threw my precious writing-table out of the window. He took down Mary Fay's picture and saved my dear little chair Mrs Sanborn gave me and my camp-stool. Then one more look as he fled before the frightful smoke. . . . It burned his hand and he rushed from the room. My bedstead & carpet were left to the flames. Now we'll begin at my coming home. I walked down from the 7.15 train. C. Cheney ran out to me and told me my parents were at the Manse and both were well & unhurt. I met Annie coming and we drove up the Manse Avenue & Father stood at the door. He looked a little moved and called me "houseless child" and wanted to know why I was so slow. . . . Father & I set out to walk down to the house. I asked how it all happened & he told me the story. My surprise & joy at seeing the house standing as of old was very great. I entered the door & saw the stairs unburnt—though the banisters were removed & looked into the study where all was unhurt though the windows were out. Next the red-room. The floor was a pond, the ceiling still dripped, but room & closet were sound as ever except where the hinges of the E. entry door had been chopped out with an axe. The parlour & dining-room ceilings were down, not on the floor but hanging & waving, and all the closets of housekeeping stood unchanged except that they were blackened with smoke. Through kitchen & back-chambers I roamed, and John took me up the East stairs to see how though they were whole & the entry, the garret stairway was charred. Then to Mrs Gregory's to see what was there. Mrs Gregory said "This isn't the way I sh'd have chosen of returning the thousand & one favours we have received from your folks, but I'm glad to have the chance of doing anything for you." There were stacks of pictures & mountains of clothes. There to my surprise I saw most of the clothes from your chest up garret. I thought the garret went bodily. I found afterward the stethoscope at the Alcott's, and a pile of your notebooks, also your cup and saucer that Alice Forbes gave you. John has your axe. Having seen the Gregory's house, we went next to the Staples's barn, where piles of books & bedding, odd bureau drawers, carpets & curtains of Mother's windows were piled. Then into the house. There in the parlour was my piano looking bright & cool. Mrs Staples presently came down, all lame & aching, she had worked so hard at the fire, she had been having a rum bath to see if it would take out the stiffness. She brought piles of blankets, and some of Mother's clothes that had been soaked & she had dried them. Then Mrs Wetherbee, full of affection, showed me all the silver & half the glass, and some beds, rugs etc. in her house, & in the barn the railing of the front stairs & the bedsteads & some carpets. Mrs Whitcomb, as usual perfectly silent but very friendly, took me up stairs to see the crockery, dining-room clock, and half the knickknacks of our establishment in one of her chambers. John brought us home to the Manse, and explained to me that it was the slate roof that saved the house by falling in and smothering the fire. When talking of the house he advised us to have it all carefully put in first rate order now, so there'd be no jobs to be done in it for the next 20 years, and reminded me of the everlasting tinkering. "Why I guess Mr Emerson's spent 100 dollars a year on it. Mr Benjamin said 'Mr Emerson 'ud ha' been a richer man if it had burnt down 20 years ago'" I treasure up all his advice and carry it to Mr Keyes. . . . Father had yesterday a visit from Mr Frank Lowell and, Edward, Mr L. gave me a letter to give Father after he had gone. It contained a check for five thousand dollars from some of Father's intimate friends to enable him to rebuild his house more as he would like or for him to use for any other purpose he preferred. Father read it to himself with a face such as you can imagine, looked at the check & exclaimed "Good heavens!" He was perfectly astonished at the vast sum. He asked me where I got it and said "Well, he did it like a great gentleman as he is, and let me have the visit without any suspicion of this!" He has written a lovely letter to Mr Lowell, asking leave to think twice about it, and to let him come to see him first. . . .

Madeleine B. Stern, "The Alcotts and the Emerson Fire," *American Transcendental Quarterly*, 36 (Fall 1977): 7–9.

    Ellen Tucker Emerson, *The Letters of Ellen Tucker Emerson*, ed. Edith E. W. Gregg, 2 vols. (Kent, Ohio: Kent State University Press, 1982), 1:676–82.

"Emerson: A Literary Interview" (1874)

ANONYMOUS

Styled as an interview, this essay provides a casual, almost gossipy, report of Emerson's Concord home and surroundings, his physical appearance and character, and his assessments of Bronson Alcott, Margaret Fuller, William Wordsworth, Thomas Carlyle, John Stuart Mill, and the American historian George Bancroft, among others. The tone of the piece indicates how by this point in his life reporters could treat Emerson with an unusual degree of familiarity, while the style of the piece anticipates that of some reminiscences published after his death, including Pendleton King's "Notes of Conversations with Emerson"† and Frank Bellew's "Recollections of Ralph Waldo Emerson."† Whether Emerson actually attacked Swinburne "as a perfect leper and a mere sodomite" as stated here is open to question; regardless of the accuracy of the report, Swinburne's honor was defended in a letter from a "personal friend" which appeared in the *New-York Daily Tribune* and characterized the derogatory remarks as "the last tricks of tongue now possible to a gap-toothed and hoary-headed ape, carried first into notice on the shoulders of Carlyle" (25 February 1874, p. 4).

The little village of Concord, which is the home of Emerson and the other Transcendentalists, is situated in Massachusetts, about an hour's ride from Boston. It is a quiet and truly rural place, resembling the suburban parts of London. . . . Little if any business is carried on, and most of the neat residences are occupied by farmers, retired merchants, or persons doing business in Boston. It is a drowsy, well-to-do and respectable sort of a village, yet with its local society, its scandals and little cliques of people, just like any other country community. . . . Close by the Revolutionary battle-field is the famous old house where Hawthorne lived for a time; . . . [his] study-window looked out on the river, and many memorials of his occupancy remain. . . . A. Bronson Alcott, the father of "Little Women," lived next door, while hard by was Thoreau's home, and that of William [Ellery] Channing, the poet. . . .

All of these famous persons, however, are of inferior importance to Emerson, who ranks as the Plato of this Yankee Athens, and towers head and shoulders above all his contemporaries. "My house," he writes in his essay on "Nature," "stands in low land with limited outlook, and on the skirts of the village." The original building before it was burnt, was a modest, old-fashioned farmhouse. . . . Yet within its portal how many earnest seekers after truth have entered to commune with its owner! Youths and sages, scholars and illiterate men, among them travelers from every land. I made one pause before following in the footsteps of so remarkable a throng: but, unabashed. I knocked, and entered within, and was soon seated in the comfortable, but simply furnished, family room, and conversing freely with Mr. Emerson. As I had met him once before in New York, I needed no further introduction. Mr. Emerson is a good host, and none find warmer welcome from him than aspiring young men. His manner is neither cold nor formal, and, though slightly reserved, it is very winning. He is kindliness and amiability personified, and he at once invites confidence by his sympathetic attention. He does not dogmatize nor monopolize the conversation, like many other famous men; but he is an admirable listener, and tempts his companion to reveal all that he knows and is; with almost ludicrous unconsciousness that meantime he is being anatomized and duly catalogued by the imperturbable but acute philosopher. I felt afterward as it I had acted like a presumptuous idiot in airing my own notions so freely in the presence of this all-wise man; but it is in vain to try to resist the mysterious fascination which forces each person to contribute to his store. As Alcott says, "Emerson absorbs from every one; and, if you are in sympathy with him, he will soon extract your secret."

No one who has watched Mr. Emerson's face can forget its lineaments. Simplicity and shrewdness are united in its lines. As some one has said, there is "an awful distance in the impersonal gray eyes," and the man seems at times as if changed to a far-off, pure, cold, intellectual iceberg. This feeling changes, however, when he begins to speak, for his face lightens with sympathy, and he is warm and human once more.

His head is long and massive, very high above the ears, with the moral faculties largely developed, while it indicates a large and strong brain. His physique is slight but wiry, and there is nothing puny about him. The firm yet sweet mouth, and the clear steady gaze, show power and courage. One would infer that this was a man who dared to say what he thought, and who cared for the opposition of neither men nor devils.

He spoke without restraint, and showed great readiness of expression. He was a little restless, and while talking he seemed unable to keep perfectly quiet, but rubbed the palms of his hands together, or tapped one foot on the floor with a nervous sort of movement. But without further preliminaries I will jot down some of his utterances. He said this is the age of science and encyclopedias, but much of our lately acquired knowledge will be dropped in the future. Literary supremacy may be transferred the same as political supremacy. England has held it the longest, but now it has left her, and become the property of Germany. Yet who knows but that it may belong to the United States before long. . . .

He thought Margaret Fuller was a great conversationalist and a fine letter-writer; but her published works are not remarkable.

Wordsworth is *the* great English poet. . . . His Ode on Immortality touches the high-water-mark of modern literature. In this connection he said that in order to really appreciate nature one should be poor and live in the country . . . and have no other means of enjoyment except communication with the physical world around.

Walter Savage Landor will always be read by the select few. Matthew Arnold is growing too diffusive. His "sweetness and light" has become heavy as lead with too much repetition. . . . Saint-Beuve is *the* great French writer. He said, "I don't meddle with August Compte," in reply to the question whether he was interested in the Positive Philosophy.

He condemned Swinburne severely as a perfect leper and a mere sodomite, which criticism recalls Carlyle's scathing description of that poet—as man standing up to his neck in a cesspool, and adding to its contents. . . . Alcott he aptly described as a man who reads Plato without surprise. When I mentioned having written to the Orphic Sage, without the letter reaching him, Mr. Emerson smiled, and said: "The Post Office authorities don't know anything about such men as he."

Thoreau was a true genius and so great was his mastery of the phenomena of nature, that it would need another Linnæus, as well as a poet, to properly edit his writings.

Matthew Arnold's appreciation of Macaulay he thought was just, while he praised Bancroft highly, rating him foremost among American historians. He was an excellent scholar and an exact writer. Thoreau, who was deeply read in Canadian history, told him that in that department of American history Bancroft was beyond criticism, and had not made a misstatement. . . .

Carlyle being mentioned, Emerson defended him from Margaret Fuller's criticism in her letters, and said that Carlyle purposely made exaggerated statements, merely to astonish his listeners. His attitude towards America during our war was unfortunate, but no more than could be expected. Emerson mentioned meeting John Stuart Mill, but he thought the latter cold and formal; which is strange, as it is said that, in conversation, Mill always spoke with admiration of Emerson's writings. I asked Mr. Emerson which was the best of the portraits or busts which have been made of him. He answered, with a smile, that he felt, as Lincoln remarked of himself, that they each took away all the natural beauty of the original. . . .

Upon leaving, Mr. Emerson courteously accompanied me to the hall, and the last glimpse which I caught of him showed him standing in the open door, holding a lamp to direct my way to the road—a picture well personifying the attitude he has maintained towards his generation.

Frank Leslie's Illustrated Newspaper, 3 January 1874, p. 275.

From *Transcendentalism in New England: A History* (1876)

OCTAVIUS BROOKS FROTHINGHAM

A member of the second generation of Transcendentalists, Octavius Brooks Frothingham felt an intellectual and theological kinship with Emerson, whom he credited as his personal source when he delivered his own protests against religious dogmatism and formalism from the various Unitarian pulpits he occupied. Frothingham recognized that Transcendentalism, especially as practiced in New England, was less a single movement than an arrangement of literary, religious, philosophical, and social movements championed by a set of quite diverse figures, and he placed Emerson primarily among the poets, not the theologians, philosophers, or reformers. In his history, Frothingham devoted chapters to those he considered the most important and durable Transcendentalists—Bronson Alcott, Margaret Fuller, Theodore Parker, and George Ripley—but he reserved his highest praise for Emerson, whose character and contributions to the movement he developed in a chapter tellingly entitled "The Seer"; there he even defended Emerson from what he took as Alcott's slights when, in his *Concord Days* (1872), he criticized the impersonal quality of Emerson's conversation (see the headnote to Alcott's "Fuller, Thoreau, Emerson. . . . The Substance of a 'Conversation' "†).

A discerning German writer, Herman Grimm, closes a volume of fifteen essays, with one on Ralph Waldo Emerson, written in 1861. . . . The essay is interesting, apart from its literary merit, as giving the impression made by Mr. Emerson on a foreigner to whom his reputation was unknown, and a man of culture to whom books and opinions rarely brought surprise. He saw a volume of the "Essays" lying on the table of an American acquaintance, looked into it, and was surprised that, being tolerably well practised in reading English, he understood next to nothing of the contents. He asked about the author, and, learning that he was highly esteemed in his own country, he opened the book again, read further, and was so much struck by passages here and there, that he borrowed it, carried it home, took down Webster's dictionary, and began reading in earnest. The extraordinary construction of the sentences, the apparent absence of logical continuity, the unexpected turns of thought, the use of original words, embarrassed him at first; but soon he discovered the secret and felt the charm. The man had fresh thoughts, employed a living speech, was a genuine person. The book was bought, read and re-read, "and now every time I take it up, I seem to take it up for the first time."

The power that the richest genius has in Shakspeare, Rafael, Goethe, Beethoven, to reconcile the soul to life, to give joy for heaviness, to dissipate fears, to transfigure care and toil, to convert lead into gold, and lift the veil that conceals the forms of hope, Grimm ascribes in the highest measure to Emerson. . . .

The reasons of Grimm's admiration . . . are good reasons, but they are not the best. They do not touch the deeper secret of power. That secret lies in the writer's pure and perfect idealism, in his absolute and perpetual faith in thoughts, his supreme confidence in the spiritual laws. He lives in the region of serene ideas; lives there all the day and all the year; not visiting the mount of vision occasionally, but setting up his tabernacle there, and passing the night among the stars that he may be up and dressed for the eternal sunrise. To such a spirit there is no night: "the darkness shineth as the day; the darkness and the light are both alike." There are no cloudy days. . . . Emerson . . . never riots and never laughs, but is radiant with a placid buoyancy that diffuses itself over his countenance and person. Mr. Emerson's characteristic trait is serenity. He is faithful to his own counsel, "Shun the negative side. Never wrong people with your contritions, nor with dismal views of politics or society. Never name sickness; even if you could trust yourself on that perilous topic, beware of unmuzzling a valetudinarian who will soon give you your fill of it." He seems to be perpetually saying "Good Morning."

This is not wholly a result of philosophy; it is rather a gift of nature. He is the descendant of eight generations of Puritan clergymen,—the inheritor of their thoughtfulness and contemplation, their spirit of inward and outward communion. The dogmatism fell away; the peaceful fruits of discipline remained, and flowered beautifully in his richly favored spirit. An elder brother William, whom it was a privilege to know, though lacking the genius of Waldo, was a natural idealist and wise saint. Charles, another brother, who died young and greatly lamented had the saintliness and the genius both. The "Dial" contained contributions from this young man, entitled

"Notes from the Journal of a Scholar" that strongly suggest the genius of his eminent brother; . . . passages from them . . . [throw] light on the secret of Emerson's inspiration. . . .

Idealism is native to [Emerson's] temperament, the proper expression of [his] feeling. Emerson was preordained an idealist; he is one of the eternal men, bearing about him the atmosphere of immortal youth. He is now seventy-three years old, . . . but his last volume, "Letters and Social Aims," shows the freshness of his first essays. The opening chapter, "Poetry and Imagination," has the emphasis and soaring confidence of undimmed years; and the closing one, "Immortality," sustains an unwearied flight among the agitations of this most hotly-debated of beliefs. The address before the Phi Beta Kappa Society at Cambridge, in 1867, equals in moral grandeur and earnestness of appeal, in faithfulness to ideas and trust in principles, the addresses that made so famous the prime of his career. There is absolutely no abatement of heart or hope; if anything, the tone is richer and more assured than ever it was. During the season of his popularity as a lyceum lecturer, the necessity of making his discourse attractive and entertaining, brought into the foreground the play of his wit, and forced the graver qualities of his mind into partial concealment; but in later years, in the solitude of his study, the undertone of high purpose is heard again, in solemn reverberations, reminding us that the unseen realities are present still; that no opening into the eternal has ever been closed. . . .

Emerson does not claim for the soul a special faculty, like faith or intuition, by which truths of the spiritual order are perceived, as objects are perceived by the senses. He contends for no doctrines, whether of God or the hereafter, or the moral law, on the credit of such interior revelation. He neither dogmatizes nor defines. On the contrary, his chief anxiety seems to be to avoid committing himself to opinions; to keep all questions open; to close no avenue in any direction to the free ingress and egress of the mind. He gives no description of God that will class him as theist or pantheist; no definition of immortality that justifies his readers in imputing to him any form of the popular belief in regard to it. Does he believe in personal immortality? It is impertinent to ask. He will not be questioned; not because he doubts, but because his beliefs are so rich, various and many-sided, that he is unwilling, by laying emphasis on any one, to do an apparent injustice to others. He will be held to no definitions; he will be reduced to no final statements. . . . He dwells in principles, and will not be cabined in beliefs. He needs the full expanse of the Eternal Reason. . . .

It is . . . worth while to dwell . . . on this point, because it furnishes a perfect illustration of Emerson's intellectual attitude towards beliefs, its entire sincerity, disinterestedness and modesty. The serenity of his faith makes it impossible for him to be a controversialist. He never gave a sweeter or more convincing proof of this than in the sermon he preached on the Communion Supper, which terminated his connection with his Boston parish, and with it his relations to the Christian ministry. . . . The rite in question was held sacred by his sect, as a personal memorial of Jesus perpetuated according to his own request. To neglect it was still regarded as a reproach; to dispute its authority was considered contumacious; to declare it obsolete and useless, an impediment to spiritual progress, a hindrance to Christian growth, was to excite violent animosities, and call down angry rebuke. Yet this is what Mr. Emerson deliberately did. That the question of retaining a minister who declined to bless and distribute the bread and wine, was debated at all, was proof of the extraordinary hold he had on his people. Through the crisis he remained unruffled, calm and gracious as in the sunniest days. On the evening when the church were considering his final proposition, with such result as he clearly foresaw, he sat with a brother clergyman talking pleasantly on literature and general topics, never letting fall a hint of the impending judgment. . . .

Mr. Emerson's place is among poetic, not among philosophic minds. He belongs to the order of imaginative men. The imagination is his organ. His reading, which is very extensive in range, has covered this department more completely than any. He is at home with the seers, Swedenborg, Plotinus, Plato, the books of the Hindus, . . . Shakspeare, Henry More, Hafiz; the books called sacred by the religious world; "books of natural science, especially those written by the ancients,—geography, botany, agriculture, explorations of the sea, of meteors, of astronomy;" he recommends "the deep books." Montaigne has been a favorite author on account of his sincerity. He thinks Hindu books the best gymnastics for the mind. . . .

. . . His thoughts are few and pregnant; capable of infinite expansion, illustration and application. They crop out on almost every page of his characteristic writings; are iterated and reiterated in every form of speech; and put into gems of expression that may be worn on any part of the person. His prose and his poetry are aglow with them. They make his essays oracular, and his verse prophetic. By virtue of them his best books belong to the sacred literature of the race; by virtue of them, but for the lack of artistic finish of rhythm and rhyme, he would be the chief of American poets.

The first article in Mr. Emerson's faith is the primacy of Mind. That Mind is supreme, eternal, absolute, one, manifold, subtle, living, immanent in all things, permanent, flowing, self-manifesting; that the universe is the result of mind, that nature is the symbol of mind; that finite minds live and act through concurrence with infinite mind. This idea recurs with such frequency that, but for Emerson's wealth of observation, reading, wit, mental variety and buoyancy, his talent for illustration, gift at describing details, it would weary the reader. As it is, we delight to follow the guide through the labyrinth of his expositions, and gaze on the wonderful phantasmagoria that he exhibits. . . .

. . . [One] is surprised to hear Mr. Alcott say, "I know of but one subtraction from the pleasure the reading of [Emerson's] books—shall I say his conversation?—gives me; his pains to be impersonal or discreet, as if he feared any the least intrusion of himself were an offence offered to self-respect, the courtesy due to intercourse and authorship." To others this exquisite reserve, this delicate withdrawal behind his thought, has seemed not only one of Emerson's peculiar charms, but one of his most subtle powers. Personal magnetism is very delightful for the moment. The exhibition of attractive personal traits is interesting in the lecture room; sometimes in the parlor. The public, large or small, enjoy confidences. But in an age of personalities, voluntary and involuntary, the man who keeps his individual affairs in the background, tells nothing of his private history, holds in his own breast his petty concerns and opinions, and lets thoughts flow through him, as light streams through plate glass, is more than attractive—is noble, is venerable. To his impersonality in his books and addresses, Emerson owes perhaps a large measure of his extraordinary influence. You may search his volumes in vain for a trace of egotism. In the lecture room, he seems to be so completely under the spell of his idea, so wholly abstracted from his audience, that he is as one who waits for the thoughts to come, and drops them out one by one, in a species of soliloquy or trance. He is a bodiless idea. When he speaks or writes, the power is that of pure mind. The incidental, accidental, occasional, does not intrude. No abatement on the score of personal antipathy needs to be made. The thought is allowed to present and commend itself. Hence, when so many thoughts are forgotten, buried be-neath affectation and verbiage, his gain in brilliancy and value as time goes on; and in an age of ephemeral literature his books find new readers, his mind exerts wider sway. That his philosophy can be recommended as a sound rule to live by for ordinary practitioners may be questioned. It is better as inspiration than as prescription. For maxims it were wiser to go to Bentham, Mill or Bain. The plodders had best keep to the beaten road. But for them who need an atmosphere for wings, who require the impulse of great motives, the lift of upbearing aspirations—for the imaginative, the pas-sionate, the susceptible, who can achieve nothing unless they attempt the impossible—Emerson is the master. A single thrill sent from his heart to ours is worth more to the heart that feels it, than all the schedules of motive the utilitarian can offer.

From *Transcendentalism in New England: A History* (New York: Putnam's, 1876), pp. 218–19, 221–22, 224–25, 227–28, 231–32, 236, 237–38, 247–48.

From *Prose Works 1892* (1881–1882)

WALT WHITMAN

Walt Whitman had sent a copy of the 1855 edition of *Leaves of Grass* to Emerson soon after its publication. He admired the older man, having heard him lecture in 1842, and he once commented to John Townsend Trowbridge that "I was simmering, simmering, simmering" until "Emerson brought me to a boil." Emerson responded with a famous letter of praise, in which he writes "I greet you at the beginning of a great career" (see *Letters*, 8:446). Whitman was so taken with the letter that he printed it in a New York newspaper, reprinted it as a broadside, stamped the line just quoted in gold on the spine of the 1856 edition of *Leaves*, and reprinted the entire letter as an appendix to the volume, all without Emerson's permission. Even though Whitman's actions upset Emerson, they did not cause him to break off the relationship. The two met in 1855 and again in 1860, when Emerson tried unsuccessfully to get Whitman to delete the "Enfans d'Adam" ("Children of Adam") poems from the third edition of *Leaves* because of their sexual content. Emerson supported Whitman's attempts to gain a government position during the Civil War. Still, the two did not meet again until late in Emerson's life, and the selection here gives Whitman's impressions of the event. After Emerson's death, Whitman continued to praise Emerson, though he also tried to distance himself from Emerson's writings, describing them as more like the traditional literature which he was in opposition to when he wrote *Leaves of Grass* than as an influence on his own works.

"A Visit, at the Last, to R. W. Emerson" (September 1881)

Concord, Mass.—Out here on a visit—elastic, mellow, Indian-summery weather. Came to-day from Boston, . . . convoy'd by my friend F. B. Sanborn, and to his ample house, and the kindness and hospitality of Mrs. S. and their fine family. Am writing this under the shade of some old hickories and elms, just after 4 P.M., on the porch, within a stone's throw of the Concord river. Off against me, across stream, on a meadow and side-hill, hay-makers are gathering and wagoning-in probably their second or third crop. The spread of emerald-green and brown, the knolls, the score or two of little haycocks dotting the meadow, the loaded-up wagons, the patient horses, the slow-strong action of the men and pitch-forks—all in the just-waning afternoon, with patches of yellow sun-sheen, mottled by long shadows—a cricket shrilly chirping, herald of the dusk—a boat with two figures noiselessly gliding along the little river, passing under the stone bridge-arch—the slight settling haze of aerial moisture, the sky and the peacefulness expanding in all directions and overhead—fill and soothe me.

Same evening.—Never had I a better piece of luck befall me: a long and blessed evening with Emerson, in a way I couldn't have wish'd better or different. For nearly two hours he has been placidly sitting where I could see his face in the best light, near me. Mrs. S[anborn].'s back-parlor well fill'd with people, neighbors, many fresh and charming faces, women, mostly young, but some old. My friend A. B. Alcott and his daughter Louisa were there early. A good deal of talk, the subject Henry Thoreau—some new glints of his life and fortunes, with letters to and from him—one of the best by Margaret Fuller, others by Horace Greeley, Channing, &c.—one from Thoreau himself, most quaint and interesting. (No doubt I seem'd very stupid to the room-full of company, taking hardly any part in the conversation; but I had "my own pail to milk in," as the Swiss proverb puts it.) My seat and the relative arrangement were such that, without being rude, or anything of the kind, I could just look squarely at E., which I did a good part of the two hours. On entering, he had spoken very briefly and politely to several of the company, then settled himself in his chair, a trifle push'd back, and, though a listener and apparently an alert one, remain'd silent through the whole talk and discussion. A lady friend quietly took a seat next him, to give special attention. A good color in his face, eyes clear, with the well-known expression of sweetness, and the old clear-peering aspect quite the same.

Next Day.—Several hours at E.'s house and dinner there. An old familiar house, (he has been in it thirty-five years,) with surroundings, furnishment, roominess, and plain elegance and fullness, signifying democratic ease, sufficient opulence, and an admirable old-fashioned simplicity—modern luxury, with its mere sumptuousness and affectation, either touch'd lightly upon or ignored altogether. Dinner the same. Of course the best of the occasion (Sunday, September 18, '81) was the sight of E. himself. As just said, a healthy color in the cheeks, and good light in the eyes, cheery expression, and just the amount of talking that best suited, namely, a word or short phrase only where needed, and almost always with a smile. Besides Emerson himself, Mrs. E., with their daughter Ellen, the son Edward and his wife, with my friend F[rank]. S[anborn]. and Mrs. S., and others, relatives and intimates. Mrs. Emerson, resuming the subject of the evening before, (I sat next to her,) gave me further and fuller information about Thoreau, who, years ago, during Mr. E.'s absence in Europe, had lived for some time in the family, by invitation. . . .

"Boston Common—More of Emerson." (October 1881)

Oct. 10-13.—I spend a good deal of time on the Common, these delicious days and nights. . . . I know all the big trees, especially the old elms along Tremont and Beacon streets, and have come to a sociable-silent understanding with most of them, in the sunlit air, (yet crispy-cool enough,) as I saunter along the wide unpaved walks. Up and down this breadth by Beacon street, between these same old elms, I walk'd for two hours, of a bright sharp February mid-day twenty-one years ago, with Emerson, then in his prime, keen, physically and morally magnetic, arm'd at every point, and when he chose, wielding the emotional just as well as the intellectual. During those two hours he was the talker and I the listener. It was an argument-statement, reconnoitring, review, attack, and pressing home . . . of all that could be said against that part (and a main part) in the construction of my poems, "Children of Adam." More precious than gold to me that dissertation—it afforded me, ever after, this strange and paradoxical lesson; each point of E.'s statement was unanswerable, no judge's charge ever more complete or convincing, I could never hear the points better put—and then I felt down in my soul the clear and unmistakable conviction to disobey all, and pursue my own way. "What have you to say then to such things?" said E., pausing in conclusion. "Only that while I can't answer them at all, I feel more settled than ever to adhere to my own theory, and exemplify it," was my candid response. Whereupon we went and had a good dinner at the American House. And thenceforward I never waver'd or was touch'd with qualms. . . .

"By Emerson's Grave" (May 1882)

May 6, '82.—We stand by Emerson's new-made grave without sadness—indeed a solemn joy and faith, almost hauteur—our soul-benison no mere
"Warrior, rest, thy task is done,"
for one beyond the warriors of the world lies surely symboll'd here. A just man, poised on himself, all-loving, all-inclosing, and sane and clear as the

sun. Nor does it seem so much Emerson himself we are here to honor—it is conscience, simplicity, culture, humanity's attributes at their best, yet applicable if need be to average affairs, and eligible to all. So used are we to suppose a heroic death can only come from out of battle or storm, or mighty personal contest, or amid dramatic incidents or danger . . . that few even of those who most sympathizingly mourn Emerson's late departure will fully appreciate the ripen'd grandeur of that event, with its play of calm and fitness, like evening light on the sea.

How I shall henceforth dwell on the blessed hours when, not long since, I saw that benignant face, the clear eyes, the silently smiling mouth, the form yet upright in its great age—to the very last, with so much spring and cheeriness, and such an absence of decrepitude, that even the term *venerable* hardly seem'd fitting.

Perhaps the life now rounded and completed in its mortal development, and which nothing can change or harm more, has its most illustrious halo, not in its splendid intellectual or esthetic products, but as forming in its entirety one of the few, (alas! how few!) perfect and flawless excuses for being, of the entire literary class.

We can say, as Abraham Lincoln at Gettysburg, It is not we who come to consecrate the dead—we reverently come to receive, if so it may be, some consecration to ourselves and daily work from him.

The first two selections originally appeared in the 3 December 1881 *Critic*, the third in the 6 May 1882 *Critic*; both were revised for inclusion in *Specimen Days & Collect* (1882). Their textual histories are presented, and the variations between printings listed, in *Prose Works 1892*, ed. Floyd Stovall, 2 vols. (New York: New York University Press, 1963–1964), 1:278–80, 281–82, 290–91, the text of which is used here.

[Emerson's Death] (1882)

ELLEN TUCKER EMERSON

Emerson's final illness occurred over the brief span of about ten days. The earliest notices of his illness and death were published in newspaper reports of the "human interest" variety with which we are familiar today. Successive headlines ran, "Ralph Waldo Emerson Sick," "Mr. Emerson Somewhat Better," "No Hope for Emerson," "Mr. Emerson Dead," "Into the Unknown, of Which He Spoke So Grandly, Ralph Waldo Emerson Has Passed," "Ralph Waldo Emerson's Funeral," "Emerson at Rest," and so forth. Accounts appearing under headings such as these originated in the Boston press and were immediately reprinted in other newspapers; many were supplemented by an editorial on Emerson's significance or with reminiscences of Emerson by persons who knew him well.

Between 24 and 25 April 1882, when notices of Emerson's final illness first appeared in the *Boston Daily Advertiser, New-York Daily Tribune, New York Evening Post, New York Herald,* and *New-York Times,* and the close of that year, more than two hundred such reports appeared in America and abroad. In all, Emerson's biography and a near-uniform set of remarks on the significance of his passing dominate the prose. Reference is typically made to his New England lineage and character, his prominence as an author of many volumes of prose and occasional poetry, his years of service as a lecturer on the lyceum circuit, and his association with virtually every American luminary of his time and with international figures such as Thomas Carlyle. Several reports also contained poignant and sometimes hyperbolic expressions of what America's imminent or realized loss of Emerson meant for the nation. When on 27 April— the day that Emerson died—the *Boston Evening Transcript* reported that hope for his recovery had entirely faded, the paper rehearsed one of the more common laments heard in the days immediately following. According to the *Transcript*'s reporter, Emerson was "the teacher, the inspirer, almost the conscience . . . of his countrymen." On the day after his death, the *Boston Daily Advertiser* considerably extended that lament, declaring America's loss of Emerson to be the loss of "the most philosophical mind and temper of this century."

Emerson's death marks a major point of transition in his recorded reputation as that reputation has been set forth thus far in the reminiscences,

(*continued*)

memoirs, and other personal writings printed in this volume. From April 1882 onward, the durability of Emerson's reputation, and his position as an intellectual and literary figure who is central to the telling of any history of the evolution of American thought or literature, are simply assumed. At the same time, however, one begins to see a different kind of personal Emerson developed in some of the writings that follow; indeed, one begins to see an Emerson in two parts. On the one hand, there is the Emerson who grows out of and extends the generally positive depictions of his character and his contributions to American culture that had been dominant up to this point; on the other hand, here and there a significantly more realistic Emerson emerges, an Emerson whose tendency to "coldness"—as it is sometimes described—is addressed, whose lack of philosophic "system" is not only acknowledged, but also seriously critiqued, and whose late-in-life infirmities are described and documented—all, really, for the first time.

For those interested in the circumstances that contributed to Emerson's emergence so quickly at the end of the nineteenth century as a fully formed canonical figure, the account of his death by his daughter Ellen Tucker Emerson is highly instructive. In her letter to her longtime friend Clara Dabney, written on 13 and 19 May 1882, Ellen depicts her father as one who moved seamlessly from this world to the next with an almost indescribable degree of sweetness and calm, who was cherished by every soul from Concord to Boston and beyond, and who to the very end cared more about the feelings of his family and closest friends than he did about his imminent demise.

Ellen Tucker Emerson to Clara Dabney, 13 and 19 May 1882

Dear Miss Clara.

I know you will all have heard that my Father has died, and I have been wanting to write you all about him. It has seemed to me that in this last year he has lost a little faster than in former years. Last summer I noticed it, and much more this winter. It had even become hard for him to understand common things that were said to him, and it was very little that he could say himself. But he was particularly strong and well and much enjoyment was still possible for him. I think I have told you that church-going was a delight lately, and many little club entertainments, readings of papers & discussion afterwards, that he has been invited to, have given him so much pleasure that he was always sorry if he heard that there had been anything of the kind which he had missed. He had walked more than usual too, for sitting still in the study had become a weariness to him, I began to think. We are glad to think that there never was a time of sadness & helplessness, and there was not, but it seemed to me to be coming very near, and I was often tempted to look forward with fear. Though how thoroughly I have been taught day by day through all these years how foolish and needless that is! Every lion that I have seen before me all the way has proved to be chained when I came to the spot. I never have once said to myself or to Mother "What shall we do when this or that becomes necessary?" and in that way distinctly impressed myself with a particular fright, that I have not remembered the question when whatever it was did become necessary, with reason to adore the gracious Providence that had prepared all for it just in time, so that there was no sorrow, no fight, no trouble of any kind. Yet the fear of all that might be when speech had wholly ceased could not be kept entirely down, though I knew it was naughty, and when after Father had been two days sick Edward told me on Saturday April 22d that he probably would not get well, it seemed a very solemn word, but not sad, I could only praise the Lord. Edith & Will came on Sunday and stayed till Tuesday morning, and Edward gave up every thing but sick babies, so that he was with Father for hours every day. So that most of the time he and Will could do everything for Father, which was a great comfort to him and them. Then Edith's confinement being very near, . . . Will took her home, but she sent up Ralph & Violet on Tuesday, . . . and Cameron & Don came on Wednesday. . . . The sight of the children each time they came into the room was sure to make Father smile, and he could say "Good boy!" "Good little girl!" always and sometimes a little more. I don't think he was ever delirious, though confused enough to think he was not at home, and to want to be carried home as fast as possible. Still he often recognized that he was at home, almost always knew us, and evidently had many natural cares on his mind, for one day when he had been talking long and trying vainly to make me understand, he at last succeeded, and I found it was the present finances of the family that he was thinking of, and when I told him that the April bills were paid . . . and that there was money in the bank as well as in the house, he was entirely content, and said no more. He was perpetually grateful for everything that was done, and often smiled and understood for a minute or two what was said. Edward saw that he liked it when Cousin Elizabeth Ripley came to see him, so on Wednesday he sent Judge Hoar, Mr Alcott, Mr Channing & Mr Staples to see him. To Mr Alcott he spoke perfectly clearly, to Judge Hoar so that it was easy to understand, and Judge Hoar said when he came out "His face is as the face of an angel." . . . The next morning when Don went Father said "Good boy! excellent boy!" "I'm going Grandpapa," said Don, "Where?" "I'm going home." "Are you going to teach or to be taught?" "I'm going to school," said Don. But after that Father did not seem to be awake to much that was said or done, much of the time not to see us or to be conscious that we spoke to him. He asked once for Mother but when she came he did not look at her. Up to that time he had been more thankful to have her with him than anyone else. But sometimes through the day it was evident that he did know us. We never asked him. At noon Mr Cabot came. I made a loud and joyful announcement of it and Father said "Who?" When I told him again he said "Mr Elliot Cabot! Praise." Edward gave him brandy & Mr Cabot came in. Father showed the old joy when he saw him, and tried to say "This is that good man who has done so much for me," but it would not come out straight, and soon what he said was no longer to be guessed at. At four Mr Cabot went, he said Father was looking beautifully. Dr Putnam arrived & Mr Sanborn came to bid Father goodbye. Father smiled and said "This is a man that is a man," but could not say anything else, and seemed to be more uncomfortable. . . . In a few minutes great pain began, Annie ran to call the doctors up. They tried in vain to relieve him, and finally gave him ether. Every time he began to come out of it he seemed still in pain, so that they renewed it, and at 10 minutes of 9 he died. Edward sent word at six o'clock to Charley Emerson and Judge Hoar and Mr Keyes and they all came. And everything that could be done for people was done for us. Dr Furness came the next day from Philadelphia. The papers will tell you about the funeral. It seemed to us most beautiful, most affecting, the great concourse, and most of the things that were said and done satisfied us. What a kindness it seems when people come to a funeral at one's own house. It never seemed to me a kindness to go to a funeral. But when people came to . . . Father's it seemed to me so friendly, so lovely of them, it did me great good. Our little Edward Forbes was very sweet. He sat during all the service at the house with tears running down his face, and after we had gone up stairs to put on our things he asked Edith's leave to go down once more to look at his grandpapa, and Mrs Cabot said he seemed not to know there was a soul in the room, he came and leaned on the coffin and looked and looked. When we came to the grave we found it all lined all the way down, with little hemlock twigs, and a bed of green at the bottom. Some of the young people had thought to do that! I had never seen anything like it done before. Now come letters, lovely letters. We have been most thankful for them. . . .

The Letters of Ellen Tucker Emerson, ed. Edith E. W. Gregg, 2 vols. (Kent, Ohio: Kent State University Press), 2:463–65.

"Reminiscences of Ralph Waldo Emerson" (1882)

LOUISA MAY ALCOTT

The daughter of Emerson's lifelong friend, the impractical reformer Bronson
Alcott, and one of the most enduring American women writers of the late nineteenth century, Louisa May Alcott knew Emerson all of her life and, as her biographers and editors have frequently remarked, she considered herself a second
Bettina von Arnim to Emerson's Goethe. Never a practicing Transcendentalist,
Alcott fully understood the practical limitations of Transcendentalism as she
was literally forced to lived through them at the hands of her father and Charles
Lane when the Alcotts settled at Fruitlands in 1843, and when she found herself, especially during and after the 1860s, having to provide for her family's financial security through the sale of her writings.

In her "Reminiscences of Ralph Waldo Emerson," Alcott directly addresses
her debt to Emerson as her intellectual and literary mentor. At the same time,
her account of their friendship over so many years does much to humanize
Emerson at a time when many writers are transforming his life into a form of
secular sainthood. For Alcott, the real measure of Emerson's character is to be
found in his devastation at little Waldo's death in 1842, his playfulness in the
company of his own and the Alcott children, his ironic understatement at seeing his house burn in 1872, and his humanitarianism in supporting reform
movements such as Women's Suffrage. By opening her account in the *Youth's
Companion* with the statement, "I count it the greatest honor and happiness of
my life to have known Mr. Emerson," Alcott, whose *Little Women* (1868–1869)
and *Little Men* (1871) already served America's rising generation as classics of
family and community life, virtually legislated a new generation's attention to
Emerson's literary and intellectual legacy.

As I count it the greatest honor and happiness of my life to have known Mr.
Emerson, I gladly accede to a request for such recollections as may be of interest for the young readers for whom I write [in the *Youth's Companion*].

My first remembrance is of the morning when I was sent to inquire for little Waldo, then lying very ill.

His father came to me so worn with watching and changed by sorrow that I was startled, and could only stammer out my message.

"Child, he is dead," was his answer.

Then the door closed and I ran home to tell the sad tidings. I was only eight years old, and that was my first glimpse of a great grief, but I never have forgotten the anguish that made a familiar face so tragical, and gave those few words more pathos than the sweet lamentation of the Threnody.

Later, when we went to school with the little Emersons in their father's barn, I remember many happy times when the illustrious papa was our good playfellow.

Often piling us into a bedecked hay-cart, he took us to berry, bathe, or picnic at Walden, making our day charming and memorable by showing us the places he loved; the wood-people Thoreau had introduced to him; or the wild flowers whose hidden homes he had discovered. So that when years afterward we read of "the sweet Rhodora in the wood," and "the burly, dozy humblebee," or laughed over "The Mountain and the Squirrel," we recognized old friends, and thanked him for the delicate truth and beauty which made them immortal for us and others.

When the book-mania fell upon me at fifteen, I used to venture into Mr. Emerson's library and ask what I should read, never conscious of the audacity of my demand, so genial was my welcome.

His kind hand opened to me the riches of Shakespeare, Dante, Goethe and Carlyle, and I gratefully recall the sweet patience with which he led me round the book-lined room, till "the new and very interesting book" was found; or the indulgent smile he wore when I proposed something far above my comprehension.

"Wait a little for that," he said. "Meantime try this, and if you like it, come again."

For many of these wise books I am waiting still, very patiently, because in his own I have found the truest delight, the best inspiration of my life.

When these same precious volumes were tumbled out of the window while his house was burning some years ago, as I stood guarding the scorched, wet pile, Mr. Emerson passed by, and surveying the devastation with philosophic calmness, only said in answer to my lamentations,—

"I see my library under a new aspect. Could you tell me where my good neighbors have flung my boots?"

In the tribulations of later life, this faithful house-friend was an earthly

Providence, conferring favors so beautifully that they were no burden, . . . and living what he wrote, his influence purified and brightened like sunshine.

Many a thoughtful young man and woman owe to Emerson the spark that kindled their highest aspirations, and showed them how to make the conduct of life a helpful lesson, not a blind struggle.

> "For simple maids and noble youth
> Are welcome to the man of truth;
> Most welcome they who need him most,
> They feed the spring which they exhaust,
> For greater need
> Draws better deed."

He was in truth, like his own Saadi, "a cheerer of men's hearts."

Friendship, Love, Self-Reliance, Heroism and Compensation among the essays have become to many readers as precious as Christian's scroll, and certain poems live in the memory as sacred as hymns, so helpful and inspiring are they.

No better books for earnest young people can be found. The truest words are often the simplest, and when wisdom and virtue go hand in hand, none need fear to listen, learn and love.

The marble walk that leads to his hospitable door has been trodden by the feet of many pilgrims from all parts of the world, drawn thither by their love and reverence for him. In that famous study his town's people have had the privilege of seeing many of the great and good men and women of our time, and learning of their gracious host the finest lessons of true courtesy.

I have often seen him turn from distinguished guests, to say a wise or kindly word to some humble worshipper, sitting modestly in a corner, content merely to look and listen, and who went away to cherish that memorable moment long and gratefully.

Here, too, in the pleasant room, with the green hills opposite, and the pines murmuring musically before the windows, Emerson wrote essays more helpful than most sermons; lectures which created the lyceum; poems full of power and sweetness; and better than song or sermon has lived a life so noble, true and beautiful that its wide-spreading influence is felt on both sides of the sea.

In all reforms he was among the foremost on the side of justice and progress. When Faneuil Hall used to be a scene of riot and danger in Anti-Slavery days, I remember sitting up aloft, an excited girl, among the loyal women who never failed to be there; and how they always looked for that serene face on the platform, and found fresh courage in the mere sight of the wisest man in America, standing shoulder to shoulder with the bravest.

When Woman's Suffrage was most unpopular, his voice and pen spoke for the just cause, undaunted by the fear of ridicule which silences so many.

His own simple, abstemious habits were his best testimony in favor of temperance in all things, while in religion he believed that each soul must choose its own aids, and prove the vitality of its faith by high thinking and holy living.

When travelling in various countries I found his fame had gone before, and people were eager to hear something of the Concord poet, seer and philosopher.

In a little town upon the Rhine, where our party paused for a night, unexpectedly delayed, two young Germans, reading the word Boston on the labels of our trunks as they stood in the yard of the inn, begged to come in and see the Americans, and their first question was,—

"Tell us about Emerson."

We gladly told them what they asked, and they listened as eagerly as we did to anything we could hear concerning their great countryman Goethe.

A letter once came to me from the far West, in which a girl asked what she should read to build up a noble character. It was a remarkable letter, and when I inquired what books she most desired, she answered, "All of Emerson's; he helps me the most."

A prisoner just from Concord jail came to see me on his release, and proved to be an intelligent, book-loving young man, who had been led into crime by his first fit of intoxication. In talking with him, he said Emerson's books were a comfort to him, and he had spent some of the money earned in prison to buy certain volumes to take with him as guides and safeguards for the future.

In England his honored name opened many doors to us, and we felt as proud of our acquaintance with him as Englishmen feel of the medals with which their Queen decorates them. So widely was he known, so helpful was his influence, so ennobling the mere reflection of his virtue and his genius.

Longfellow was beloved by children, and of Emerson it might be said, as of Plato, "He walks with his head among the stars, yet carries a blessing in his heart for every little child."

When he returned from his second visit to Europe after his house was burned, he was welcomed by the school-children, who lined his passage from the cars to the carriage, where a nosegay of blooming grandchildren awaited him; and escorted by a smiling troop of neighbors, old and young, he was conducted under green arches to his house.

Here they sang "Sweet Home," gave welcoming cheers, and marched away to come again soon after to a grand house-warming in the old mansion which had been so well restored that nothing seemed changed.

Many a gay revel has been held under the pines, whole schools taking possession of the poet's premises; and many a child will gladly recall hereafter the paternal face that smiled on them, full of interest in their gambols, and of welcome for the poorest.

Mrs. Emerson, from her overflowing garden, planted flowers along the roadside and in the plot of ground before the nearest school-house to beautify the children's daily life. Sweeter and more imperishable than these will be the recollections of many kindnesses bestowed by one who, in the truest sense of the word, was a friend to all.

As he lay dying, children stopped to ask if he were better, and all the sunshine faded out of the little faces when the sad answer came. Very willing feet roamed the woods for green garlands to decorate the old church where he would come for the last time; busy hands worked till midnight that every house should bear some token of mourning; Spring gave him her few early flowers and budding boughs from the haunts that will know him no more, and old and young forgot for a little while their pride in the illustrious man to sorrow for the beloved friend and neighbor.

Life did not sadden his cheerful philosophy; success could not spoil his exquisite simplicity; age could not dismay him, and he met death with sweet serenity.

He wrote, "Nothing can bring you peace but yourself. Nothing can bring you peace but the triumph of principles;" and this well-earned peace transfigured the beautiful dead face, so many eyes beheld with tender reverence, seeming to assure us that our august friend and master had passed into the larger life for which he was ready, still to continue,—

"Without hasting, without rest.
Lifting Better up to Best:
Planting seeds of knowledge pure,
Thro' earth to ripen, thro' heaven endure."

Youth's Companion, 55 (25 May 1882): 213–14.

[Reminiscences of Emerson] (1882)

Frederic Henry Hedge

The son of Harvard professor Levi Hedge, Frederic Henry Hedge was the Transcendentalist most familiar with German literature, and the only one who had studied in Germany. He met Emerson in 1828, when both were in the Harvard Divinity School. One of the leading lights of what became the Transcendentalist movement, his March 1833 article on Samuel Taylor Coleridge in the Unitarian journal, the *Christian Examiner*, is considered the first major confrontation between those who favored the intuitive philosophy of Immanuel Kant and those who believed in John Locke, who had made sensory experience the prime means by which we learn. In 1835, partially through Emerson's assistance, Hedge became pastor to a congregation in Bangor, Maine, where he stayed until 1850. His return visits to Boston became the occasion for the social gatherings known as the Transcendental Club. But the influence of Hedge's essentially conservative parish, his support of the American Unitarian Association, his desire to find a moderate middle ground in the current theological debates, and his own antipathy toward the more radical aspects of Transcendentalism, all soon distanced him from the movement and his friends in it. He later served as editor of the *Christian Examiner*, president of the American Unitarian Association, and professor of German language and literature at Harvard University. Hedge's reminiscences of Emerson, written for James Elliot Cabot shortly after Emerson's death, present a useful overview of Emerson and his ideas that spans half a century.

Frederic Henry Hedge to James Elliot Cabot, 14 September 1882

Dear Mr. Cabot,

I send you herewith, at your suggestion some reminiscences of our friend Emerson, written at the first leisure moment since the receipt of your letter. . . .

I have brought them down to the time when he began to be famous & when as I suppose your acquaintance with him commenced. . . .

Reminiscences of Emerson

My acquaintance with Emerson began in 1828. He was then living in Divinity Hall Cambridge, & though not a member of the Divinity School was understood to be a candidate for the ministry preparing himself in his own way for the function of preacher. There was no presage then, as I remember, of his future greatness. His promise seemed faint in comparison with the wondrous brilliancy of his younger brother, Edward Bliss Emerson, whose immense expectation was doomed never to be fulfilled. A still younger brother, Charles Chauncy, had also won admiration from contemporary youth while Waldo as yet had given no proof of what was in him.

He developed slowly. Yet there was notable in him then, at the age of twenty five, a refinement of thought & a selectness in the use of language which gave promise of an interesting preacher to cultivated hearers. He never jested; a certain reserve in his manner restrained the jesting propensity & any license of speech in others.

He kept a diary in which he recorded whatever he had heard that seemed to him memorable during the day. I remember his coming to me one evening to learn some particulars in an anecdote with which Professor Norton had illustrated his remarks on a sermon just preached by one of the students in Divinity Hall chapel. He could not sleep until he had made a note of the whole.

As I kept no diary myself I can recall but little of our talk. I tried to interest him in German literature but he laughingly said that as he was entirely ignorant of the subject he should assume that it was not worth knowing.

Later he studied German mainly for the purpose of acquainting himself with Goethe to whom his attention had been directed by Carlyle.

He was slow in his movements as in his speech. He never through eagerness interrupted any speaker with whom he conversed, however prepossessed with a contrary opinion. And no one, I think, ever saw him run.

He told me that he never went from home on even the shortest journey without leaving his papers & other matters as he would have them found if suddenly overtaken by death.

In ethics he held very positive opinions. And here his native independence of thought was manifest. "Owe no conformity to custom," he said, "against your private judgement." "Have no regard to the influence of your example, but *act always from the simplest motive*."

Once I was giving him a lift in my chaise on his way to Boston. West Boston bridge was then a toll bridge & on that day the toll was taken at the further end. I proposed to take him half the way across & let him walk the rest. This he would not accept; it would be getting half the benefit of the bridge without paying toll.

In the spring of 1829 he was ordained minister of the Second Church in Boston then located at the North end, & soon after married Miss Ellen Tucker of Concord N. H. The pair set up house keeping in a court off Chardon St. which, I believe has since been destroyed. In the summer they occupied a house in Brookline, a quaint, old fashioned mansion near the site of St Paul's church.

I recall the first Mrs. Emerson as a beautiful, fragile figure apparently just out of her "teens," with a complexion that indicated feeble health & foreboded early death.

Emerson's early sermons were characterized by great simplicity & an unconventional, untheological style which brought him into closer *rapport* with his hearers than was commonly achieved by the pulpit in those days. Hearers of an orthodox turn were shocked by what seemed to them unsanctified discourse; but those who listened with unprejudiced & appreciative minds, especially the young, were charmed by his preaching as by no other. He won his first admirers in the pulpit. I wish that some of his sermons might he printed; they would be interesting, if only as curiosities.

He sometimes spoke to me of the repugnance he felt to the communion service & I was not surprised when we heard that he had asked to be excused from that part of the pastoral office. The sensation caused by this step was prodigious. Even friends were shocked by it. Hints of insanity were not wanting.

This led to the resignation of his office. His wife meanwhile had died & he went abroad. It was during this first visit to Europe in 1833 that he became acquainted with Carlyle then residing at Craigenputtoch whither, with some difficulty, Emerson found his way.

His first course of lectures in Boston was given, I think, during the winter of 1834–35. He was then living in Concord in the house known as the "Old Manse" with . . . Dr Ezra Ripley who had married the widow of his grandfather & was called "grandfather" by the Emersons. I saw him frequently during that winter & was much impressed with the intellectual progress he seemed to have made during the two preceding years. I felt as never before the overweight of his genius. For some years after his removal to Concord he continued to preach, supplying the pulpit at East Lexington. His brother Edward died at Porto Rico in 1834, Charles in New York in 1836. In 1835 he married Miss Lydia Jackson, the present Mrs. Emerson, & bought the house which [they] thenceforward occupied until his death. In 1836 he published his first printed volume "Nature." A new epoch in American literature dates from that publication. . . .

Frederic Henry Hedge to James Elliot Cabot, 30 September 1882

Dear Mr. Cabot,

I think it not unlikely that Emerson was more rapid in his movements in after life than he was at the time of my first acquaintance with him when he was more of a dreamer. His character gained in decision as the exigencies of life forced him to become more a man of affairs, especially after the death of his brother Charles on whom he had leaned for aid in practical matters. And decision favors rapid motion. But my impression of the slow-moving youth remains.

I was well acquainted with Edward B[liss Emerson]. He was of the class before me in college & we were fellow members of some college clubs. I have never known a more brilliant youth.[1] A beautiful countenance full of force & fire, yet of an almost feminine refinement. He was a favorite in society, especially in feminine society, & a welcome partner in the dance. He was not merely the first scholar in his class but first by a long interval. His orations were epochs in college history; the one he delivered on taking his degree contained an eloquent allusion to Lafayette then present which I still recall after the lapse of nearly sixty years. He was looking to political life for his career but the overwrought brain gave out; he fell into conscious & irrecoverable ruin. His death, I fancy, was hastened by grief for his failed ambition.

Charles too I knew very well. He was also a youth of wonderful promise, but more practical than Waldo, with a more ready tongue, a good extempore speaker, somewhat sarcastic, strong in independence & moral courage, a frank confessor of religious faith, speaking freely of sacred things, without a shadow of cant, & without the shyness & shamefacedness with which men of the world are apt to approach such topics. "Always do the thing you are afraid to do"—he was a man who would not have shunned to affront the

1. Not so tall as Waldo but of full middle size. [Hedge's note]

highest dignitary at the bidding of truth. I think he rather dominated Waldo while thoroughly appreciating his genius. It is certain that Waldo was much influenced by him.

I suppose it is true that E. was not a faithful pastor; he had no real vocation for the pastoral office; he was not sympathetic, sickness & the house of mourning repelled him. It was the instinct of heredity, or perhaps the consciousness of having something to say for which the pulpit furnished the best opportunity, rather than a due consideration of its claims that led him into the ministry. I am not surprised to learn that there was a falling off in the attendance at his church. The average, formal churchgoer missed the unction, with a relish of sanctimoniousness, (though unquestionably honest & sincere) of his predecessor. Emerson's piety was of a different type & the old people, used to certain phrases & tones, could not "see it." But I am sure that the young, for the most part, & unbiased minds, heard him gladly & felt themselves edified by him.

His want of fluency in prayer was due in part to his great fastidiousness in the choice of words. He shrank from the use of stereotyped phrases. So the aesthetic hampered the emotional. I remember his speaking to me of the difficulty he experienced in that function, & how the necessity of saying something & not stopping abruptly led him to say what he would not have said— a kind of insincerity. But later, when he had acquired more confidence, in his services at East Lexington, his prayers were said by an intelligent listener to be something wonderful. A prayer, he said, is "a sally into the Infinite"; & such, this listener told me were the prayers she heard from him.

I can't say who first proposed the Dial. The project of a literary organ which should represent the "new ideas" was discussed for a year or more by the so called "Transcendentalists" at their meetings before it ripened into deed. It might have been Alcott who suggested "Dial" for its title, but I never heard that it was. Geo. Ripley had nothing to do with the editing of it. So far as I rem[em]ber, Margaret Fuller & Emerson were the only responsible editors. . . .

I suppose you know about "Aunt Mary" who had such influence over E. in his early days. . . .

Frederic Henry Hedge to James Elliot Cabot, 20 November 1883

Dear Mr. Cabot,

. . . As to Emerson's voice, I don't think he ever took pains to improve it. Nor

[99]

did it materially improve from the first use of it in public speaking. It developed somewhat but without any effort or practising for effect. It gained a little in depth & richness as, I suppose, a barytone voice always does with the intellectual & moral growth of the speaker. But that is all. It reached its perfection, I think, when he entered on the thirties. I never heard it finer than in 1835....

Frederic Henry Hedge to James Elliot Cabot, 8 December 1883

Dear Mr. Cabot,

... The "Transcendental" business, so far as I remember, had this origin. In Sept. 1836 on the day of the Celebration of the bicentennial anniversary of the founding of Harvard College, Mr. Emerson, George Ripley & myself with a fourth [George Putnam] who so soon withdrew from the connection that 'tis not worth the while to mention his name, chanced to confer together on the state of current opinion in theology & philosophy, which we agreed in thinking very unsatisfactory. Could anything be done in the way of protest & introduction of deeper & broader views? What precisely we wanted it would have been difficult for either of us to state. What we strongly felt was dissatisfaction, with the reigning sensuous philosophy dating from Locke, on which our Unitarian theology was based. The writings of Coleridge recently edited by Marsh & some of Carlyle's earlier essays, especially the "Characteristics" & the "Signs of the Time" had created a ferment in the minds of some of the young clergy of that day. There was a promise in the air of a new era of intellectual life.

We four concluded to call a few like minded seekers together on the following week. Some dozen of us, including the three already named, met in Boston at the house, I believe of Mr Ripley. Among them I recall the names of Orestes Brownson (not yet turned Romanist), C. A. Bartol, Theodore Parker, [Charles Stearns] Wheeler & [Robert] Bartlett tutors in Harvard College. There was some discussion but no conclusion reached, on the question whether it were best to start a new journal as the organ of our views or to work through those already existing.

The next meeting, in the same month of September, was held, by invitation of Emerson, at his house in Concord.

A large number assembled; beside some of those who met in Boston I remember Mr. Alcott, J. S. Dwight, Ephraim Peabody, Dr Francis, Mrs Sarah Ripley, Miss E. P. Peabody, Margaret Fuller, Mr. C. Stetson, J. F. Clarke.

There was conversation, entertaining, instructive, on many topics, but no action taken.

These were the earliest of a series of meetings held from time to time as occasion prompted for seven or eight years. Jones Very was one of those who occasionally attended, . . . Thoreau another. There was no club, properly speaking, no organization, no presiding officer, no vote ever taken on any question. How the name "Transcendental" [was] given to these gatherings & the set of persons who took part in them, originated I cannot say. It certainly was never assumed by the persons so called. I suppose I was the only one who had any first hand acquaintance with the German transcendental philosophy at the start. The Dial was the product of the movement & in some sort its organ. With the expiration of that journal the meetings, so far as I remember, ceased. I can think of nothing more concerning this matter that would interest you at present.

Matthew Fisher, "Emerson Remembered: Nine Letters by Frederic Henry Hedge," in *Studies in the American Renaissance 1989*, ed. Joel Myerson (Charlottesville: University Press of Virginia, 1989), pp. 318–19, 322–23, 325, 326–27.

"Some Recollections of Ralph Waldo Emerson" (1882)

[Edwin Percy Whipple]

Prolific American essayist and literary critic Edwin Percy Whipple advocated for a national literature free from British and other influences and a national critical theory informed by ethics and an appreciation of the essential intellectual relationship between authors and their readers. Although he enjoyed a close friendship with Nathaniel Hawthorne, helping him to select the title for *The House of the Seven Gables* and offering him useful commentary on the manuscript of *The Blithedale Romance*, in the richly anecdotal piece that follows, Whipple clearly identifies Emerson as his premier model of the ideal writer and critic. Written from complete devotion to Emerson, the essay describes their first meeting and emphasizes Emerson's lofty character and Franklinesque practicality, his antipathy toward spiritualism, and his abilities as thinker and lecturer. Although the accuracy of his memory has never been proven, in this reminiscence Whipple states that he thinks he may have been the source of the characterization of Emerson as a "Greek-Yankee—a cross between Plato and Jonathan Slick," while at the same time he confesses his own doubt about whether he may also have been the source of the characterization of Emerson as "a Hindoo-Yankee—a cross between Brahma and Poor Richard."

It is impossible for those who only knew Emerson through his writings to understand the peculiar love and veneration felt for him by those who knew him personally. Only by intercourse with him could the singular force, sweetness, elevation, originality, and comprehensiveness of his nature be fully appreciated; and the friend or acquaintance, however he might differ from him in opinion, felt the peculiar fascination of his character, and revolved around this solar mind in obedience to the law of spiritual gravitation—the spiritual law operating, like the natural law, directly as the mass, and inversely as the square of the distance. The friends nearest to him loved and honored him most; but those who only met him occasionally felt the attraction of his spiritual power, and could not mention him without a tribute of respect. There probably never was another man of the first class, with a general system of thought at variance with accredited opinions, who exercised so much gentle, persuasive power over the minds of his opponents. . . . To his readers in the closet, and his hearers on the lecture platform, he poured lavishly out from his intellectual treasury . . . the silver and gold, the pearls, rubies, amethysts, opals, and diamonds of thought. If his readers and his audiences chose to pick them up, they were welcome to them; but if they conceived he was deceiving them with sham jewelry, he would not condescend to explain the laborious processes in the mines of meditation by which he had brought the hidden treasures to light. . . .

[Everybody] who intimately knew this seer and thinker had the good sense never to intrude into the inward sanctities . . . of his individual meditations, and vulgarly ask questions as to the doubts and conflicts he had encountered in that utter loneliness of thought, where his individual soul, in direct contact, as he supposed, with the "Over-Soul," was trying to solve problems of existence which perplex all thoughtful minds. He would do nothing more than make affirmations regarding the deep things of the spirit, which were to be accepted or rejected as they happened to strike or miss the point of inlet into the other intellects he addressed. . . .

The native elevation of Emerson's mind and the general loftiness of his thinking have sometimes blinded his admirers to the fact that he was one of the shrewdest of practical observers, and was capable of meeting so-called practical men on the level of the facts and principles which they relied upon for success in life. When I first had the happiness to make his acquaintance I was a clerk in a banking house. I have a faint memory of having written in a penny paper a notice of his first volume of Essays which differed altogether from the notices which appeared in business journals of a higher rank and price. The first thing that struck me was the quaint, keen, homely good sense which was one of the marked characteristics of the volume; and I contrasted the coolness of this transcendentalist, whenever he discussed matters relating to the conduct of life, with the fury of delusion under which merchants of established reputation sometimes seemed to be laboring in their mad attempts to resist the operation of the natural laws of trade. They, I thought, were the transcendentalists, the subjective poets, the Rousseaus and Byrons of business, who in their greed were fiercely "accommodating the shows of things to the desires of the mind," without any practical insight of principles or foresight of consequences. . . .

[103]

As far as my memory serves me at this time, I think to me, in my youthful presumption, belongs the dubious honor or dishonor of calling him our "Greek-Yankee—a cross between Plato and Jonathan Slick." I am less certain as to the other statement that he was "a Hindoo-Yankee—a cross between Brahma and Poor Richard." . . . But I always wondered that the Franklin side of his opulent and genial nature did not draw to him a host of readers who might be repelled by the dazzling though puzzling sentences in which his ideal philosophy found expression. It is to be supposed that such persons refused to read him because they distrusted his constant tendency to combine beauty with use. The sense of beauty, indeed, was so vital an element in the very constitution of his being that it decorated everything it touched. He was a thorough artist, while inculcating maxims of thrift far beyond those of Poor Richard. His beautiful genius could not be suppressed even when he discoursed of the ugliest sides of a farmer's life; he shed an ideal light over pots and cans, over manure heaps and cattle-raising; and when he announced that maxim of celestial prudence, "Hitch your wagon to a star," the transcendentalist was discovered peeping through the economist, and it became hard to believe that he was in ordinary affairs a really practical man. . . .

The raciest testimony . . . to the soundness of Emerson in practical matters was delivered by a sturdy, stalwart Vermonter in a car on the Fitchburg Railroad. My journey was to be a tedious one of three hundred miles, and when I took my seat in the car, I felt that my fellow-passengers would give me no such glimpses into their characters as would be afforded by a ride of ten miles in a stage-coach. . . . There were two persons in front of me, mighty in bulk, but apparently too much absorbed in their own reflections to speak to each other. The train, as usual, stopped at Concord. Then one of the giants turned to the other, and lazily remarked, "Mr. Emerson, I hear, lives in this town."

"Ya-as," was the drawling rejoinder; "and I understand that, in spite of his odd notions, he is a man of *con-sid-er*-able propity."

This apposite judgment was made when Emerson's essays had been translated into most of the languages of Europe, and when the recognition of his genius was even more cordial abroad than it was among his few thousands of appreciative admirers at home; but the shrewd Yankee who uttered it was more impressed by his thrift than by his thinking. He belonged to the respectable race of *des*cendentalists, and was evidently puzzled to understand how a *trans*cendentalist could acquire "propity."

On one occasion, in my early acquaintance with Emerson, I was hastily summoned to lecture at a country town some five miles from Boston, because Emerson, who had been expected to occupy the desk, had not signified his acceptance of the invitation. He either had neglected to answer the letter of the committee, or his own note in reply had miscarried. About ten minutes before the lecture was to begin, Emerson appeared. Of course I insisted on having the privilege of listening to him, rather than compel the audience to listen to me. He generously declared that as the mistake seemed to have arisen from his own neglect, I had the right to the platform. When I solemnly assured him that no lecture would be heard that evening in that town unless he delivered it, he, still somewhat protesting, unrolled his manuscript, and took his place at the desk. The lecture, though perhaps not one of his best lyceum discourses, was better than the best of any other living lecturer. When it was over, he invited me to take a seat in the chaise which had brought him from Boston. I gladly accepted. The horse was, fortunately for me, one of the slowest beasts which ever had the assurance to pretend to convey faster, by carriage, two persons from one point to another than an ordinary pedestrian could accomplish in a meditative walk. The pace was, I think, about two miles an hour. As soon as we got into the chaise, I began to speak of the lecture, and referring to what he had said of the Puritans, I incidentally alluded to the peculiar felicity of his use of the word "grim," and added that I noticed it was a favorite word of his in his published essays. "Do you say," he eagerly responded, "that I use the word often?" "Yes," I replied, "but never without its being applicable to the class of persons you are characterizing." He reflected a minute or two, and then said, as if he had experienced a pang of intellectual remorse, "The word is probably passing with me into a mannerism, and I must hereafter guard against it—must banish it from my dictionary."

. . . Emerson was in his happiest mood. He entered into a peculiar kind of conversation . . . in which reverie occasionally emerged into soliloquy, and then again became a real talk. . . . I shall never forget that evening. The moon was nearly at its full, undisturbed by a cloud, and the magical moonlight flooded the landscape and skyscape with its soft, gentle, serene, mystical radiance, . . . and I never felt its mystical charm more profoundly than on this ride of two hours with Emerson. . . .

Emerson's voice had a strange power, which affected me more than any other voice I ever heard on the stage or on the platform. It was pure thought translated into purely intellectual tone, the perfect music of spiritual utterance. It is impossible to read his verses adequately without bearing in mind his peculiar accent and emphasis; and some of the grandest and most uplifting passages in his prose lose much of their effect unless the reader can recall the tones of his voice. . . . There was nothing sensual, nothing even sensuous, nothing weakly melodious, in his utterance; but his voice had the stern, keen, penetrating sweetness which made it a fit organ for his self-centered, commanding mind. Yet though peculiar to himself, it had at the same time an impersonal character, as though a spirit was speaking through him. . . .

He had, from the start, a strong antipathy to "spiritism." When departed spirits, by "knockings" and moving furniture, first began to inform us poor mortals that they were still alive—alive, however, in a world which appeared, on the whole, to be worse than that from which death had released them, the great question of immortality was considered by many pious persons to have obtained new evidences of its truth from these materialistic manifestations. . . .

Emerson's impatience when the subject came up for discussion in a company of intelligent people was amusing to witness. He was specially indignant at the idea of women adopting spiritism as a profession, and engaging to furnish all people with news of their deceased friends at a shilling a head. The enormous vulgarity of the whole thing impressed him painfully, especially when he was told that some of his own friends paid even the slightest attention to the revelations, as he phrased it, of "those seamstresses turned into sibyls, who charged a pistareen a spasm!" Brougham's well-known remark that the idea of Campbell's writing his life added a new horror to death, was a just anticipation of a terrible fact; for Campbell did write his life, and made a dreadful wreck of Brougham's reputation. Happily, Emerson's last days were clouded by a failure of memory, or he might have mourned that his spirit would be called by "mediums" from "its golden day" to furnish the public with information detailing his present "gossip about the celestial politics." . . .

In all Emerson's experience as a lecturer there was only one occasion when he received that tribute to a radical orator's timely eloquence which is expressed in hisses. The passage of the Fugitive Slave Law stirred him into unwonted moral passion and righteous wrath. He accepted an invitation to deliver a lecture in Cambridgeport, called for the purpose of protesting

against that infamous anomaly in jurisprudence and insult to justice. . . .
Those who sympathized with him were there in force; but a score or two of
foolish Harvard students came down from the college to the hall where the
lecture was delivered, determined to assert "the rights of the South." . . .
They were the rowdiest, noisiest, most brainless set of young gentlemen that
ever pretended to be engaged in studying "the humanities." . . . Their only
arguments were hisses and groans whenever the most illustrious of American men of letters uttered an opinion which expressed the general opinion
of the civilized world. . . . It was curious to watch him as, at each point he
made, he paused to let the storm of hisses subside. The noise was something
he had never heard before; there was a queer, quizzical, squirrel-like or bird-
like expression in his eye as he calmly looked round to see what strange human animals were present to make such sounds; and when he proceeded to
utter another indisputable truth, and it was responded to by another chorus
of hisses, he seemed absolutely to enjoy the new sensation he experienced,
and waited for these signs of disapprobation to stop altogether before he resumed his discourse. The experience was novel; still there was not the
slightest tremor in his voice, not even a trace of the passionate resentment
which a speaker under such circumstances and impediments usually feels,
and which urges him into the cheap retort about serpents, but a quiet waiting for the time when he should be allowed to go on with the next sentence.
During the whole evening he never uttered a word which was not written
down in the manuscript from which he read. . . .

Emerson's good sense was so strong that it always seemed to be specially
awakened in the company of those who were most in sympathy with his loft-
iest thinking. Thus, when "the radical philosophers" were gathered one evening at his house, the conversation naturally turned on the various schemes
of benevolent people to reform the world. Each person present had a pana-
cea to cure all the distempers of society. For hours the talk ran on, and before
bed-time came, all the sin and misery of the world had been apparently ex-
pelled from it, and our planet was reformed and transformed into an abode
of human angels, and virtue and happiness were the lot of each human being. Emerson listened, but was sparing of speech. Probably he felt, with La-
mennais, that if facts did not resist thoughts, the earth would in a short time
become uninhabitable. At any rate, he closed the *séance* with the remark: "A
few of us old codgers meet at the fireside on a pleasant evening, and in

thought and hope career, balloon-like, over the whole universe of matter and mind, finding no resistance to our theories, because we have, in the sweet delirium of our thinking, none of those obstructive facts which face the practical reformer the moment he takes a single forward step; then we go to bed; and the pity of it is we wake up in the morning feeling that we are the same poor old imbeciles we were before!" . . .

Many of Emerson's friends and acquaintances thought that his sense of humor was almost as keen as his sense of Beauty and his sense of Right. I do not remember an instance in my conversations with him, when the question came up of his being not understood, or, what is worse, misunderstood by the public, that he did not treat the matter in an exquisitely humorous way, telling the story of his defeats in making himself comprehended by the audience or the readers he addressed as if the misapprehensions of his meaning were properly subjects of mirth, in which he could heartily join. . . . For example, on one occasion I recollect saying that of all his college addresses I thought the best was that on "The Method of Nature," delivered before the Society of the Adelphi, in Waterville College, Maine, August 11, 1841. He then gave me a most amusing account of the circumstances under which the oration was delivered. . . . At that time a considerable portion of the journey to Waterville had to be made by stage. He arrived late in the evening, travel-worn and tired out, when almost all the sober inhabitants of Waterville had gone to bed. It appeared that there was some doubt as to the particular citizen's house at which he was to pass the night. "The stage-driver," said Emerson, "stopped at one door; rapped loudly; a window was opened; something in a night-gown asked what he wanted; the stage-driver replied that he had inside a man who *said* he was to deliver the lit-ra-rye oration to-morrow, and thought he was to stop there; but the night-gown disappeared, with the chilling remark that he was not to stay at *his* house. Then we went to another, and still another, dwelling, rapped, saw similar night-gowns and heard similar voices at similar raised windows; and it was only after repeated disturbances of the peace of the place that the right house was hit, where I found a hospitable reception. The next day I delivered my oration, which was heard with cold, silent, unresponsive attention, in which there seemed to be a continuous unuttered rebuke and protest. The services were closed by prayer, and the good man who prayed, prayed for the orator, but also warned his hearers against heresies and wild notions, which appeared to me of that kind for which I was held responsible. The address was really written in the heat and happiness of what I thought a real inspiration; but all the warmth was extinguished in that lake of iced water." . . .

. . . Emerson's greatness came from his character. Sweetness and light streamed from him because they were *in* him. In everything he thought, wrote, and did we feel the presence of a personality as vigorous and brave as it was sweet, and the particular radical thought he at any time expressed derived its power to animate and illuminate other minds from the might of the manhood which was felt to be within and behind it. To "sweetness and light" he therefore added the prime quality of fearless manliness.

If the force of Emerson's character was thus inextricably blended with the force of all his faculties of intellect and imagination, and the refinement of all his sentiments, we have still to account for the peculiarities of his genius, and to answer the question, why do we instinctively apply the epithet "Emersonian" to every characteristic passage in his writings? We are told that he was the last in a long line of clergymen, his ancestors, and that the modern doctrine of heredity accounts for the impressive emphasis he laid on the moral sentiment; but that does not solve the puzzle why he unmistakably differed in his nature and genius from all other Emersons. An imaginary genealogical chart of descent connecting him with Confucius or Gotama would be more satisfactory. At the time he acquired notoriety but had not yet achieved fame, it was confidently asserted in all Boston circles that his brother Charles, the "calm, chaste scholar" celebrated by Holmes, was greatly his superior in ability, and would, had he not died early, have entirely eclipsed Ralph; Emerson himself, the most generous and loving of brothers, always inclined to this opinion; but there is not an atom of evidence that Charles, had he lived, would have produced works which would be read by a choice company of thinkers and scholars all over the world, which would be translated into all the languages of Europe, and would be prized in London and Edinburgh, in Berlin and Vienna, in Rome and Paris, as warmly as they were in Boston and New York. What distinguishes *the* Emerson was his *exceptional* genius and character, that something in him which separated him from all other Emersons, as it separated him from all other eminent men of letters, and impressed every intelligent reader with the feeling that he was not only "original but aboriginal." Some traits of his mind and character may be traced back to his ancestors, but what doctrine of heredity can give us the genesis of his genius? Indeed, the safest course to pursue is to quote his own words, and despairingly confess that it is the nature of genius "to spring, like the rainbow daughter of Wonder, from the invisible, to abolish the past, and refuse all history."

Harper's New Monthly Magazine, 65 (September 1882): 576–87.

ORDER OF PERFORMANCES

AT THE

LATIN SCHOOL,

August 25, 1815.

1. "De Æstate Carmen," imitation of Thomson.

   A. Young.

2. A Greek Dialogue, "Pyrrho and his Neighbour." Translated from Fenelon.

   W. H. Furness & L. P. Curtis.

3. A Latin Dialogue, "The Two Robbers." Translated from Dr. Aiken.

   T. G. Bradford & E. G. Loring.

4. An English Poem, "Independence."

   R. W. Emerson.

5. An English Dialogue, "Cicero and Chesterfield." Knox.

   G. R. M. Withington & I. Winslow.

6. A Latin Oration, "De Literis Græcis."

   F. P. Leverett.

The names of the performers are placed in the order in which they will speak.

Program for the exercises at the Boston Public Latin School in 1815, showing a poem, "Independence," by Emerson.

Emerson's letter of 28 February 1816 to Mary Moody Emerson.

lead him astray after Will.o'the.wisp · over wilderness
& fen; fright him with ghostly hobgoblins · wreak
your vengeance as you will — He gives you free
leave on this sole condition. = if you can. —

Junio.

August 24
1820.

Emerson's drawing of his college room, 1820.
From *The Journals of Ralph Waldo Emerson*, ed. Edward Waldo Emerson and Waldo Emerson
Forbes, 1909–1914, vol. 1.

"Bush," the Emerson house in Concord.

ORDER OF EXERCISES

FOR

COMMENCEMENT,

XXIX AUGUST, MDCCCXXI.

Exercises of candidates for the degree of Bachelor of Arts.

.*. *The performers will speak in the order of their names.*

1. A Salutatory Oration in Latin.   NATHANIEL WOOD.

2. A Conference, "On the character of John Knox, William Penn, and John Wesley."
   RALPH WALDO EMERSON.
   AMOS GIDDON GOODWIN.
   WILLIAM POPE.

3. A Latin Dialogue, "On the Roman Triumph."
   JOHN LOWELL GARDNER.
   BENJAMIN TUCKER.

4. Forensic Disputation.   "Whether there be an ultimate standard of taste."
   RALPH FARNSWORTH.
   JOHN BOYNTON HILL.

5. A Dissertation, "On Popular Superstitions."
   MELLISH IRVING MOTTE.

6. A Philosophical Disputation, "On the relative physical advantages of the Eastern and Western Continents."
   HENRY LANE.
   FREDERICK PERCIVAL LEVERETT.

7. A Conference, "On natural scenery, the powerful passions, and moral and religious topics, as subjects of poetry.
   GEORGE WASHINGTON ADAMS.
   WILLIAM PARKER COFFIN.
   FREDERICK GORE KING.

8. A Literary Discussion, "On the elegant literature of England and France."
   WARREN BURTON.
   JOSIAH QUINCY.

9. A Colloquial Discussion, "On attachment to established usages, and a fondness for innovation."
   SAMUEL HATCH.
   GEORGE ALEXANDER OTIS.

10. A Dissertation, "On the effects of Tragedy on the intellectual and moral character."
    WILLIAM WITHINGTON.

11. A Conference, "On the state of physical science, oratory, fine writing, and metaphysics in England during the reign of Queen Anne."
    ENOCH FRYE.
    DAVID WOOD GORHAM.
    EDWARD KENT.
    WILLIAM FOSTER OTIS.

12. An Oration in English, "On Sacred Eloquence."
    CHARLES WENTWORTH UPHAM.

13. A Forensic Disputation.   "Whether the equal distribution of property among the children of intestates be beneficial to society."
    JOHN MILTON CHENEY.
    JOSEPH BANCROFT HILL.

14. An Oration in English.   "The importance of a national literature to national virtue."
    ROBERT WOODWARD BARNWELL.

—————

Exercises of candidates for the degree of Master of Arts.

1. An Oration in English, "On Genius"
   Mr. SAMPSON REED.

2. A Valedictory Oration in Latin.   Mr. JOHN FLAVEL JENKINS.

Commencement program for Harvard's graduation in 1821, with Emerson participating in a conference "On the character of John Knox, William Penn, and John Wesley."

Ellen Louisa Tucker Emerson in 1829.
From *The Journals of Ralph Waldo Emerson*, ed.
Edward Waldo Emerson and Waldo Emerson
Forbes, 1909–1914, vol. 2.

Painting of Emerson by Sarah Good-
ridge in 1829.
From a copy in the Joel Myerson Collection
of Nineteenth-Century American Literature,
University of South Carolina.

The Old Manse, where Emerson wrote *Nature* (1836).
From *Concord: A Pilgrimage to the Historic and Literary Center of America*, 1922.

Christopher Pearse Cranch's caricature of Emerson's passage about the transparent eyeball in *Nature*.

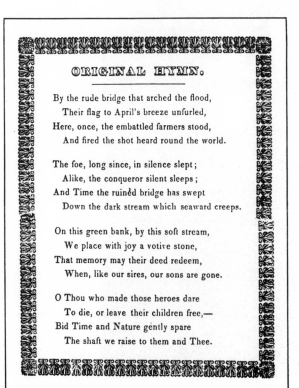

ORIGINAL HYMN.

By the rude bridge that arched the flood,
  Their flag to April's breeze unfurled,
Here, once, the embattled farmers stood,
  And fired the shot heard round the world.

The foe, long since, in silence slept;
  Alike, the conqueror silent sleeps;
And Time the ruinèd bridge has swept
  Down the dark stream which seaward creeps.

On this green bank, by this soft stream,
  We place with joy a votive stone,
That memory may their deed redeem,
  When, like our sires, our sons are gone.

O Thou who made those heroes dare
  To die, or leave their children free,—
Bid Time and Nature gently spare
  The shaft we raise to them and Thee.

Broadside printing of the "Concord Hymn," 1837.
From a copy in the Joel Myerson Collection of Nineteenth-Century American Literature, University of South Carolina.

Drawing of Emerson in 1844 by
Caroline Neagus Hildreth.
From *The Journals of Ralph Waldo Emerson*, ed.
Edward Waldo Emerson and Waldo Emerson
Forbes, 1909–1914, vol. 1.

Lidian Jackson Emerson in 1844.
From *The Journals of Ralph Waldo Emerson*, ed. Edward Waldo Emerson
and Waldo Emerson Forbes, 1909–1914, vol. 4.

Mr Munroe

I send some more Copies [struck] to be sent as fast as may be, to their several destinations,

W. A. Tappan care of Lewis Tappan. There is some [one] in Kirby St. which is agent for Lewis and this parcel might perhaps be sent there if you know them.

W. M. Prichard, Esq care of C. S. Francis New York

Benj Rodman, Esq. New Bedford] If you send books to N. Bedford, where there ought to be a maker for many of mine, let this go so; otherwise, Mr Weld in [W—] [Boston] [—] is son in law of Mr R. & it might be sent there.

C. P. Cranch: New York] Mr Greeley or Mr Francis will know his address.

Yours respectfully, R W Emerson

Emerson's letter of 18 October 1844 to his publisher, James Munroe, with instructions for sending copies of *Essays: Second Series* to his friends.

Crayon sketch of Emerson by Eastman Johnson, 1846.
From F. B. Sanborn, "Portraits of Emerson," *New England Magazine*, 1896.

T. M. Brewer. Esq

    Dear Sir,

        I have begged Mr Channing to send a copy of his new Poems to you, that you may look at "New England" & "Wachusett" at least which I hope may entitle him to a friendly line in the critical column of the Atlas. Yours respectfully,

      R. W. Emerson.

Concord, Dec. 18, 1846.

Emerson's letter of 18 December 1846 to Thomas Mayo Brewer promoting Ellery Channing's *Poems*.

Emerson in 1848.

Emerson in 1850.

Emerson in the 1850s.

Emerson in 1856.

Emerson in 1854.
From Mary Miller Engel, *I Remember the Emersons*, 1941.

Emerson in 1863.

Emerson with his children Edward and Edith discussing "A Virgil Lesson" in 1858.

From *The Journals of Ralph Waldo Emerson*, ed. Edward Waldo Emerson and Waldo Emerson Forbes, 1909–1914, vol. 10.

Emerson's study in Concord.
From a copy in the Joel Myerson Collection of Nineteenth-Century American Literature, University of South Carolina.

Emerson in 1868.

Part of Emerson's letter of 13 November 1870 to F. B. Sanborn concerning
Ellery Channing's *The Wanderer* (1871).

From F. B. Sanborn, *The Personality of Emerson*, 1903.

Emerson in 1873.

Emerson's letter of 1 March 1874 to
Miss Ware about his favorite hymns.

Emerson's letter of 16 March 1879 to
Edward Everett Hale about Harvard.
From *Booklover's Magazine*, 1903.

From *Concord Lectures on Philosophy . . . at the Concord School of Philosophy in 1882*

Julia Ward Howe and Ednah Dow Cheney

Established in 1879, the Concord School of Philosophy has been described as "the last flowering of the Transcendentalist movement." The major figures involved in the school were Bronson Alcott, Franklin Benjamin Sanborn, and William Torrey Harris. The school convened each summer between 1879 and 1887, and then one last time in 1888 for a memorial service for Alcott, who had died the previous March.

After Emerson's death in April 1882, lecturers for that summer were invited to memorialize him by writing under one of two categories that were broad enough to accommodate various interpretations of his life and significance: "immortality" and "Emerson." On 22 July, Sanborn gave an "Introductory Address," and Julia Ward Howe—writer, composer of "The Battle Hymn of the Republic," and biographer of Margaret Fuller—and Ednah Dow Cheney—abolitionist and woman suffragist—were joined by Cyrus A. Bartol, speaking on "The Nature of Knowledge—Emerson's Way"; Joel Benton, speaking on "Emerson as a Poet"; Harris, speaking on "Dialectic Unity in Emerson's Prose Writings"; and Alexander Wilder, who, while speaking on "Emerson as a Philosopher," named him the "Plato of America." Additionally, Alcott read "Ion: A Monody" in remembrance of Emerson and John Albee delivered a "Reminiscence and Eulogy."

In his brief introduction to the lectures, Raymond L. Bridgman describes the setting for "The Emerson Commemoration":

> For the special exercises of the school . . . the town hall of Concord was opened. Forenoon and afternoon sessions were held, and a large audience was present, . . . including many of Emerson's townsmen and many persons from abroad. Evergreen decorations upon the walls and platform, the national colors behind the desk, and constant reminders of Emerson, made the outward appearance symbolize the inner feeling toward the departed. A portrait of Emerson as an old man hung in front of the desk. One representing him in middle life was on the wall behind the speakers, and upon an evergreen-covered table was [Daniel Chester] French's bust representing him in advanced years.

"Reminiscences"

JULIA WARD HOWE

I first remember Emerson as the author of "Nature." When I first saw the little book, which had no external attractions, I thought nothing of it; I said to myself, "Here is some American pretender. Have we not the great thinkers in England and can we rival them in America?" I next heard of Emerson apart from his book. I heard him spoken of as a heretic, a man nobody could understand. I thought him an irreligious man. At a later day I was introduced to him by a Boston friend, but shrank from the acquaintance. I next saw him in a waiting-place where all of us were shivering with the cold. In the company was a child two years old, whom he put on his shoulders and presented to me, saying in his original way, "This is a young traveller." The steamer we were to take was belated and we had most of our journey by day. Mr. Emerson sought me out. I was charmed by his manner, but still I thought that he was only a more charming personification of Satan in the world than I had before seen. He asked me if I knew Margaret Fuller. I told him I thought her an ugly person. He then dwelt upon her mind and conversation. I was still impressed by what he said and the sweetness of his manner of saying it.

I next heard him deliver one of his lectures, and the voice and words brought their own explanation. I then understood how a man's previous reputation may fail to explain him to the public. He was universally laughed at then in high society, and it is not pleasant to remember that ridicule now. I was pleased to hear him called Christ-like by Dr. Bartol. He had a look of power that did not show itself in the garb of power. Who can give us that look of inward meaning again? Even in his serenity, what a charm! He had genuine honesty of speech. Had he been St. Peter, so just was he that he would have administered exact justice at the gate of heaven, and if he had not liked the company he had admitted there, he would have escaped to a heaven of his own.

Mr. Emerson has given us sunshine. Once, very weary, after a long western journey, and going to a cheerless hotel at an early morning hour, the only refuge from weariness I could find was a stray volume of his that happened to be at hand, and then I was truly warmed and fed by him. He had power to take people into realms of thought and life. It is a pleasant thing that most of us have seen and known him, but to others who have not, the legacy of his thought will be permanent. The lessons he taught will be kept and understood and appreciated more and more.

"Reminiscences"

EDNAH DOW CHENEY

It seems to me that those of us who heard what Mrs. Howe said, must agree that the age owes a sacred debt to the coming generation to preserve for it, as far as possible, the influence and the memory of the wonderful life that has been lived among us. As we look back over forty years, to the time when I can remember Mr. Emerson as the strongest, most spiritual, and most intellectual influence of my life, and know what he was to me, and what he was to every hungry, earnest and true heart which came near him, I feel a sense of pity and responsibility to all young people who are growing up, who cannot know him as we knew him; who cannot hear that voice which penetrated so to the very portals of the soul; who cannot look into those eyes, which always seemed to look into infinity and eternity. Though that life has been lived here among us, in the midst of us all, yet there has never been breathed upon it a spot of blame. There is no tarnish on it.

I regret very much that you could not have heard today the eloquent words of Mr. James, such as he used to speak while Mr. Emerson was living. I wish you could have heard what I suppose he would have spoken, for, although not agreeing with him in many points of doctrine, yet he recognized Mr. Emerson as a representative, unfallen man; a man inspired with earnestness and purity, tempered with wisdom, sanity, strength, and manhood. One of his most remarkable qualities, that quality of temperance, of moderation combined with enthusiasm and power, was one great charm and power, which he preserved always the same. He was ever the same to us. Those who sat at his feet once really sat there all their lives. As the prophet, when he came down from the mountains, having been fed by the birds of God, lived on the strength of that meat forty days, so those who had really eaten of that feast which he furnished us, could live in its strength all their lives. That temperance, that common sense which never allowed him to be extravagant, never allowed him to pass beyond the bounds of moderation, reason and sanity, was one cause why we can never fail to find wisdom in his words, and health and strength in his acts.

. . . He published years ago a lecture on slavery, in the darkest hours of the struggle. He spoke then from the highest point of view—that of the right of every man to freedom. Yet he said also: "I must not disdain to say to the slaveholder that his cotton and his sugar will be safe even when the slave is free." It seems to me this truth has not been sufficiently recognized—that he did not despise the common things of life. He did not refrain from using all those arguments which would be worthy of his cause. He came down from his high plane of poetry and philosophy to use statistics, to use any lawful argument by which he might win in the great cause of anti-slavery. And, although many fancied that his life was one of mere thought,—mere poetry and philosophy,—yet there never has been a single good cause or a single battle that we have struggled through in these years, in which his voice has not sounded like a trumpet, while he was in the van, the bravest and purest of leaders, working in his own way, but working earnestly. One of his most remarkable addresses was at the time when Sumner was stricken down. . . . At that time Mr. Emerson came to a meeting held in Boston, and he spoke of the outrage in such words as changed the whole aspect of the case. The man who struck him down, he said, was only, as it were, an accident of mere brute force. The man Sumner, the patriot, would rise above it all,—and he showed how even that brutal assault was an incident, and that nothing could touch the immense influence of Sumner's name or destroy his power. Mr. Emerson had even forgotten those brave words when Sumner came to die. But at a memorial Southern meeting the words were brought forward which Emerson had forgotten. In South Carolina a colored man had remembered them as they were reported in the newspapers of the time, and he told how they had been an inspiration and a strength to him ever afterward.

One thing that has given him such a constant and persistent influence is that he did not rest in dogmas. It has been questioned whether he believed in immortality. He did not speak about it; he lived in it. We do not talk about our homes, the shelter of the mother's arms and the father's love which has surrounded us all our lives. We live in them and grow strong in that love and protection. So he believed in immortality with his heart. Every line and every thought of his writings presuppose it, if they do not state it.

Mr. Sanborn has handed me a short letter he wishes me to read at this point, and it endorses what I have said. Miss Sarah E. Chase of Worcester writes:

"The last time I saw Emerson was in Rome, and our last conversation was on immortality. And, though I have listened to the arguments of many eminent men in the old world and the new on this subject, besides reading all I could find in ancient and modern literature, I found him more convincing than all others. How his countenance glowed, as he triumphantly concluded: 'I am so sure that the hereafter will be so much better than the possibility of imagining that the manner does not occupy my thought, so wonderful is the goodness and wisdom of the ordering of the hour.' "

It was here, it was now, it was in this life that, like Michael Angelo, he found immortality. So with our acquaintance with his religious thought and life,—if we could cherish those words and read them in their depth, we should find that we could not be beyond the faith and trust which his life so richly presents to us all.

It was astonishing, in all these many years, to see how Emerson always had the same audience around him. The last time I heard him speak in public was in the Old South Church in Boston, when entertainments were given there for the sake of increasing the fund for its preservation. Old, gray-headed men and women were there who used to listen to him in middle age, whom I had not seen in public for years. But they must come out to hear Emerson. Some of them felt that they must hear him every time they had an opportunity. When we were young girls, nothing in our list of entertainments was to be compared with Emerson,—no party, no singing, no theatre. To hear him was pure and perfect delight. His pleasure in young men has been spoken of. His delight in persons was one of his great joys. He noticed young men and women who listened to his lectures, and came to know them before he ever spoke to them. After Mr. Alcott started the Town and Country Club, I remember the eagerness with which he would turn and look at each speaker. Nothing was found uninteresting by him. He found something good in every one who spoke. It was that which made him so near to all and to each one. And so to every one who has lived with him, and to those who have known him so intimately, it is that which makes him so infinitely dear and so infinitely precious. . . . [Of] Emerson we say "is," not "was." . . . It seems as if he were always in the present and future. He is with us now, and it is for us who had the blessing of his presence and influence to preserve them for those who come after us.

From *Concord Lectures on Philosophy: Comprising Outlines of All the Lectures at the Concord School of Philosophy in 1882, with an Historical Sketch*, ed. Raymond L. Bridgman (Cambridge, Mass.: Moses King, 1883), pp. 62–63, 72–74.

From *Reminiscences and Memorials of the Men of the Revolution and Their Families* (1883)

A. B. MUZZEY

Artemas Bowers Muzzey, a prolific author of religious and inspirational tracts and a Unitarian minister and pastor of churches in Framingham, Cambridge, and Newburyport, Massachusetts, and Concord, New Hampshire, first met Emerson at Harvard in 1820, was married by him at the Second Church, and attended his funeral. Muzzey explains in his opening paragraph that he included a chapter on Emerson in his *Reminiscences and Memorials of the Men of the Revolution and Their Families* because of the Emerson family's association with the Revolution; however, it is apparent in the body of the essay that his real reason for including Emerson was to pay homage to the character of a valued, lifelong friend. The essay is significant for its range of reference across a broad span of time and for its wealth of anecdotes, including this remark by "Father" Edward Thompson Taylor, preacher at the Seamen's Methodist Bethel in Boston and the original for Melville's character Father Mapple in *Moby-Dick*: "You Unitarians are awfully honest. . . . What is to become of your heretic Emerson? I don't know where he will go when he dies. He is hardly good enough to be accepted in Heaven, and yet . . . Satan wouldn't know what to do with him." In the essay, Muzzey also provides a rare description of his Harvard classmate Edward Bliss Emerson, remembering him as "gifted with rare personal beauty, an eye large and beaming with genius, and a face radiant but not more with surpassing intellect than a fascinating sweetness" (p. 347).

Ralph Waldo Emerson . . . demands a prominent notice in these pages, partly for his Revolutionary family. Within a half-century the most varying epithets have been applied to him. In his early life admired as a preacher, denounced ere long as a heretic, to-day his numerous eulogists give him diverse designations. Men of all denominations unite in calling him a prophet, and—if not altogether yet almost—a Christian. Thinker, genius, philosopher, poet, essayist, leader, and king in how many realms, there is one more name which I think he richly deserves. He was, by eminence, a Patriot. . . .

My recollection of Emerson extends back to his seventeenth year, when I entered Harvard College, he being then in the senior class. His fine face and figure attracted the attention of us Freshmen; his poem on Class Day gave indication of his future success in verse, no less than prose; and his eloquent words in his "conference part" at commencement, on the "Character of John Knox" indicated in simple, terse, and forcible periods the claims of the great Scottish reformer. In 1826 Mr. Emerson began to preach; and it was while he occupied a room in Divinity Hall, that, as his neighbor in the same building, I became personally acquainted with him. He had then, as ever, great faith in the promptings of nature, which gave him a strong individuality. I saw clearly, from that time, that Mr. Emerson was to be a marked man, in private as in public. His language was keen and piquant in conversation, no less than in his writings. Speaking of one in the building, he said, "S—— is queer: he talks in scraps."

He was sought as a candidate for many pulpits. A new society had been formed in Boston, and four preachers were asked to fill the desk for successive Sundays, that one of them might be selected as a candidate for settlement. Mr. Emerson was invited to preach on one of these Sundays. Referring to this circumstance, I asked him which day he should accept: "I shall decline to go at all," was his prompt reply; "this competition is rather too close." His conceptions of personal dignity and self-respect were here, as everywhere, very delicate; and his manner, though modest, could be pronounced and decided. He was sometimes thought by strangers to be proud. Nothing was more unjust. I have heard him speak to a domestic in his house with as much kindness and consideration as he would manifest to a near member of his own family.

He was settled as colleague pastor with Rev. Henry Ware, in the Second Church of Boston. . . . [After] Mr. Ware had resigned and become a professor in the Cambridge Divinity School, Mr. Emerson married me to a member of his society. I can never forget the impressive manner in which that service was performed; and the remembrance of that hour, to which he often referred with his genial smile when we met, has been to me no ordinary privilege and pleasure.

When Mr. Emerson resigned his office as pastor, many hearts were grieved at the cause of it, while every one accorded him praise for his sincerity and conscientiousness. He had come to the conclusion that the communion service was not intended to be a perpetual rite, and not believing in its value and efficacy, he made known to his church that he could no longer conscientiously administer this ordinance. They differed from him so decidedly in regard to its authority and value that he felt constrained, on this account, finally to resign his office, and with a tender farewell, in the tone of which with one heart they united, he left his society.

Soon he became noticed for his suspected heresies, and I recollect witnessing the effect of his standing which showed itself on one particular occasion. At the annual Unitarian festival, among those invited to give addresses was Father Taylor, of the Methodist Bethel Church in Boston. "You Unitarians," he said in his speech, "are awfully honest. . . . What is to become of your heretic Emerson? I don't know where he will go when he dies. He is hardly good enough to be accepted in Heaven, and yet . . . Satan wouldn't know what to do with him." . . .

Mr. Emerson felt a deep interest in all that pertains to the life and health of our nation. One of our best critics says of him: "He is the most republican of republicans." Lowell . . . affirms that "to him, more than to all other causes, did the young martyrs of our Civil War owe the sustaining strength and thoughtful heroism that is so touching in every record of their lives." In a letter written during that sad yet needful struggle Emerson gives this decided testimony of a custom of nations, which . . . is abhorrent to some of the best instincts of our higher nature: "I shall always respect war hereafter. The cost of life, the dreary havoc of comfort and time, are overpaid by the vistas it opens of eternal life, eternal law, reconstructing and uplifting society,— breaks up the old horizon, and we see through the rifts a wider."

All his essays, notably those on Character, Politics, and New England Reforms, one in the "Atlantic," entitled, "American Civilization," and that read in the Old South, February, 1878, entitled "Fortune of the Republic," abundantly show his public spirit. He aided every measure designed to educate the community in liberal principles, broad views, and a thorough personal culture. "We should cling," said he, "to the common school. . . . Let us educate every soul." He thought highly of the system of public lectures, and gave at least three for the purchase of the Old South Church, as a memorial of the Revolution. To the lyceum in his own town, Concord, he gave . . . one hundred lectures. I recall an occasion, when, after my reading in that lyceum a lecture on the importance of training and securing good teachers for our public schools, he, in his earnest manner, said to me, "A good teacher is as rare as a good poet."

It was a treat to attend the lectures of Mr. Emerson. . . . It was a special pleasure to listen to him year by year. At first, by his quaint, terse, and richly laden sentences, he seemed to perplex some of our wisest men. I sat, one evening, quite near the Hon. Jeremiah Mason,—a man who could penetrate into the deepest depths of the law so long as the speaker or writer kept to the "dry light." But Emerson, I saw, sorely tried him. Two ladies by his side evidently enjoyed every word they heard. The next day Mr. Mason, it is said, being asked how he liked Emerson, replied: "Oh, I couldn't understand him at all. You must ask my daughters about him; they took it all in."

Meeting him one day, after one of his lectures, at the store of Little & Brown, where Rev. Dr. Francis and others were present, we were expressing our satisfaction at what we had heard from him, when Dr. Francis remarked: "You must have spent a long time in preparing your lectures, they are so full of thought and of historical material." "Oh, no," said Mr. Emerson; "I never write until I am driven to it by the time each week." And sometimes, while listening to his lectures, they seemed almost extemporaneous. They struck one as full of thoughts entirely fresh and original, and in some passages as if the inspiration of the hour. There was sometimes, in the beginning of a sentence, a little hesitancy, as if he was waiting for a word or words to be given him for utterance at the moment. Still they must have been . . . the result of long premeditation as well as extensive reading. If there was ever an appearance of disregard of manner in his utterances, this was not true of him. I recollect hearing him, while he was a student in Divinity Hall, reading aloud, evidently for the benefit of his voice; and he would occasionally take up a volume from his table in which he had the speeches of Webster and Everett bound together. "Everett," he once said to me, "is a great word-catcher." . . .

Mr. Emerson's interest in antislavery was profound and unremitting. I remember only one instance in which his sweet serenity seemed for an instant to leave him. After the execution of John Brown, a meeting was called in Boston for indignant denunciation of that act. Mr. Emerson was one of the speakers. Sitting quite near the platform and in front of him, I saw his face wore a passing shade and a slight frown, as if the terror of the deed we had met to consider and comment upon was too great for human endurance. . . .

Meeting Mr. Emerson occasionally toward his last days, and finally at the funeral of a kindred poetic genius, the lamented Longfellow,— . . . I saw no change, save that the smile of his youth and manhood had become sweeter with his approaching end, and the grasp of his hand had become warmer.

[119]

And when, at his own so soon following obsequies, I looked on that noble form, fitly robed in his angel apparel of white, the placid face spoke of the upper serenities in which he had trusted, and on which he had now entered.

From *Reminiscences and Memorials of the Men of the Revolution and Their Families* (Boston: Estes and Lauriat, 1883), pp. 337, 340–48.

From *Ralph Waldo Emerson* (1884)

Oliver Wendell Holmes

The Boston Brahmin, physician, and satirist Oliver Wendell Holmes knew Emerson for over fifty years. Although Holmes and Emerson counted each other as friends, with Emerson often sending Holmes a copy of his latest publication, Holmes, whose formalism undoubtedly stemmed from his scientific training, was contemptuous of Emerson's brand of Transcendentalism and its underlying intuitive and analogical methodology. Throughout his biography of Emerson, which appeared in the influential American Men of Letters series edited by Charles Dudley Warner, Holmes challenged his friend's philosophy and attacked Transcendentalism by reference to the eccentricities of individuals such as Bronson Alcott and Henry Thoreau. Thus, even though he approved of Emerson as a person, and, indeed, even though he believed, as he wrote, that "his power" was "to inspire others, to make life purer, loftier, calmer, brighter," in the biography Holmes calls Emerson's reputation and contributions to American intellectual history into question by association. The selection that follows is taken from "Emerson—A Retrospect," the concluding chapter of Holmes's biography.

Emerson's earthly existence was in the estimate of his own philosophy so slight an occurrence in his career of being that his relations to the accidents of time and space seem quite secondary matters to one who has been long living in the companionship of his thought. Still, he had to be born, to take in his share of the atmosphere in which we are all immersed, to have dealings with the world of phenomena, and at length to let them all "soar and sing" as he left his earthly half-way house. It is natural and pardonable that we should like to know the details of the daily life which the men whom we admire have shared with common mortals, ourselves among the rest. But Emerson has said truly "Great geniuses have the shortest biographies. Their cousins can tell you nothing about them. They lived in their writings, and so their home and street life was trivial and commonplace." ...

Emerson's personal appearance was that of a scholar, the descendant of scholars. He was tall and slender, with the complexion which is bred in the

alcove and not in the open air. He used to tell his son Edward that he measured six feet in his shoes, but his son thinks he could hardly have straight-
ened himself to that height in his later years. He was very light for a man of
his stature. He got on the scales at Cheyenne, on his trip to California, com-
paring his weight with that of a lady of the party. A little while afterwards he
asked of his fellow-traveler, Professor Thayer, "How much did I weigh? A
hundred and forty?" "A hundred and forty and a half," was the answer. "Yes,
yes, a hundred and forty and a half! That *half* I prize; it is an index of better
things!"

Emerson's head was not such as Schopenhauer insists upon for a philosopher. He wore a hat measuring six and seven eighths on the *cephalometer*
used by hatters, which is equivalent to twenty-one inches and a quarter of
circumference. The average size is from seven to seven and an eighth, so that
his head was quite small in that dimension. It was long and narrow, but lofty,
almost symmetrical, and of more nearly equal breadth in its anterior and
posterior regions than many or most heads.

His shoulders sloped so much as to be commented upon for this peculiarity by Mr. Gilfilan, and like "Ammon's great son," he carried one shoulder a little higher than the other. His face was thin, his nose somewhat ac-
cipitrine, casting a broad shadow; his mouth rather wide, well formed and
well closed, carrying a question and an assertion in its finely finished curves;
the lower lip a little prominent, the chin shapely and firm, as becomes the
cornerstone of the countenance. His expression was calm, sedate, kindly,
with that look of refinement, centring about the lips, which is rarely found in
the male New Englander, unless the family features have been for two or
three cultivated generations the battlefield and the playground of varied
thoughts and complex emotions as well as the sensuous and nutritive port of
entry. His whole look was irradiated by an ever active inquiring intelligence.
His manner was noble and gracious. Few of our fellow-countrymen have
had larger opportunities of seeing distinguished personages than our present minister at the Court of St. James. In a recent letter to myself, which I
trust Mr. Lowell will pardon my quoting, he says of Emerson:—"There was
a majesty about him beyond all other men I have known, and he habitually
dwelt in that ampler and diviner air to which most of us, if ever, only rise in
spurts."

From members of his own immediate family I have derived some particulars relating to his personality and habits which are deserving of record.

[122]

His hair was brown, quite fine, and, till he was fifty, very thick. His eyes were of the "strongest and brightest blue." The member of the family who tells me this says:—

"My sister and I have looked for many years to see whether any one else had such absolutely blue eyes, and have never found them except in sea-captains. I have seen three sea-captains who had them."

He was not insensible to music, but his gift in that direction was very limited, if we may judge from this family story. When he was in College, and the singing-master was gathering his pupils, Emerson presented himself, intending to learn to sing. The master received him, and when his turn came, said to him, "Chord!" "What?" said Emerson. "Chord! Chord! I tell you," repeated the master. "I don't know what you mean," said Emerson. "Why, sing! Sing a note." "So I made some kind of a noise, and the singing-master said, 'That will do, sir. You need not come again.'"

Emerson's mode of living was very simple: coffee in the morning, tea in the evening, animal food by choice only once a day, wine only when with others using it, but always *pie* at breakfast. "It stood before him and was the first thing eaten." Ten o'clock was his bed-time, six his hour of rising until the last ten years of his life, when he rose at seven. Work or company sometimes led him to sit up late, and this he could do night after night. He never was hungry,—could go any time from breakfast to tea without food and not know it, but was always ready for food when it was set before him.

He always walked from about four in the afternoon till tea-time, and often longer when the day was fine, or he felt that he should work the better. . . .

He thought too much of his bodily insufficiencies, which, it will be observed, he only refers to in his private correspondence, and in that semi-nudity of self-revelation which is the privilege of poetry. His presence was fine and impressive, and his muscular strength was enough to make him a rapid and enduring walker.

Emerson's voice had a great charm in conversation, as in the lecture-room. It was never loud, never shrill, but singularly penetrating. He was apt to hesitate in the course of a sentence, so as to be sure of the exact word he wanted; picking his way through his vocabulary, to get at the best expression of his thought, as a well-dressed woman crosses the muddy pavement to reach the opposite sidewalk. It was this natural slight and not unpleasant semicolon pausing of the memory which grew upon him in his years of decline, until it rendered conversation laborious and painful to him.

He never laughed loudly. When he laughed it was under protest, as it were, with closed doors, his mouth shut, so that the explosion had to seek another respiratory channel, and found its way out quietly, while his eyebrows and nostrils and all his features betrayed the "ground swell," as Professor Thayer happily called it, of the half-suppressed convulsion. He was averse to loud laughter in others, and objected to Margaret Fuller that she made him laugh too much.

Emerson was not rich in some of those natural gifts which are considered the birthright of the New Englander. He had not the mechanical turn of the whittling Yankee. I once questioned him about his manual dexterity, and he told me he could split a shingle four ways with one nail,—which, as the intention is not to split it at all in fastening it to the roof of a house or elsewhere, I took to be a confession of inaptitude for mechanical works. He does not seem to have been very accomplished in the handling of agricultural implements either, for it is told in the family that his little son, Waldo, seeing him at work with a spade, cried out, "Take care, papa—you will dig your leg." . . .

There are stories which show that Emerson had a retentive memory in the earlier part of his life. It is hard to say from his books whether he had or not, for he jotted down such a multitude of things in his diary that this was a kind of mechanical memory which supplied him with endless materials of thought and subjects for his pen.

Lover and admirer of Plato as Emerson was, the doors of the academy, over which was the inscription . . . —Let no one unacquainted with geometry enter here,—would have been closed to him. All the exact sciences found him an unwilling learner. He says of himself that he cannot multiply seven by twelve with impunity.

. . . Emerson is reported as saying, "God has given me the seeing eye, but not the working hand." His gift was insight: he saw the germ through its envelope; the particular in the light of the universal; the fact in connection with the principle; the phenomenon as related to the law; all this not by the slow and sure process of science, but by the sudden and searching flashes of imaginative double vision. He had neither the patience nor the method of the inductive reasoner; he passed from one thought to another not by logical steps but by airy flights, which left no foot-prints. This mode of intellectual action when found united with natural sagacity becomes poetry, philosophy, wisdom, or prophecy in its various forms of manifestation. Without that gift of natural sagacity (*odoratio quædam venatica*),—a good scent for truth and beauty,—it appears as extravagance, whimsicality, eccentricity, or insanity, according to its degree of aberration. Emerson was eminently sane for an idealist. He carried the same sagacity into the ideal world that Franklin showed in the affairs of common life.

He was constitutionally fastidious, and had to school himself to become able to put up with the terrible inflictions of uncongenial fellowships. We must go to his poems to get at his weaknesses. The clown of the first edition of "Monadnoc" "with heart of cat and eyes of bug," disappears in the after-thought of the later version of the poem, but the eye that recognized him and the nature that recoiled from him were there still. What must he not have endured from the persecutions of small-minded worshipers who fastened upon him for the interminable period between the incoming and outgoing railroad train! He was a model of patience and good temper. We might have feared that he lacked the sensibility to make such intrusions and offences an annoyance. . . .

Of Emerson's affections, his home-life and those tender poems in memory of his brothers and his son give all the evidence that could be asked or wished for. His friends were all who knew him, for none could be his enemy; and his simple graciousness of manner, with the sincerity apparent in every look and tone, hardly admitted indifference on the part of any who met him, were it but for a single hour. Even the little children knew and loved him, and babes in arms returned his angelic smile. Of the friends who were longest and most intimately associated with him, it is needless to say much in this place. Of those who are living, it is hardly time to speak; of those who are dead, much has already been written. . . .

How nearly any friend, other than his brothers Edward and Charles, came to him, I cannot say, indeed I can hardly guess. That "majesty" Mr. Lowell speaks of always seemed to hedge him round like the divinity that doth hedge a king. What man was he who would lay his hand familiarly upon his shoulder and call him Waldo? No disciple of Father Mathew would be likely to do such a thing. There may have been such irreverent persons, but if any one had so ventured at the "Saturday Club," it would have produced a sensation like Brummel's "George, ring the bell," to the Prince Regent. His ideas of friendship, as of love, seem almost too exalted for our earthly conditions, and suggest the thought as do many others of his characteristics, that the spirit which animated his mortal frame had missed its way on the shining path to some brighter and better sphere of being.

Not so did Emerson appear among the plain working farmers of the village in which he lived. He was a good, unpretending fellow-citizen who put on no airs, who attended town-meetings, took his part in useful measures, was no great hand at farming, but was esteemed and respected, and felt to be a principal source of attraction to Concord, for strangers came flocking to the place as if it held the tomb of Washington.

What was the errand on which he visited our earth,—the message with which he came commissioned from the Infinite source of all life?

Every human soul leaves its port with sealed orders. These may be opened earlier or later on its voyage, but until they are opened no one can tell what is to be his course or to what harbor he is bound. . . .

. . . He might have been an idol, and he broke his own pedestal to attack the idolatry which he saw all about him. He gave up a comparatively easy life for a toilsome and trying one; he accepted a precarious employment, which hardly kept him above poverty, rather than wear the golden padlock on his lips which has held fast the conscience of so many pulpit Chrysostoms. Instead of a volume or two of sermons, bridled with a text and harnessed with a confession of faith, he bequeathed us a long series of Discourses and Essays in which we know we have his honest thoughts, free from that professional bias which tends to make the pulpit teaching of the fairest-minded preacher follow a diagonal of two forces,—the promptings of his personal and his ecclesiastical opinions.

Without a church or a pulpit, he soon had a congregation. It was largely made up of young persons of both sexes, young by nature, if not in years, who, tired of routine and formulæ, and full of vague aspirations, found in his utterances the oracles they sought. To them, in the words of his friend and neighbor Mr. Alcott, he

"Sang his full song of hope and lofty cheer."

Nor was it only for a few seasons that he drew his audiences of devout listeners around him. Another poet, his Concord neighbor, Mr. Sanborn, who listened to him many years after the first flush of novelty was over, felt the same enchantment, and recognized the same inspiring life in his words, which had thrilled the souls of those earlier listeners.

"His was the task and his the lordly gift
Our eyes, our hearts, bent earthward, to uplift."

This was his power,—to inspire others, to make life purer, loftier, calmer, brighter. Optimism is what the young want, and he could no more help taking the hopeful view of the universe and its future than Claude could help flooding his landscapes with sunshine.

From *Ralph Waldo Emerson* (Boston: Houghton, Mifflin, 1884), pp. 357–69, 372–73.

"Notes of Conversations with Emerson" (1884)

PENDLETON KING

Pendleton King's visit to Concord in the summer of 1870 shows Emerson's vitality and mental awareness two years before the fire that devastated his house and took so a great toll on his mind. Like so many who met Emerson, King found him a man who "devoted his life to noble ends, and of being perfectly willing to leave the result to time." King's record of Emerson's comments in 1870 on his own writings; on Thoreau, Ellery Channing, the Alcotts, and Hawthorne; on Coleridge, Carlyle, and other English writers; and on philosophers who influenced his ideas are unusually detailed and informative. King's second reminiscence, of a visit following Emerson's lecture on "Eloquence" (called by King "Orators and Oratory") in Philadelphia in 1875, continues Emerson's comments on these subjects.

I called on Mr. Emerson at his home in Concord toward the last of June, 1870. I found him just finishing dinner . . . about half-past one o'clock. After a short conversation in his library, he requested me to remain there till he changed his coat and got a cane and a pair of easy shoes, and we would take a walk. In answer to my apologies and expressions of unwillingness to take more of his time, he assured me that it would do him good and give him pleasure to walk.

He led me from place to place, stopping now and then to express himself more fully or more clearly on some point of our conversation, so that it was twilight when we returned. . . .

In our long walk he showed me much of the neighborhood of Concord, and told me many interesting things about it. He showed me the springs that he and his literary friends always visited in their walks, and from which they drank, generally keeping some old cup there for that purpose. "Thoreau invariably visited these springs."

There was a certain awkwardness about Mr. Emerson's movements, but there was no lack of vigor in them, considering he was sixty-seven years old. We talked the whole time we were together, on a great variety of subjects.

But, from the great interest which his conversation had for me, I was able to write out much of it, often retaining his exact expressions. I had no intention whatever of publishing this, so that I wrote it out in outline only, and in the elliptical language of conversation. But in such a case it is very desirable to have, as nearly as may be, his own words and shades of expression: so that I consider it better to give my notes as made a few days after our conversation, rather than any relation of it from memory. Of course, in a conversation in which he spoke much of literary men, some of his criticisms would be unfavorable to others. . . . But there was in his conversation, tone, and manner no tinge of envy or jealousy, but a remarkable charity and kindness. He left the impression on me of having no illusions as to his own position in the literary world, of having devoted his life to noble ends, and of being perfectly willing to leave the result to time. He seemed to me one of the truest gentlemen I have ever met. . . . His unfavorable, like his favorable, criticism seemed to spring wholly from a desire to get at the truth and to express himself in an accurate manner, and, in most cases, could hardly have pained the persons criticised had they been present. . . .

"Concord is a little milk-town, and sends a great deal to Boston. Recently it has been found that grape-vineyards make the most profitable crop for autumn, and strawberries for the spring: so we send many to Boston daily. Many have lost their fruit,—their apples by a total destruction of the crop by the canker-worm. Many farmers neglect their trees and put not even tar on them. Printers' ink is the best remedy: I have saved my trees with it.

"Mr. Channing lives here in Concord. He was with Thoreau a great deal, and nearly always in the latter's long walks. He is a very subtle man, and one has to bear with him and understand him by degrees before one likes him. But he is a very valuable man. So is Mr. Alcott, who is a thinker, but has not to the same extent the power of expressing himself on paper. Consequently, he has written little or nothing of value. He is two or three years my senior. He lives here in this house, and takes much pleasure in arranging his fences, gates, and garden. He would walk a great distance to get these knots which you see on his gate. He is, as you know, the father of Miss Alcott, whose books you see everywhere,—books whose popularity pleases us all, especially as the father's income is limited. I have not read the books myself. Mr. Conway has written of Mr. Alcott, and narrated several anecdotes of him, every one of which he reports incorrectly.

"The English make many mistakes about Americans. For instance, some

English journalist has asserted that the person referred to in my essay on 'Shyness,' meaning 'Society and Solitude,' was Hawthorne. But it was not; neither was it Thoreau. They take many of these points from Mr. Conway, who is a Unitarian minister in London, originally from Virginia, educated, became a Methodist minister, came to Massachusetts, studied divinity at Harvard, and gave up Methodism and became a Unitarian; a quite worthy man, but unable to tell anything as he hears it. He wrote, I think for *Fraser's Magazine*, an article on Concord, to which my attention was called, and on reading it I found that many things were very inaccurately told.

"I think highly of Thoreau. He is now read by a limited number of men and women, but by very ardent ones. They were dissatisfied with my notice of him in the *Atlantic* after his death: they did not want me to place any bounds to his genius. He came to me a young man, but was so popular with young people that he quite superseded his old master. But now and then I come across a man that scoffs at Thoreau and thinks he is affected. For example, . . . Lowell is constantly making flings at him. I have tried to show him that Thoreau did things that no one could have done without high powers; but to no purpose. I am surprised to hear that you have read Thoreau. Neither his books nor mine are much read in the South, I suppose. . . .

"Thoreau was unacquainted with the technical names of plants when I first knew him. On my telling him the name of a flower, he remarked that he should never see the *flower* again, for if he met it he would be able only to see the *name*. He, however, afterward became quite accurate in botany. His cabin, or hut, stood on this very spot. There is a pious mark (a cross) on that tree which indicates the place. I don't know who made the mark; I did not. Daily before taking his walk he would examine his diary to see what flowers should be out. His hut was in full view of Walden Pond: these trees here have grown up since then. He could run out on awaking and leap right into the water, which he did every morning.

"Walden was then very quiet. The passing of the railroad and the workmen have introduced more company around it, seriously interfering with the pleasure and quietness of the place. Perhaps to Mr. Alcott, Mr. Channing, and myself this is more annoying than to others, as we frequently walk here and bathe; but now we know not but some boat may approach at any time. Last winter a man of tastes somewhat similar to those of Thoreau, partly from having read his books, got permission of me and built a hut on Walden also, and actually remained here alone some two or three months. He was very heroic in it. He ate no meat. We sent him some, but he refused. He gladly, however, accepted fruit. Mr. Channing liked him, and was often with him. I will gladly introduce you to Mr. Channing or Mr. Alcott, if you have time to remain. Mr. Alcott will willingly assist you in solving any problems of philosophy in which you may need assistance. He is a very valuable thinker. . . .

"There are many writers more or less popular that I don't at all read. Gail Hamilton, for instance, I have not read. I read only as my pleasure leads me to, disregarding the fame of the book.

"The best men, you will find, are hidden men: few will improve by seeing. In England, perhaps none will improve by being seen except two,—Tennyson, with his broad culture, and Carlyle. If you go to England, these you must see, and likewise James Hutchinson Sterling. He is very highly recommended by Carlyle and others as a philosopher. I have read his essays on some of the poets, and his criticism is quite good. No, men do not improve on seeing them. You would scarcely believe that some of the best poetry of this century could come from Wordsworth, after seeing him,—such a simple man, and with such strange notions,—a regular English churchman, and with old politics,—cockney politics. He seemed altogether unlike a great poet. . . .

"Coleridge, too, was very unlike the 'divinely inspired' that you hear so much about. I am glad you have his 'Biographia Literaria': it was to me, when young, a great work. It contained very sound notions of criticism, and is about the best of the century, along with Carlyle's. He has given us more definitions that any other man,—for example, the difference between the fancy and the imagination. As valuable as is the 'Biographia Literaria,' he gets on his high horse in parts of it. . . .

"I place, without hesitation, Plato above Aristotle. The philosophy of the former is of a higher kind than that of the latter. In my view, the systems of Bain, Spencer, and other scientific investigators run too much toward materialism. Spencer I regard as a mechanical writer. Dr. Holmes is a friend of mine, but nevertheless I think his way of investigating philosophical problems runs into materialism.

"Mr. Carlyle is not coming to this country, as some of the papers state. I have long been in correspondence with him. I don't really know his religious creed. He always upholds realities in opposition to shams. . . .

"Come into my dining-room and see a head of Carlyle better than either of these in my study. It was taken by the sister of Tennyson's wife. It is very good indeed. Some pictures of him are horrible. She took this picture of Tennyson also, which is evidently, you see, so arranged as to show Tennyson with a Shakespearian head. . . .

"[Carlyle] always writes to me in the midst of his works how thoroughly sick he is of them and disgusted with them; he only wishes to get them off his hands. In conversation he breaks out into rich eloquence in a deep voice; he knows that he is superior to those he meets, and when he finishes a sentence he would willingly have others speak; but, they not willing to risk themselves in a warfare with such a one, he again goes on, and thus monopolizes the conversation, with no wrong motives and with no determination to crush out the conversation of others. His persistence in wearing some old-fashioned clothes . . . is probably the reason why the boys sometimes notice him. I don't fully see why the critics should compare Carlyle and myself: we agree, however, in both being idealists.

"In my works I like the articles 'Fate' and 'Worship' in my 'Conduct of Life' very well. The article 'Culture' I wished to make a good thing, but there crept into it a wrong tone or ring which I could never get out: so that I can never read it without making corrections,—never with perfect satisfaction. You have read, you say, my 'Representative Men.' Perhaps it would pay you to re-read my article on 'Swedenborg.' At the time I wrote it I regarded it as the best on Swedenborg that had appeared in this country. . . .

"I don't see why the clergy or religious congregations should have much opposition to me, except, perhaps, those where the old Calvinistic influence is strong. . . . For I have not opposed, but been very friendly to their success, except where they go for baking or burning their babes. . . .

"Hawthorne lived in that house. He was a good listener, but did not talk much, even with his friends. After many fruitless efforts to get him to talk, I told him one day that this would never do, and proposed to him a little tour together, hoping that this would loosen his tongue a little. It would be well for you to call on Mr. Longfellow. You would find him very hospitable and kind to strangers."

Our walk lasted some hours, carrying us as far as a height of some distance south of Walden Pond, where we sat an hour or more. It was there that he spoke of Plato at some length, much in the strain in which he has written of him. Besides these philosophical heights and depths, he pointed out to me Monadnock, Wachusett, and the wide extent of country visible to us, "waiting for a population."

We talked of various other literary and philosophical subjects, but went not deep into theology. I thought I could notice some reticence on his part in expressing himself as to his creed, probably not due to any want of clearness in his own mind, but to a fear of disturbing me by doubts suddenly and abruptly awakened. I observed that he was at times somewhat slow from age in recalling the names of books and authors. He twice told me wrongly the date of the removal of Thoreau's hut, and on my delicately hinting a mistake he quickly saw his error.

As we approached his quiet home on our return, I remarked to him that in his "English Traits" he had described the difficulty he had found in approaching distinguished men. . . .

"I confess, Mr. Emerson," I said, "that I had misgivings lest I should find you somewhat reserved. I must thank you that, instead of cold and distant, I have found you ——."

"An old farmer. You didn't expect to find that. Yes, I have been a farmer these twenty years."

He invited me into his library again, and gave me one of his books, in which he wrote, "With kind remembrances of our walk," over his name. Then, after a glass or two of wine together, I went my way rejoicing.

In the spring of 1875 I heard Mr. Emerson lecture at the Academy of Music in Philadelphia, before a large audience, on "Orators and Oratory." His delivery was not impressive, his voice not strong or pleasing. Age had much changed him in those respects. Yet he read certain passages well, and especially brought out in several sentences a delicate humor that might have escaped another reader. The audience seemed well enough satisfied, though not enthusiastic. In Philadelphia he stopped with his friend Dr. Furness, at whose house I saw him two days after his lecture. I found him in the library, smoking a cigar, which he laid on the table during our conversation. He recalled my visit to him in Concord and his having previously seen me in Cambridge. But I noticed in him the same inability now and then in recalling the names of authors and their books. This indication of failing powers was more noticeable than in 1870, and he himself spoke of it. . . .

He said that he was always interested in Swedenborgians.

"There is Mr. Samson Reed, who wrote a right good book, 'The Growth of the Mind,' many years ago, who was a Swedenborgian. He is now a Boston merchant, whom I occasionally meet. In reading Swedenborg and others,—Blake, for example,—one must be able to distinguish between the inspired parts and the errors."

He did not know that Swinburne had written on Blake or admired him. He spoke of Swinburne as "unclean," "a man of the flesh purely," "crazy, in a way."

He spoke highly of Dr. Holmes,—how bright he was yet, "the boy; and a fine man he has grown up into," as if they were boys together only yesterday.

"Selden's Table-Talk is good. Sydney's version of the Psalms is good and poetical." He took "Parnassus" from the book-case and pointed out to me three of these that he particularly liked and so had included them in this book of selections.

"There was something fine in Thoreau. I have tried to convince Lowell, Longfellow, and Judge Hoar of this. There is left now only a sister of Thoreau, the only one of the name. He has left behind him much manuscript on natural history, beautiful and as fine as Linnæus; but I get no encouragement from the publishers to bring it out. From Thoreau might be collected a book of proverbs or sentences that would charm the Hindoos.

"I have had various interruptions that have delayed me bringing out a new volume of my writings,—'Poetry and Criticism'" (afterward published as "Letters and Social Aims"). "I must go back home and attend to it soon, as I am getting very old. Please write me your address here, and I will send it to you when it appears." ...

He thought his "Parnassus" would be valuable to the lovers of old poetry especially; and I gathered from his talk that he had taken a great deal of pains in preparing it.

"Lowell's 'Fable for Critics' is good. . . . He is happy in his humorous poetry, but not so much so in his longer poems that are not humorous.

"Carlyle disliked to buy books, and has no large library, but has a few hundred good books, which are to come to Harvard College. It is not generally known, but he instructed Mr. Charles Norton and myself to offer them to Harvard, and they have been gladly accepted. Carlyle has kinder feelings toward America than appears in his writings, I think.

"Thoreau once took charge of my garden, and on the occasion of a visit from Theodore Parker I sent Thoreau to the station for him, hoping that he would like Parker; but he did not, and expressed a contempt for the man. Haughtiness of manner was frequently a characteristic of Thoreau."

This was the last conversation I had with Mr. Emerson, though I had the pleasure of seeing him once more,—in Washington Street, Boston,—about a year before his death. I stopped and looked at him as long as he was in sight. Outwardly he appeared much the same man as six years before, but his friends knew that the end was not far off.

Lippincott's Magazine, 33 (January 1884): 44–50.

"Glimpses of Emerson" (1884)

[ANNIE ADAMS FIELDS]

Annie Adams Fields and her husband James T. Fields—Emerson's publisher—
were close friends of the Emersons. Fields is probably best remembered today
as a social reformer and the keeper of a literary *salon* in her Charles Street home
on Boston's fashionable Beacon Hill. There, from the early 1870s to her death
in 1915, she entertained international guests such as Charles Dickens, hosted
evening dinners during which luminaries such as Oliver Wendell Holmes and
Emerson held intellectual or literary "conversations" with a select company,
and managed an extensive support network for American women writers that
included Rebecca Harding Davis, Mary E. Wilkins Freeman, and Sarah Orne
Jewett (who became Annie's companion after James's death in 1881), among
many others.

In "Glimpses of Emerson," Fields writes a touching tribute to a valued
friend. Her interest is to define Emerson's character, which she does by describing his hospitality, generosity, and extraordinary efforts on behalf of the careers of his friends and of young writers with whom he had little or no acquaintance other than through their works. Fields elaborates on Emerson's service in
securing an American readership for Carlyle, his editing of Thoreau's and Jones
Very's works, and his admiration of Ellery Channing's poetry and that of
Forceythe Willson, the now-obscure writer from Geneva, New York. She also
describes his transition in 1872 from a public lecturer to a conversationalist before private audiences, remarking on his reading of "Amita," an unpublished
paper on his aunt, Mary Moody Emerson, on 22 March, before Oliver Wendell
Holmes, Henry James Jr., and others at her Charles Street home and on his performance between 15 April and 20 May, when he presided over six "Conversations on Literature" at Mechanics' Hall in Boston, which she and James had,
in fact, arranged.

Fields's "Glimpses of Emerson" is a richly anecdotal essay developed from
familiarity with Emerson and his many literary friends and acquaintances over
an extended period of time. While most of Emerson's letters cited by Fields
have been published in Rusk's and Tilton's standard edition of his *Letters*,
Fields drew many of her stories about Emerson from her diary, which remains
unpublished in the collections of the Massachusetts Historical Society.

The perfect consistency of a truly great life, where inconsistencies of speech appear at once harmonized by the beauty of the whole, gives even to a slight incident the value of a bit of mosaic which, if omitted, would leave a gap in the picture. Therefore we never tire of "Whisperings" and "Talks" and "Walks" and "Letters" relating to the friends of our imagination, if not of our fireside, and in so far as such fragments bring men and women of achievement nearer to our daily lives, without degrading them, they warm and cheer us with something of their own beloved and human presences.

This feeling explains the publication of so many of these side lights on the lives of what Emerson himself calls "superior people," and the following glimpses will only confirm what he expresses of such natures when he says, "In all the superior people I have met I notice directness, truth spoken more truly, as if everything of obstruction, of malformation, had been trained away."

In reading the correspondence between Carlyle and Emerson, few readers could fail to be impressed with the generosity shown by Emerson in giving his time and thought without stint to the publication of Carlyle's books in this country. Nor was this the single instance of his devotion to the advancement of his friends. In a brief memoir, lately printed, of Jones Very, as an introduction to a collection of his poems, we find a like record there.

After the death of Thoreau, Emerson spared no trouble to himself that his friend's papers might be properly presented to the reading world. He wrote to his publisher, Mr. Fields: "I send all the poems of Thoreau which I think ought to go with the letters. These are the best verses, and no other whole piece quite contents me. I think you must be content with a little book, since it is so good. I do not like to print either the prison piece or the John Brown with these clear sky-born letters and poems." . . .

Emerson stood, as it were, the champion of American letters, and whatever found notice at all challenged his serious scrutiny. The soul and purpose must be there; he must find one line to win his sympathy, and then it was given with a whole heart. He said one day at breakfast that he had found a young man! A youth in the far West had written him, and inclosed some verses, asking for his criticism. Among them was the following line, which Emerson said proved him to be a poet, and he should watch his career in future with interest:

'Life is a flame whose splendor hides the base.'

We can imagine the kindly letter which answered the appeal, and how the future of that youth was brightened by it. "Emerson's young man" was a constant joke among his friends, because he was constantly filled with a large hope; and his friend of the one line was not by any means his only discovery.

His feeling respecting the literary work of men nearer to him was not always one of satisfaction. When Hawthorne's volume of *English Sketches* was printed, he said, "It is pellucid, but not deep"; and he cut out the dedication and letter to Franklin Pierce, which offended him. The two men were so unlike that it seemed a strange fate which brought them together in one small town. An understanding of each other's methods or points of view was an impossibility. Emerson spoke once with an intimate friend of the distance which separated Hawthorne and himself. They utterly disagreed upon politics and every theory of life.

Mr. Fields was suggesting to Emerson one day that he should give a series of lectures, when, as they were discussing the topics to be chosen; Emerson said: "One shall be on the Doctrine of Leasts, and one on the Doctrine of Mosts; one shall be about Brook Farm, for ever since Hawthorne's ghastly and untrue account of that community, in his *Blithedale Romance*, I have desired to give what I think the true account of it."

Sometimes, also, he had keen discussions and differences with Henry James. One day he appeared shocked at some of the doctrines advanced by Mr. James, and the conversation was dying, when Emerson's sister, who was present, took a chair, and planting it directly in front of James, said, "Let me confront the monster"; whereupon the topic was resumed, and they parted great friends.

He had many reservations also with regard to Dickens. He could not easily forgive any one who made him laugh immoderately. The first reading of *Dr. Marigold* in Boston was an exciting occasion, and Emerson was invited to assist. After the reading he sat talking until a very late hour, for he was taken by surprise at the novelty and artistic perfection of the performance. His usual calm had quite broken down under it; he had laughed as if he might crumble to pieces, his face wearing an expression of absolute pain; indeed, the scene was so strange that it was mirth-provoking to those who were near. But when we returned home he questioned and pondered much upon Dickens himself. Finally he said: "I am afraid he has too much talent for his genius; it is a fearful locomotive to which he is bound, and he can never be freed from it nor set at rest. You see him quite wrong evidently, and

would persuade me that he is a genial creature, full of sweetness and ameni-
ties, and superior to his talents; but I fear he is harnessed to them. He is too
consummate an artist to have a thread of nature left. He daunts me. I have
not the key." . . .

I find a record of one very warm day in Boston in July when, in spite of the
heat, Mr. Emerson came to dine with us:

"He talked much of Forceythe Willson, whose genius he thought akin to Dante's,
and says E[lizabeth]— H[oar]— agrees with him in this, or possibly suggested it,
she having been one of the best readers and lovers of Dante outside the reputed
scholars. 'But he is not fertile. A man at his time should be doing new things.'
'Yes,' said ___, 'I fear he never will do much more.' 'Why, how old is he?' asked
Emerson; and hearing he was about thirty-five, he replied, with a smile, 'There is
hope till forty-five.' He spoke also of Tennyson and Carlyle as the two men connected with literature in England who were most satisfactory to meet, and better
than their books. His respect for literature in these degenerate days is absolute. It
is religion and life, and he reiterates this in every possible form. Speaking of Jones
Very, he said he seemed to have no right to his rhymes; they did not sing to him,
but he was divinely led to them, and they always surprised you." . . .

When the lecture on Brook Farm really came, it was full of wit and charm,
as well as of the truth he so seriously desired to convey. The audience was
like a firm, elastic wall, against which he threw the balls of his wit, while they
bounded prettily back into his hand. Almost the first thing he said was
quoted from Horatio Greenough, whom he esteemed one of the greatest
men of our country. But there is nothing more elusive and difficult to retain
than Emerson's wit. It pierces and is gone. Some of the broader touches,
such as the clothes-pins dropping out of the pockets of the Brook Farm gentlemen as they danced in the evening, were apparent to all, and irresistible.
Nothing could be more amusing than the boyish pettishness with which, in
speaking of the rareness of best company, he said, "We often found ourselves
left to the society of cats and fools."

Emerson was always faithful to his appreciation of Channing's poems.
When "Monadnock" was written, he made a special visit to Boston to talk it
over, and the fine lines of Channing were always ready in his memory, to
come to the front when called for. His love and loyalty to Elizabeth Hoar
should never be forgotten in however imperfect a rehearsal of his valued
companionships. . . .

Emerson was no lover of the sentimental school. The sharp arrow of his wit found a legitimate target there. Of one person in especial, whom we all knew and valued for extraordinary gifts, he said: "___ is irreclaimable. The sentimentalists are the most dangerous of the insane, for they can not be shut up in asylums."

The labor bestowed upon his own work before committing himself to print was limitless. . . . Sometimes in joke a household committee would be formed to sit in judgment on his essays, and get them out of his hands. The "May-day" poem was long in reaching its home in print. There were references to it from year to year, but he could never be satisfied to yield it up. In April, 1865, after the fall of Richmond, he dined with us, full of what he said was "a great joy to the world, not alone to our little America." That day he brought what he then called some verses on Spring to read to us, but when the reading was ended, he said they were far "too fragmentary to satisfy him," and quietly folded them up and carried them away again. . . .

It was seldom he showed a sincere willingness or desire to print. One day, however (it was in 1863), he came in bringing a poem he had written concerning his elder brother, who, he said, was a rare man, and whose memory richly deserved some tribute. He did not know if he could finish it, but he would like to print *that*. It was about the same period that he came to town and took a room at the Parker House, bringing with him the unfinished sketch of a few verses which he wished Mr. Fields to hear. He drew a small table into the centre of the room, which was still in disorder (a former occupant having slept there the previous night), and then read aloud the lines he proposed to give to the press. They were written on separate slips of paper, which were flying loosely about the room and under the bed. A question arose of the title, when Mr. Fields suggested "Voluntaries," which was cordially accepted and finally adopted. . . .

His painstaking never relaxed, even when he was to read a familiar lecture to an uncritical audience. He had been invited by the members of the Young Ladies' Saturday Morning Club to read one of his essays in their parlor. This he kindly consented to do, as well as to pass the previous night with his friends in Charles Street, and read to them an unpublished paper, which he called "A[m]ita."[1] . . . This is not the place to speak of the charm of that reading[,] . . . but Emerson's enjoyment of his own wit, as reflected back from the

1. "Amita" was Emerson's pen name for his aunt, Mary Moody Emerson. (Editors' note)

faces of his listeners, can not be reproduced, nor a kind of squirrel-like shyness and swiftness which pervaded it. . . .

During [one] season Emerson consented to give a series of readings in Boston. He was not easily persuaded to the undertaking until he felt assured of the very hearty co-operation which the proposed title of "Conversations" made evident to him. . . . In spite of all [his] terrors, the "Conversations" were an entire success, financially as well as otherwise. I find in the diary:

> . . . [22 April] "To-day is the second of Mr. Emerson's 'Readings,' or 'Conversations,' and he is coming with Longfellow and the Hunts to have dinner afterward. . . . We had a gay, lovely time at the dinner; but—first about the lecture. Emerson talked of poetry, and the unity which exists between science and poetry, the latter being the fine insight which solves all problems. The *un*written poetry of to-day, the virgin soil, was strongly, inspiringly, revealed to us. He was not talking, he said, when he spoke of poetry, of the smooth verses of magazines, but of poetry itself wherever it was found. He read favorite single lines, also, from Byron's 'Island,' giving Byron great praise, as if in view of the injustice which has been done him in our time. After Byron's poem he read a lyric written by a traveler to the Tonga Islands, which is in Martin's *Travels*, also a noble poem called 'The Soul,' and a sonnet, by Wordsworth. We were all entranced as the magic of his sympathetic voice passed from one poetic vision to another." . . .

Emerson was perfectly natural and at ease in manner and speech during these readings. He would sometimes bend his brows and shut his eyes, endeavoring to recall a favorite passage, as if he were at his own library table. One day, after searching thus in vain for a passage from Ben Jonson, he said: "It is all the more provoking as I do not doubt many a friend here might help me out with it." . . .

The apprehensions which assailed him before his public addresses or readings were not of a kind to affect either speech or behavior. He seemed to be simply detained by his own dissatisfaction with his work, and was forever looking for something better to come, even when it was too late. His manuscripts were often disordered, and at the last moment, after he began to read, appeared to take the form in his mind of a forgotten labyrinth through which he must wait to find his way in some more opportune season. . . .

Opportunities for social communication were sacred in his eyes, and never to be lightly thrown aside. He wore an expectant look upon his face in company, as if waiting for some new word from the last comer. He was himself the stimulus, even when disguised as a listener, and his additions to the evenings called Mr. Alcott's Conversations were marked and eagerly expected. Upon the occasion of Longfellow's last departure for Europe in 1869, a private farewell dinner took place, where Emerson, Agassiz, Holmes, Lowell, Greene, Norton, Whipple, and Dana all assembled in token of their regard. Emerson tried to persuade Longfellow to go to Greece to look after the Klephs, the supposed authors of Romaic poetry, so beautiful in both their poetic eyes. Finding this idea unsuccessful, he next turned to the Nile, to those vast statues which still stand awful and speechless witnesses of the past. He was interesting and eloquent, but Longfellow was not to be persuaded. It was an excellent picture of the two contrasting characters—Longfellow, serene, considerate, with his plans arranged and his thought resting in his home and his children's requirements; Emerson, with eager, unresting thought, excited by the very idea of travel to . . . the strange world where the thought of mankind was born.

This lover of hospitalities was . . . king in his own domain. In the winter of 1872 Mr. Fields was invited to read a lecture in Concord, and an early invitation came bidding us to pass the time under his roof-tree. . . .

After the lecture the old house presented a cheerful countenance. . . . [F]ires blazed, friends sent flowers, and Mr. Alcott joined in conversation. "Quite swayed out of his habit," said Emerson, "by the good cheer." The spirit of hospitality led the master of the house to be swayed also, for it was midnight before the talk was ended. It was wonderful to see how strong and cheerful and unwearied he appeared. . . .

But the days came when desire must fail, and the end draw near. One morning he wrote from Concord: "I am grown so old that, though I can read from a paper, I am no longer fit for conversation, and dare not make visits. So we send you our thanks, and you shall not expect us."

It has been a pleasure to rehearse in my memory these glimpses of Emerson, and, covered with imperfections as they are, I have found courage for welding them together in the thought that many minds must know him through his work who long to ask what he was like in his habit as he lived, and whose joy in their teacher can only be enhanced by such pictures as they can obtain of the righteousness and beauty of his personal behavior.

Harper's New Monthly Magazine, 68 (February 1884): 457–67.

"Recollections of Ralph Waldo Emerson" (1884)

FRANK BELLEW

The son of an officer in the British Army, illustrator and caricaturist Frank Henry Temple Bellew (1828–1888) was born in Calcutta, India, spent his early years in France and England, and moved to New York City in 1850, where he counted newspapermen Ed Underhill, Frank Cahill, and Walt Whitman among his friends. His illustrations were well known to American newspaper readers, and in 1881 he became the "special" artist for *Canadian Illustrated News* in Quebec. Bellew's "Recollections of Ralph Waldo Emerson," which concentrates on their initial acquaintance in 1855, offers rare glimpses—narrated with characteristic British humor—into Emerson's professional life, light side, hospitality, and home life at the time. Of special interest in the essay are Bellew's descriptions of Emerson's frustration at correcting the proofs of *English Traits*, his ease at taking advantage of Hawthorne's shyness, his interactions with his children, and his surprise on learning from Bellew that, without his permission, Whitman had published Emerson's congratulatory letter on the appearance of *Leaves of Grass* in the *New-York Tribune*.

It was in July, 1855, that I first I walked up the nave of Concord, and, though I have visited many old-land cathedrals, . . . not one ever impressed me more than this sanctuary of thought and learning, with its broad aisle of arching elms, its teeming memories of New-World history, and its thousand associations with the evangelists of our new religion of humanity. The scene itself was beautiful. The vaulted roof of green, nearly half a mile in length, belittled any temple of mere masonry. The comfortable New-England homes on either side, with their gardens of flowers in front and their peeps of orchards behind, seemed to incarnate the spirit of the apostle of the place.

Here I met Emerson, and, being from a land of which he had formed many good opinions, he treated me perhaps with a larger measure of graciousness than was his wont with strangers. At all events, shortly after my introduction, he invited me to accompany him in his afternoon rambles through the woods and fields, which I learned was a most distinguished honor, rarely, if ever, accorded to any one, and for which I might thank my nationality. On the occasion of our first tramp,—I think it was the first, but the spoon of time has so stirred up the pudding of my brain that the ingredients are tolerably mixed; but the time is not of the remotest consequence—on one occasion he took me to Walden Pond, to which Thoreau gave renown. It appeared to be an extinct gravel-pit, filled with the most exquisitely pure water, and was often used by himself and a few others as a bath. I think he claimed that its purity and coldness gave it special tonic properties for this purpose. He asked me if I would not like to take a plunge.

"But we have no towels," I suggested.

"Oh," he replied, "that is of no consequence: we can dry ourselves in the sun. I rarely trouble myself about towels."

But I, not being familiar with the rare dryness of the American climate, and recalling some damp recollections of having once or twice, as a boy, tried a similar experiment in England, which resulted in my shivering on the bank for some time after my swim and then with much difficulty dragging my wet body into my clothes and going home in great discomfort, did not dare to venture, and so missed an opportunity of something akin to baptism at the hands of the prophet.

Near this pond he showed me a few acres of shrubbery he had planted as an investment for the benefit of his son, and he considered it the most profitable one he could make. The saplings were then about the thickness of a man's wrist, and he calculated that by the time his son reached the age of twenty-one the timber would be of considerable value. His son was then, I think, about nine years of age. It would at least, he thought, pay better than railway-shares, in which he had invested some money, but from which, up to that time, he had received no dividends.

On our way home he plucked a pod of the milk-weed, and broke it open to show me the shining silver-fish inside, and told me a good deal, which I have forgotten, about the plant. He had a reverential sympathy for everything that was nature, and a great admiration for the man who helped to remove the obstacles in the way of the perfect development of any of its forms. He often spoke with enthusiasm of Mr. [Bull], who had developed the Concord grape. He took great pride in his own roses. He loved beauty in a woman: it mattered not, he thought, about her intellect. He was passionately fond of children, and was wont to entertain them in large numbers at garden-parties at his own place, on which occasions all classes were invited. I remember once a swarm of little ones holding high jinks in his barn and amusing themselves with little dolls made of corn-cobs, and Emerson was one of the children, and enjoyed it more than any of the rest. He loved health and strength in men, and health in all things.

As illustrating his appreciation of the robust qualities in the male, a remark he made to me about his son struck me forcibly. We were talking about phrenology, and at the same time about the talent and character of his son Eddy, to whom I had been giving some lessons in drawing, when I said that I thought he had a well-developed organ of combativeness.

Emerson replied, "I hope so; though I have been afraid that he was rather deficient in that respect. However, he is doing better now: he has been fighting the street-boys a good deal lately."

I noticed in our walks that he was exceedingly respectful to all the weeds and insects: nothing was insignificant to him. He spoke almost with reverence of the pumpkin, saying that it had done a great deal for the settlers in early days, who would doubtless have starved without it, and that New England owed a great deal to the pumpkin. Once, when I had the temerity to question the status of the American apple, he knocked me down with a monster brought from his own garden, which was, I think, the most beautiful member of the family I have ever seen. On another occasion, when I was speaking admiringly of some model barns and out-buildings erected by a Mr. Samuel G. Wheeler on his estate near the village, he waved the subject gently aside with, "Oh, yes, the buildings are without doubt most excellent of their kind; but Mr. Wheeler has conferred a far greater benefit than that on Concord,—he has planted two rows of elms on the highway all along the front of his property. Those trees will be a boon to countless generations to come." To him the barns and stables were very good things in their way; but his mind was on the growth of the trees. The barns, I believe, have been burned down, but the trees now form a stately avenue and one of the great ornaments of Concord.

Returning from our rambles one day, we were overtaken by a thunderstorm when within about a furlong of Mr. Emerson's house. For a few minutes we took refuge under the eaves of a hay-stack; but, this protection being only partial, and there seeming to be a Hebridean prospect of our gradually getting soaked to the skin in that position, Mr. Emerson begged me to remain where I was, while he ran up to the house and sent back his man with an umbrella. I, however, being young and of robust instincts, did not dread a wetting, and thought I could stand it at least as well as he, and so protested against this arrangement. Still he persisted, and started off for the house. As I saw him, with his hat pulled down over his eyes, his collar drawn up round his ears, his black raiment and long legs, skipping over the wet grass, somehow a vision of . . . gentle spirits . . . flitted before me, with the Sage of Concord . . . bent on his mission of kindness. I followed, and we reached the shelter of his porch almost simultaneously, with every stitch of our clothing as full of water as it could possibly be. He seemed nearly vexed that I had been so stupid as to thwart his amiable plan. I assured him that I had not the slightest objection to a drenching. . . . But he, having passed that period of life when a man sees fun in being soaked, treated my honest asseverations as merely wordy complaisance, and forthwith insisted on my changing my clothes for a suit of his own dry ones. At first I resolutely resisted, representing that my own house was only a mile off, and I could easily walk up there and make the necessary change when the rain abated. He . . . persisted with such force and firmness—thrusting me into his bedroom, dragging from wardrobes, bureaus, and other places of concealment coats, socks, cravats, boots, shirts, everything, and insisting that I should put them on then and there—that I felt my resolution waver; and . . . I at last, for the sake of peace, was fain to submit to the change. . . . On reaching home my family did not at first recognize me, and, when it did, every member thereof was seized with violent hysteria. . . . When it is borne in mind that Mr. Emerson was a philosopher and I a caricaturist, he fifty, I twenty-five, that we were differently built, that his attire was that of a Puritan divine, while I was a bit of a dandy, my transmogrification and general appearance must have fully justified the merriment which greeted me.

Emerson was at this time correcting the proofs of "English Traits." He told me that "No brochure ever cost so much trouble, so much correcting, revising, and mending. These are the fourth set of proofs," he said, "which I am now going to send to the printers, and I hope they are the last." Apropos of this he quoted some author whose maxim was, "Write with fury and correct with phlegm." He asked me to give him my idea of the salient trait in the English character. I reflected for some time, and then said that the more I thought of it the more it seemed to me to have every trait.

"Ah!" replied he quickly, "you must catch it on the wing, catch it on the wing." He had a habit of repeating the last word or two of his sentences when he wished to emphasize them.

Thoreau said he thought the keynote of the English character was some variation of the quality of firmness or obstinacy, and I am inclined to think that Emerson was of the same opinion. Emerson was a decided admirer of the English on the whole, but he was greatly shocked when the news reached us, about that time, of the ovation which had been given to Louis Napoleon by the people on the occasion of his visit to England. He seemed really distressed that he must lose so much of the good opinion he had entertained of a great people. He told me how when he first went to London . . . little known to the world, but recognized by a few thinkers, it so happened that a member of the Athenæum Club had just died, thus leaving a vacancy for the election of a new member. Two names were proposed,—those of Guizot and himself. Now, though Guizot, to be sure, was in exile, he *had* been prime minister of France, was one of the foremost statesmen of Europe, and a man of the highest social position, while Emerson was but a country dominie from a little-esteemed land across the ocean. But, when it came to the vote, the members elected the plain New-England schoolmaster to the high honor they had at their disposal. This he considered grand, as indicating a people too independent to be influenced by rank, reputation, or wealth. . . .

He had a great relish for humor, and enjoyed the grotesque phases of character. I remember his telling of some young Englishman who was one of his fellow-passengers on the steamer coming to this country, and who amused them all with his endless pranks. Emerson admired his exuberant vitality and animalism, from which all his fun and spirits were generated. On the voyage the two became very good friends, and Emerson had many complaisant things to say to his young companion about his country, but he only told him pleasant things, for it was not according to his creed or his nature to act the censor in social intercourse. Some time after they had landed, Emerson delivered a lecture on England. Here on the rostrum, of course, his position was far different from that he had occupied on the deck of a steamer. He was here to report truthfully and criticise impartially; consequently he had many things to say that were not complimentary of the subject of his discourse. The young Englishman had never before heard these harsher criticisms from Emerson, and was greatly astonished: however, he soon came to the conclusion that it was all a piece of clap-trap on the part of the lecturer, to tickle his American audience; for on meeting Emerson after the lecture he slapped him on the back, and, with a hearty laugh of self-complacency, said,—

"Didn't you humbug those fellows nicely the other night?"

Emerson enjoyed telling this story very much, as an illustration of English character. He said,—

"It was utterly impossible for this young man to comprehend the complaisance which would restrain me, in our social intercourse, from using the dissecting-knife." . . .

I once met Hawthorne at Emerson's house. I had been invited to a little tea-entertainment, and Hawthorne, not knowing that any visitors were expected, had dropped in to make a casual visit. When I arrived, Emerson told me that Hawthorne was there. "But I will not tell him that you are here, or he would run away at once; and I want to introduce you." Presently Hawthorne sauntered round the corner of the house, and was upon us before he suspected his danger. There was no help for it then, so we were introduced. Just at that moment some ladies came out of the house and distracted our attention for a few seconds. When we turned round, Hawthorne was gone.

"There," said Emerson, "I knew how it would be: he has slipped off. The sight of a stranger frightens him away at once." . . .

Emerson often expressed surprise at the fact that most people in making for themselves a home seemed to think last of that of which they ought to think first. "They will build their houses with infinite care, seeing to the heating, lighting, supply of water, postal, railway, school, and church facilities; but of their society, their companionship, the very thing they should think of first, they never think at all."

He believed that old people were often mischievous and generally childish, and that they should be restrained like children. Quoting some one else, he used to say, "When I grow old, rule me."

As I said before, his mind was most hospitable to humor. . . . He was not of that cool-blooded class who affect to think that a story once told should never be alluded to again, that it should be cast out into utter darkness, never more to touch the tongue or ring the ear again: no, when a story was good he grew to love it, and liked fondle it and enjoy its company again and again. Dull men acting on this principle are liable to become bores, but Emerson was too strong to fear anything of that sort.

One day, when I was calling upon Emerson, he drew my attention to an unbound volume of poems he had just received from New York, over which he was in raptures. It was called "Leaves of Grass," by Walt Whitman. "I have just written off post-haste to thank him," he said. "It is really a most wonderful production, and gives promise of the greatest things, and if, as he says, it is his first writing, seems almost incredible. He must have taken a long run to make such a jump as this."

He read me some passages, raising his eyebrows here and there, remarking that it was hardly a book for the seminary or parlor table. Shortly after this I went off to the Wachusett Mountain, where I remained two months. On my return to Concord I again met Emerson, who was still enthusiastic over "Leaves of Grass." "I wrote at once," he said, "a letter to the author, congratulating him."

"Yes," I replied, "I read it."

"How? When? Have you been to New York?"

"No; I read it in the New York 'Tribune.'"

"In the New York 'Tribune'? No, no! impossible! he cannot have published it!" he exclaimed, with much surprise. I assured him that I had read it a few weeks before in that paper.

"Dear! Dear!" he muttered, "that was very wrong, very wrong indeed. That was merely a private letter of congratulation. Had I intended it for publication I should have enlarged the *but* very much,—enlarged the *but*," repeating "enlarged the *but*" twice and biting the "*but*" off with his lips, and for a moment looking thoughtfully out of the window. . . .

Emerson had a most benign manner, and a most sweet, wholesome nature. His instincts helped his principles, and his principles helped his instincts, to make him a good man in the best sense of the word. Still, I fancy he was capable of being stern, and even petulant, at times; but on these points I have no positive evidence, and only base my conjecture on an occasional look or gesture I observed in his demeanor toward men.

Lippincott's Magazine, 34 (July 1884): 45–50.

"Emerson as Preacher" (1885)

E. P. Peabody

An educational and social reformer, Elizabeth Palmer Peabody assisted Bronson Alcott in the Temple School in Boston in the 1830s, began a book store and circulating library in Boston in 1840, and published several of her brother-in-law Nathaniel Hawthorne's works under her own imprint. In the late 1830s and early 1840s Peabody became active in the Transcendentalist movement. She joined the Transcendental Club, continued a sometimes strained friendship with Emerson's aunt Mary Moody Emerson which began in the 1830s, published the *Dial* between 1841 and 1843, established friendships with Margaret Fuller (who conducted several "Conversations" at Peabody's book store) and George and Sophia Ripley, and brought newcomers such as Jones Very to the attention of Emerson and his circle. In her middle and later years, Peabody continued to experiment with new pedagogical practices, opened the first English-speaking kindergarten in America in Boston in 1860, and wrote numerous articles for the *Kindergarten Messinger*. She lectured at Alcott's Concord School of Philosophy in the 1880s, and her essay "Emerson as Preacher" was first delivered there as a lecture.

Although they did not become formally acquainted until the 1830s, Peabody met Emerson in 1822, when he tutored her in Greek in his mother's home; from the 1830s until his death, Peabody maintained a reasonably continuous relationship with Emerson. Once called Transcendentalism's "Boswell" by Theodore Parker, in "Emerson as Preacher" Peabody demonstrates how she earned the title. Mixing family and social history with criticism in her reminiscence of Emerson, Peabody sympathetically portrays her subject in an account that is balanced in its judgments and extraordinary for its breadth of biographical detail about, among other things, Emerson's family life, his relationships with fellow Transcendentalists, his emergence as a major challenger to the theological status quo in America in the late 1830s, his rise to international fame as an American intellectual of the first order in the 1840s and 1850s, and his interest in the poetic possibilities of Eastern religion and philosophy.

When Mr. Sanborn wrote to me that I was appointed to this lecture, he told me that the subject assigned to me was "Mr. Emerson as Preacher,"—not "Mr. Emerson in the Pulpit," as it stands in the printed programme. But I hold on to what I had immediately agreed to do, for I think Mr. Emerson was always pre-eminently the preacher to his own generation and future ones, but as much—if not more—out of the pulpit as in it; faithful unto the end to his early chosen profession and the vows of his youth. Whether he spoke in the pulpit or lyceum chair, or to friends in his hospitable parlor, or *tête-à-tête* in his study, or in his favorite walks in the woods with chosen companions, or at the festive gatherings of scholars, or in the conventions of philanthro-pists, or in the popular assemblies of patriots in times and on occasions that try men's souls,—always and everywhere it was his conscious purpose to utter a "Thus saith the Lord." It was, we may say, a fact of his pre-existence. Looking back through eight generations of Mr. Emerson's paternal ancestry, we find there were preachers in every one of them. . . . Considering these an-tecedents, it is not surprising that [Emerson and his] brothers all naturally gravitated to the profession of preacher. The outlook at the time, however, was not alluring. . . . Although William Emerson, the eldest brother, went to Germany to study for the Christian ministry, he had not the nerve of his great ancestor[s]; and, on his return, shrank from the battle that he had dis-cernment enough to see was impending, and took up what he deemed the kindred profession of law. Edward and Charles also entered the latter pro-fession, with the most serious conceptions of its ideal, and neither for fame nor fortune,—both being strong Christians of the heroic old type. Our Mr. Emerson always spoke of these brothers as his spiritual and intellectual superiors; but I was told, by one who knew them all intimately, that both of them regarded him as the high-priest of their Holy of holies, reverencing his every intuition as a sacred oracle. Mr. Emerson's poem, entitled "The Dirge," is the memorial of this rare fraternal relation.

My own acquaintance with Mr. Emerson dated from 1822, when I took a few private lessons from him in Greek,—a study that he was at the time im-mersed in, having just graduated from Harvard University, and being an as-sistant in the young ladies' school kept in his mother's house in Federal Street by his brother William. Mr. Conway mentions this circumstance in his very beautiful apotheosis of Mr. Emerson; and, as usual, entirely transforms, by his imaginative memory, something I probably did tell him, which I will take leave to repeat here, as I have often told it myself. It is true that both of us were very shy (Mr. Emerson then nineteen and I eighteen years old), and we did not get into a chatting acquaintance, but sat opposite each other at the study table, not lifting our eyes from our books,—I reciting the poems of the "Græca Majora," and he commenting and elucidating in the most instructive manner; and we were quite too much afraid of each other to venture any other conversation. When about to leave the city for what proved a two years' sojourn on the Kennebec, I sent for his bill, through his cousin George B. Emerson, who had introduced him to me. He came with that gentleman to say that he had no bill to render, for he found he could teach me nothing. It was then that, protected by his cousin's presence, he ventured to speak freely; and he poured out quite a stream of eloquence in praise of Mr. Edward Everett's oratory, of which I happened to express my admiration, and was delighted to find him as great an admirer of it as I was. . . . After this our acquaintance lapsed for ten years, comprehending all the time Mr. Emerson was studying divinity and preaching at the Second Church in Boston. Then he resumed it (in 1833) on occasion of reading a little paper of mine which his aunt, Miss Mary Emerson,—who was my great friend, and bent on bringing us into intimate acquaintance,—had found among some loose papers of a journal of thoughts I fitfully kept, on the same principle that Mr. Emerson kept a journal all his life. This paper was a very free paraphrase of the first chapter of the Gospel of Saint John. . . .

He was on the eve of his first voyage to Europe, soon after the death of his first wife and the relinquishment of his Boston pulpit. He was at the time too feeble in health to make visits, and sent to me to come to his house in Chardon Street, where I found him quite absorbed in Goethe and Carlyle; but he immediately turned his attention to Saint John's grand peroration, and we discussed every phrase of it. It was one of those conversations which "make the soul," to use a favorite expression of his aunt Mary's. It was, therefore, on the highest plane of human thought that we first met, our theme being the Eternal Relations of God, Nature, and Man; beginning an intercourse that continued there with more or less interval during his lifetime. . . .

. . . In 1835 or 1836, when he was still supplying the pulpit at East Lexington, it was my privilege to make frequent visits to his house in Concord, and he would always invite me to go down with him in his chaise on Sundays. In one of these precious seasons for conversation, as we were returning to Concord, I repeated to him the reply of an unconsciously wise and pious woman of the congregation, with whom I had walked to the afternoon meeting, and had asked her why the society did not call to settle over them an eminent preacher that Mr. Emerson had sent in his stead on a previous Sunday. ... "Oh, Miss Peabody," her words were, "we are a very simple people here; we cannot understand anybody but Mr. Emerson." "There is a 'tell' for a Transcendentalist," said I to him playfully, thinking he would laugh in contrasting it with the current cant in Boston among the Philistines, who said they "could not understand Mr. Emerson." But he did not laugh. On the contrary, with an accent that was almost pathetic, he replied, "If I had not been cut off untimely in the pulpit, perhaps I might have made something of the sermon." "It is evident from this attentive Lexington audience," I said, "that you have already made something of the sermon." "Did you observe," he replied, "that row of venerable, earnest faces of old men who sit just in front of the platform? It would be rather difficult to be frivolous when speaking to them. But in the back part of the hall there were some young men turning over the leaves of a hymn-book. No preacher can be satisfied with himself when he leaves any of his audience at leisure to turn over the leaves of a book." "That is a high standard," I replied. And soon he added, in a livelier tone, "Henceforth the lyceum chair must be my pulpit. The word of moral truth makes one of any place." ...

... [It] was Mr. Emerson's conscious life-purpose to minister the Living Spirit, whom he sought alike in the material universe and in human history, in literature and in ethics, in art, and, above all, in his own heart and imagination. In every form of his utterance he touched the profound depth of poetry, whether he sung in verse or spoke in prose. Much of his prose is as melodious as his verse,—witness his first publication on "Nature," his lecture on the "Method of Nature," and the opening, and indeed the whole, of his Address at Divinity Hall, ... which was not to me alone the apocalypse of our Transcendental era in Boston. For, if the lifeless understanding of the day mistook it for a denial of Christ, we now see that upon those whose hearts "the forms of young imagination had kept pure," and whom the pulpit entirely ignored or seldom addressed, it flashed the first light of the revelation of "the friend of man," whom he then affirmed that an effete ecclesiasticism had made "the enemy of man." ...

And here I take leave to introduce another personal reminiscence. I had the happiness of listening to this truly prophetic discourse; and when, soon after, he was correcting the proof-sheets of it for the press, I was visiting at his house. One day he came from his study into the room where his wife and myself were sitting at our needle-work, and said, "How does this strike your Hebrew souls?" proceeding to read the paragraph containing the above expression, which begins with the words, "This Eastern monarchy of a Christianity," etc. I said, "You will put a capital 'F' to the word 'friend'?" He seemed to reflect a few moments, and then deliberately replied, "No; directly I put that capital 'F' my readers go to sleep!"

He then went on to read another paragraph, which he remarked he had omitted to deliver because he thought he "was getting too long." It came immediately after the paragraph in which he accused the "historical Christianity" of corrupting all attempts to communicate living religion, "making Christianity a mythus, and founding the Church not on Jesus' principles, but on his tropes." . . .

I can recall only one word of this omitted paragraph, but remember perfectly the sense. It was a *caveat* anticipating the development of a new party, only half understanding him, which would fall into what he called the "puppyism" of a criticism irreverent of the person of Jesus. And this party did soon appear, and has not entirely passed away yet; some of our free religionists being guilty of this lack of just conception of "the one man who, alone in all history," as Mr. Emerson says, "estimated the greatness of man!" . . . I said, interrogatively, "You will certainly print that passage, for it will convict Mr. Ware of misunderstanding and so misrepresenting you in his sermon." . . . This was an unlucky suggestion of mine; for, after a moment's silence, he replied: "No, it would be shabby to spring upon Mr. Ware this passage now. I must abide by what I delivered, whatever was its lack of full expression." I was struck silent at the moment by this exhibition of an exquisite gentlemanly loyalty, the very poetry of self-respect and politeness. But some months later, irritated by many exhibitions of the "puppyism" he had predicted, and which stupidly professed itself to be Emersonian, I said to him, "Are you quite sure you did not sacrifice a greater duty to a less, when you decided not to publish that paragraph which defined your exact meaning, lest it should put Mr. Ware in the awkward predicament of having fought a shadow?" He replied, deliberately but emphatically, "No." . . . [He] expressed that gentlemanly courtesy was simply social justice, and that anxiety to be personally understood, rather than to have the truth understood, was the special weakness of the hour. Apology, and even explanation, were the blunders of egotism. . . .

. . . Mr. Emerson said that it was the duty of the individual to affirm all that his experience had proved to be true, and never to be satisfied short of a generalization covering a principle. He had the faith that our growing experience would contain the solution of all questions, the consummation of all hopes, the satisfaction of all unselfish desires, inasmuch as the social law was intercommunication of experiences forevermore. His humility was a quickening hope, not a weak agnosticism,—the humility of a son of God who feels that all that his Father has will duly become his. He never presumes to call the Unknown unknowable. . . .

. . . Mr. Emerson in his use of the words Brahm, Pan, Apollo, the Greek Bacchus, Uriel, and other burning personifications of the Persian Muse, revivifies the Pentecostal Muse and brings home to the imagination of this duller modern time the various attributes of the Eternal Spirit; making a language of his own, that creates unity of understanding in all who speak the differing and therefore imperfect languages of man in their partial creeds. Do we not hear this in [his] great lyric utterances? . . .

I will not attempt to read the whole of what is to me the most profoundly touching of all Emerson's divine songs, the "deep Heart's" reply in the "Threnody," when he himself came up from the most transforming personal experience of his life, expressed in that wild wail over the child lost to him for "the forever of this world," that for a long time plunged him into a deep of sorrow of which the first part of the poem is the all but unequalled expression. But at length he found what fully developed the human tenderness, that gave the last divine touch to the decline of his life. . . . [This] rich strain of poetry was of all his utterances the most touching to me. For several years before this season of his personal experience he was struggling to bear the loss of his brother Charles with the dignity of a man. To the question I had put to him, "Is there not something in God corresponding to and justifying this human sensibility?" he had replied, " No!" And at that period of his life he seemed to measure spiritual strength by a man's stoical denial of the fact of pain. His intellectual fire could not smelt the ore of human suffering. A gentleman who stood with him at his brother Charles's grave, said he turned away from it with the words, "Death is an absurdity!" . . .

Not only do all his great apocalyptic chants, but nearly all his smaller pieces,—such as, "Rhea," "Each and All," "The Rhodora," "Hamatreya," "Lines to J. W." . . . seem a true preaching, . . . sometimes catching up our spirits into the vision of principles, sometimes kindling private virtue and patriotic heroism, and sometimes plunging the soul into the unfound infinite. In one of his lectures he defined prayer as, "a plunge into the unfound infinite." It seems to me, therefore, that I am not irreverent, but reverent, when . . . I say of him, more and more "the multitude hears him gladly," for, like Jesus, he preaches "with authority," and not as the Scribes.

Postscript

There was no time for a conversation after I closed my reading, . . . but to a question that was asked just as we broke up, "What was Mr. Emerson's attitude towards religious institutions?" I will here take leave to reply. It was an essentially temporary one, like that he held to the technics of the pulpit of his day. His attitude towards the Lord's Supper naturally brought him into sympathy with the Quakers on the point of stated times for public prayer; and he actually ceased to go to meeting on Sundays because church-going also had at that time become merely perfunctory. But I heard him say, at that very date, that to meet together to consider all our duties in the light of the Divine Omnipresence was by far the most legitimate of human assemblies; and he considered it a great misfortune to society that it had become such a routine that "a devout person" (he meant his own ardently Christian wife) said, "It seems wicked to go to church."

At the time he ceased to go to church he was making a pulpit of the study-table where he composed his lectures. He never abandoned his office of preacher. I heard him say, in the last half of his life, "My special parish is young men inquiring their way of life." . . .

In the last of his life, when the infirmities of old age tied his tongue, and he could no longer minister the word of moral truth to others, he resumed his early habit of going to church himself on Sundays; and his wife told me he thanked her for bringing up his children to do so.

"Emerson as Preacher," from *The Genius and Character of Emerson: Lectures at the Concord School of Philosophy*, ed. F. B. Sanborn (Boston: James R. Osgood, 1885), pp. 146–47, 149–52, 156–62, 167–68, 169–72.

[Emerson as Remembered by His Children]
(1889 and 1897, 1902, 1921)

EDWARD WALDO EMERSON, ELLEN TUCKER EMERSON,

AND EDITH EMERSON FORBES

Although he did not have children with his first wife Ellen Louisa Tucker, Emerson had four with his second wife Lydia (Lidian) Jackson: Waldo (1836–1842), Ellen Tucker (1839–1909), Edith (1841–1929), and Edward Waldo (1844–1930). In their respective reminiscences that follow, the Emerson children represent their youth as a happy time, and they are balanced in their portrayal of the influence of both their mother and their father on their lives and the quality of their home life. These reminiscences are extremely valuable for showing Emerson in his primary domestic setting.

Ellen, who was named for Emerson's first wife, never married. As typically happened to the first daughter born in households in nineteenth-century America, Ellen spent most of her adult years living at home, looking after her parents' health and managing most household affairs. In the 1870s she served as her father's private secretary, his traveling companion, and, with James Elliot Cabot, his editor. After Emerson's death she continued to care for her mother until Lidian's death in 1892.

Edith married William Hathaway Forbes in 1865, and she lived in Milton, Massachusetts, where she raised seven children: Ralph Emerson Forbes, Edith (nicknamed "Violet"), William Cameron ("Cam"), John Murray ("Don"), Edward Waldo, Waldo Emerson, and Alexander. During the long period of Emerson's declining health after the burning of his house in 1872, Edith stepped forward to serve as her father's editorial assistant on *Parnassus* (1874), an anthology of poetry and poetic excerpts that had been some fifty years in the making, while her husband took over all of Emerson's financial affairs.

Finally, Edward, who like his sister Edith was schooled in Concord by Frank Sanborn, was graduated from Harvard University's medical school and practiced medicine in Concord from 1874 to 1882. In 1874, he married Annie Keyes of Concord; they had six children. As a youngster, he had accompanied Thoreau (whom he treated as an older brother or uncle) on many nature walks, and later

(continued)

wrote a tribute, *Henry Thoreau as Remembered by a Young Friend* (1917). After his father's death, Edward devoted himself to painting, to writing about his father's literary contemporaries, and to editing his father's writings. *Emerson in Concord* (1889) is a eulogistic account of his father's life, but one filled with so many personal observations that it is one of the best extended accounts we have of Emerson the man. *The Early Years of the Saturday Club* (1918) is still the standard history of the group that Emerson belonged to for nearly thirty years. Edward edited and annotated the twelve-volume centenary edition of his father's *Works* (1903–1904) and, with Waldo Emerson Forbes, the ten-volume *Journals of Ralph Waldo Emerson* (1909–1914). Edward's son Raymond collected his best pieces (including two on Waldo) in *Essays, Address, and Poems* (1930).

Edited by Edith Emerson Webster Gregg, Emerson's great-granddaughter, these reminiscences are drawn from several sources: Ellen's manuscript, begun in 1902, "What I can remember about Father"; Edith's manuscript address delivered on 15 November 1921 before the Women's Alliance at the Unitarian Church, Milton, Massachusetts; and Edward's *Emerson in Concord* and "Ralph Waldo Emerson" in *The Youth's Companion*, 9 September 1897. The text below follows Gregg's arrangement of the sources as she edited them for publication in 1980.

Ellen Tucker Emerson's Reminiscences

I must . . . begin with my own memories of Father. I know he told me stories, and when they ended and I asked what happened next he used to say, "Then I came away."

I know I was surprised, and felt as if the ground was taken from under my feet, when, terrified by a thunderstorm, I asked for him and was [told] by the nurse that he couldn't help. I had always supposed that with him was absolute safety and defence from every ill.

I don't remember his ever carrying me. We all remember his taking us up on the hills on the other side of the road and running down the back of them with us. His way of taking hold of our hands was not by the hand, but round the arm just above the wrist with a very firm, strong hold, and he always did the same as long as he lived in guiding me through a crowd or across a brook on a plank or any such passage. It always felt very good. And when we ran down the hills with him it was a fearful delight; it seemed as if we shouldn't be able to keep our feet, but we always did, and the speed was something glorious. One of the great pleasures was going down to the brook with him, and seeing him throw stones in for us to enjoy the splash.

Whenever we walked with him he told us the name of every flower, and showed us how many pine-needles in each sheath the two kinds of pines had, and how the lichens grew thickest on the north side of every tree, how the ferns came up crozier-shaped, and how their seeds were on their leaves, how pretty the milk-weed seeds were with the silverfish inside, and how the gold-finches surrounded the thistles. He told us every time what bird it was that was singing, so that we learned the notes of many, and when the brown thrasher sang he said the Indian came one day in old times and said that bird had said "Indian, Indian! Go white man. White man give corn, beer, beer, beer, beer!"

Every time we came across the lespideza in our walks he would say "Your Uncle Charles was pleased with what he called the *elegance* of that flower," and Father liked the name and often after passing it would repeat it again and again, "Lespideza, lespideza." Once he said "*That* is the 'flower of silken leaf that erst our childhood knew.'" And once at the Cliffs he said "Hark! That is the huckleberry-bird. Like a teaspoon ringing in a tumbler! I used to think it was the pine-warbler." About this last sentence I am not absolutely sure, but my impression and association are that it was that song he spoke of in the Dirge.

He used to show us loose-strife when we walked to Flint's Pond, and take us to a spot where a certain kind of golden-rod grows, and have us bruise the stem and smell the sweet fennel-like smell, and tell us that was the Solidago odora, and he used to rub the root of both kinds of polygala that we might notice its checkerberry-scent, or crossing the poor-soiled hills to go to Caesar's he showed us the pinweed that smells like lemon. We always despised the botanical names, but he never failed to give them, and I still know a good many.

Often he would recite over and over certain verses of his:

> "In Walden woods the chickadee
> Runs round the pine and maple tree
> Intent on insect slaughter:
> O tufted entomologist!

> Devour as many as you list,
> Then drink in Walden water."

I used to hear in very early days, and in my teens:

> "And many a thousand summers
> My apples ripened well
> And light of meliorating stars
> With firmer glory fell."

Also the Romany Girl, most of it, and:

> "In my Garden three ways meet,
> Thrice the spot is blest."

All of these we loved to hear. But quite as often he would go through Leigh Hunt's Song [to Ceres]. Later he would sometimes say:

> "He smote the lake to feed his eye
> With the beryl beam of the broken wave."

When once as a little girl I found his poems and tried to read them I was immensely interested in the "Forerunners" and seized the first opportunity to inquire about them and who they were. "I never caught up with them," he said, and foiled all my attempts to learn more about them with the same reply.

After we were old enough to walk to Baker Farm, to Conantum, to Anursnack, he said, "I don't know but you will deserve to have an entrance into the sacred order of Professors of Walking. Very few belong to it." And when we had again and again met a gray-haired Mr. Pulsifer (who boarded at Mrs. Phineas How's) far from home, he said "He seems also to be a Professor of Walking." Edith however did not love the long walks; Father occasionally to encourage her would lead her (by the wrist) part of the way.

When from 1848 to 1853 we had plenty of plums we children always went out after dinner with him into the garden. There was a large tree full of apricot plums and a smaller beside it of green Gages. At first he used to shake the tree, but as the fall bruised and often split the plums Mother fastened an indelible-ink-box to a slender pole, and he used that to pick them by pushing it up against the stem. We gazing up detected those that were glowing with ripeness, and he would gather them. If one fell in spite of his utmost care, he would involuntarily do what in those days we learned to call *bushing*, a sort of whistle of compunction which always came when he spilled ink or dropped a book, or met with any such mistake or awkwardness which he thought injured anything. We all greatly enjoyed hearing it and were well pleased with our new name for it. . . . I remember that one thing led us to call it "bushing." Father used to say when he tasted a fine plum "Good wine needs no bush," and as he of course "bushed" most when he let a beauty fall on the ground it didn't take our nonsensical minds long to twist it into saying as we devoured the remains of the wrecked plum "Good wine needs no bush"—meaning his lament. Very happy times we had under the plum-trees, eating the plums and being together and with Father.

He liked to have us sit on his knee, and Edith did until she went to Cambridge to school.

By the time I was eleven I began to ask questions. I remember not only the immense pleasure I was having meanwhile, but the standing off, so to speak, in my mind to consider it, and to think what a full and fit use of a Father and his study it was, and how good it was of Father to go into the business so minutely and faithfully, and evidently to have as good a time as I did over it. My question might be, for I shall have to make one up, "What is a phaeton?" "A carriage." "What a funny name!" "Yes, it was named for Phaeton, who tried to drive the chariot of the Sun." Then I would ask about that, and Father . . . would get out Lemprière's Classical Dictionary and show me. Then that would refer to Ovid, and he would find Ovid and read me the place, and that would lead to more questions, which required another book, and another. We never stopped till we had hunted out the subject in every book that bore on it. Perhaps this didn't happen more than two or three times, but it has given me a feeling that it was a custom, and is my happiest association with the study. About this time he used to let me bring a French book and sit on his knee and try to translate it, without knowing more than ten words of French besides the irregular verbs, so that he had to tell me most of them. That was delightful. . . . He brought home Michelet's books and others from the Athenaeum, and would let me sit by him and look over while he read them to me—scraps of French history they were, which made me love it, or about Savonarola and Michael Angelo. I think I never had any Latin with him, but as soon as Eddy began to translate it, he used to read Erasmus' Colloquia with him, . . . and when he and Edith studied Virgil they quite regularly read the lesson with Father.

When I was fourteen and fifteen I went to Lenox to school. . . . Mrs. Sedgwick asked me in beginning a term what lessons my Father wished me to take. "I suppose he has had you read this," or "Will he be willing you should drop that?" or "Does he care to have you go far with this study?" I was surprised that she should imagine Father would know or care what I studied. . . . I remember his buying Cleveland's Latin Grammar and giving it to me. . . and saying "Now you are five years old it is time for you to begin Latin." Accordingly I did, and went on with it always as *the* study of most importance as long as I went to school. He seemed to feel much interest in my reading Horace, but I do not think he showed it towards Virgil, Livy, Tacitus, Catullus, or Lucretius. He used to speak of the elegance of Horace and to wish I should feel it, but I did not.

When I was sixteen I went to Mr. Agassiz's school [in Cambridge]. When Mr. Felton said he would teach a class in Greek if the girls wished to study Greek, I asked Father whether I should. I don't remember his words, but he said yes, he thought I must know Greek, it refined the mind, it made a woman what she ought to be. . . . But I never advanced in Greek. He certainly did have Edith and Edward begin Greek early and never give it up. And with their compositions he helped them somewhat as he used to help his brothers; he would talk over the subject with them, and by the time they were in their teens and going to Mr. Sanborn's school he began to drill them in speaking their pieces. It was an enchanting part of our family life. Every fortnight he chose a new piece for each, and evening after evening they recited them, and were shown how, and again shown how. (Father said that before the fortnight was over he often acquired new skill himself in rendering the piece.) Then after the children began to do well, the last few days, he said "Now we must polish the work and remove all signs of the labour"—I do not mean that he always said this, only that this finish was an important part of the work, never omitted.

When one of the children was to recite Mr. Allingham's poem "The Touchstone," and Father had laboured over teaching it the whole fortnight, he said "I have brought the recitation of 'The Touchstone' to such perfection now that I think I must read it at my lecture tomorrow night (he was lecturing in Boston then) and introduce my audience to it." He came home much pleased with the interest in the poem that the audience had showed, and the remarks and questions of people after the lecture. People who knew him were pretty sure to go up afterwards to see him, and Edith and I meanwhile, when we were at the lectures, had often little talks with his friends or ours that were no small part of our happiness. Often there were very funny stories and remarks in his lectures, and he would read them over and over at home—sometimes, he said, twenty times—to get through laughing at them himself, that he might be sure not to laugh at the lecture. Lecturing was his business; he had to work at it as other men do at their business. He said he wished he could give it up, that Mrs. Tappan was ashamed to have him travel peddling lectures all over the country. But we told him we weren't ashamed, we felt he was trying to benefit and to teach his country, as well as to make his living.

Edith Emerson Forbes's Reminiscences

In thinking over my Father's happy life, it seems to me that the ancestral ties, which led him to settle in Concord for life, were a signal good fortune to him, giving him in his boyhood a love of the country, and an intimacy with the river and meadows, the woods and ponds, the hills, and from them the western horizon line, on which blue Nobscot, Wachusett, Watatac, Uncano-mac, and best of all Monadnoc's much-loved sapphire peak are seen. . . .

Our Mother was a queenly woman, tall and graceful, and as my Father desired me to notice, walked beautifully. Years after the Plymouth days he showed me with pleasure a letter from a lady who had known her there, who wrote to him on some question of her own, and after it added a message of greeting to my Mother, and then followed this sentence: "I never hear the word *grace* without seeing Miss Jackson crossing the room in her white dress." She was courageous and never afraid to speak. She was wise and witty too. But she was also a mother to all our poor neighbors, of whom there were many, living in tenements in the oldest houses under the hill opposite. Her sympathy with distress of any kind was unfailing, and she suffered deeply in the thought of Slavery. The sufferings of animals were to her what seemed to us more bitterly pathetic than to the creatures them-selves. . . .

I like to recall one evening when my Father was giving a course of lectures in Boston. These courses of his were the very best occasions of hearing him. The audience was made up entirely of *his own* people—those who loved him and *must* hear him—very different from the times when he gave one lec-ture in a course by many speakers. There was in these an atmosphere of fel-lowship, of certainty of pleasure in the hearing, of little rustlings when in

[163]

their joy in a happy line people turned in sympathy to look at each other. Rufus Choate had recently spoken of the "Glittering Generalities" of the Declaration of Independence, and my Father alluded to it, repeating "Glittering Generalities—they are Blazing Ubiquities!" standing erect and commanding with a flash in his eyes. I think nobody could forget that moment. . . .

My Father respected and praised the useful domestic animals, though utterly unskilful with them, a lack which he regretted, and he enjoyed seeing the tact and courage of others in managing them. Pet animals he cared nothing for and shrank from touching them, though he admired the beauty and grace of cats.

My brother once received a letter from a lady who wished him to tell her, for an article in St. Nicholas on the canine friends of our authors and statesmen, some anecdotes showing his Father's liking for dogs, and the names, colour and breed of his canine friends. He answered that he was only able to tell her of the delight and sympathy with which his Father read to the family how when the Rev. Sydney Smith was asked by a lady for a motto to be engraved on the collar of her little dog Spot, the divine suggested the line from Macbeth "Out, damned Spot."

We had cats, one at a time, for a mouser, and we enjoyed them, and Father listened respectfully to what we chose to tell of them. But our Mother was always befriending unfortunate animals, and suffering in sympathy for them. After I was married my sister reported that a new cat had come in the night and jumped into the window of Mother's room. She wrote to me "Father says that when she came in the window she told Mother she was an Acton cat, and wanted a home, and one day in Acton she met a cat who said 'Why, haven't you heard? There's a Mrs. Emerson down Concord way what's kind to cats.' And so she had run and neither stinted nor stopped, and all the cats could direct her, so that here she was, ready to be cosseted." Of course, Mrs. Emerson justified her confidence.

Someone gave us a green parrot. It was not a brilliant or original talker, learning nothing new, but skilful in making as much variation as possible of her three phrases "Poor Polly," "Polly wants a cracker" and "O the pretty bird," which last she only used in a gust of affection when she heard the step of the seamstress in the entry. . . . She used to sit on the scraper on the stone doorstep most of the time in summer, her wings being clipped, and the doorstep too high for her to climb up. She used to hop down and walk in the grass, and climb a very thorny sweetbrier. Father was interested in her quaint ways, and the varieties she made in her small stock of language. But his knowledge of her limitations, and her want of aptitude and wit, such as we hear of in most parrot stories, made him say that it was a test of the truthfulness of a family to keep a parrot. One summer day a thunderstorm came up and I was out. When I came home he said "Your green cat was much troubled by the storm, and tried to get in. I offered her her cage and she stepped into it with gratitude." I believe that was the sole occasion when he took care of a pet personally.

My sister kept some bees and he was much interested in their ways. He was delighted on a very hot day to see their custom of setting half a dozen or so bees just inside their door to fan in air with their wings. Father came in much amused and reported that these had had their orders "Fan, you dogs, fan!"

Once in the last years my sister wrote me this anecdote. He was standing in the bay-window of the dining-room after breakfast, reading the morning paper which had just come, when a half-grown kitten came in and rubbed against his boots, a thing which had never happened to him before. Absorbed in his paper he was not aware of it. Then she sat down close to his feet and looked up at him with so funny an expression of adoration that my sister said "Father, look down." He moved his paper aside and looked. The little cat was gazing still and he could not but see the rapt expression and exclaimed "*Poor creature! I wish* I were worthy of it!"

Of course he watched with joy the wild birds that crowded round our fir-balsam trees near his study window. Their fresh purple cones jeweled with clear drops of pitch caught all kinds of little insects, attracting birds of many kinds. All the bright orioles, blue-birds, purple finches, swallows and yellow-birds we saw at leisure, and very near. One day he called me to see a purple finch dancing on the ground with every show of its grace and beauty, fluttering its wings, skipping forward and back before a little brown sparrow-looking bird, who stood still watching critically with little head on one side, the splendor of his swaying, dainty fanciful dance, and her modest calm inspection of his antics struck Father as such a contrast he said "It looks as if he was eloping with the *cook!*" This rather under his breath, for few things raised his shoulders so high or brought such a look of annoyance as any remark that could possibly grate on the ears of the waitress who might be within hearing. He could not bear stories to be told that could offend "one of these working ones.". . .

At four o'clock on Sundays Father came from his study, and called at the foot of the stairs "four o'clock," or he whistled for us, and then took us for long walks in the woods, showing us pretty flowers he had found in his daily walks. Oftenest we went to Walden and his loved pine grove by the Cove, where Mr. Thoreau had his leave to build his cabin. I remember that little cabin, though it was soon moved away after he returned to his home. Mr. Thoreau was a dear playmate of ours, for he occasionally lived with us, especially when Father was lecturing, sometimes in New York or as far south as Baltimore in early days, and Mr. Thoreau came as protector. He or Mr. Channing used to guide my Father to see rare flowers in hidden places, and then Father took us the next Sunday. In these walks he often crooned his verses lately written, and though he knew nothing of music, and had been emphatically rejected by the singing master who tried each freshman's capacity, yet when he chanted his own verses his voice was so sweet it was always a pleasure to hear. When he was rowing us on the river, he chanted the Canadian Boat Song in a way that made the tune seem familiar to me when I first heard it sung.

He used to choose for us the poetry for declamation day at school, when parents and friends were free to come to hear the recitations and compositions on alternate Thursdays. Many hours I spent in his study, for he loved to teach us how to learn the poetry and how to recite it, hearing it over and over with inexhaustible patience, until he had trained us to use the inflection that would best bring out the meaning, or the *pauses,* which are often as telling.

We told him of the boys and girls of the school, and he was always wise and helpful in his interest and advice. When the boys of the School Boat Club asked me to go with them (a passenger only) when they took their afternoon practice on the river, I asked my Father what I should say or do. "Tell them you will go if they ask Lizzy (my special friend) to go too." The boys agreed, and we went. They asked me to steer, and we often went with them, so I had a good chance to learn in our wandering river where were the rocks and shallows, and the best course. One of the boys used to make very clever drawings on peppermints, of about an inch across in size, perhaps a little more. They were made by very short straight lines, and would represent a ball-room with a chandelier, and one or two couples dancing in the foreground and smaller ones in the background. I wanted to show one to Father, and told the boy I wished he would give me one of these works of art. He said he would make one for me and bring it to me "at church if the teacher was not there." When I told my Father of this promise he smiled and said "You should have told him that *you* would be there" with an inflection that I translated in my mind that *I* should have such dignity as would compel him to observe the same propriety that the teacher's presence would require.

When I asked him if I might have a white dress made to wear at our teacher's wedding: "Yes, every lady ought to have a white dress in her wardrobe." When I repeated this to the dress-maker who was sewing in the house, she laughed that he should call me a lady. But I fancied that he too remembered Miss Jackson's white dress crossing the room. Of course it was not his habit to know anything of our clothes. My Mother was the Queen of the house, and it was only a chance that I happened to speak of it to him. He was apt to say to her, "What does the Queen say?" when he would like to have her answer a proposition, or conversation of a guest, or "What do *you* think, O Queen?" When they were old, and his memory for words failed him, he used to go with her and my sister to a Saturday Evening Club, where friends met and some paper was read and discussed. Father delighted to hear her give her views, and to rejoice that they were so wise and fine, and said to me how good it was—"the perfect security with which she speaks"— and what pleasure everyone had in hearing her.

Edward Waldo Emerson's Reminiscences

He had love and tenderness for very small children, and his skill in taking and handling a baby was in remarkable contrast to his awkwardness with animals or tools. The monthly nurse, who drew back instinctively when he offered to take a new-born baby from her arms, saw in another moment that she had no cause to shudder, for nothing could be more delicate and skilful and confident than his manner of holding the small scrap of humanity as delighted and smiling he bore it up and down the room, making a charming and tender address to it.

A baby's cry or its joyful little crow would instantly bring my father from his books or writing. Many men are rather afraid to take a little baby; the younger the better for him. His skill in handling and amusing them was great, and it was strange to see how this was divined in advance by those somewhat shapeless beings of whom Artemus Ward said: "How beautiful is babes; so like human beings—only so small!" They were pretty sure to stretch out their small, pudgy hands to him.

A very little child always had the entrance and the run of his study, where it was first carried around the room and shown the Flaxman statuette of Psyche with the butterfly wings, the little bronze Goethe, the copy of Michael Angelo's Fates which, because of the shears and thread, were always interesting. The pictures in the old "Penny Magazine" were the next treat, and then, if the child wanted to stay, pencil and letter-back were furnished him to draw with. After a time, if the visitor became too exacting, he was kindly dismissed, the fall being softened by some new scheme suggested. Entire sweetness and tact and firmness made resistance and expostulation out of the question.

If a child cried at table Mr. Emerson sent it out to see whether the gate had been left open or whether the clouds were coming up, so sure was he that the great calm face of Nature would soothe the little grief, or that her brilliant activity of wind and sun would divert the childish mind. The small ambassador, a little perplexed as to why he was sent then, returned, solemnly reported and climbed back into his high chair.

[Father] always expected that Sunday should be observed in the household, not with the old severity, but with due regard for a custom which he valued for itself as well as for association, and also for the feelings of others. We could read and walk . . . but were not expected to . . . play games or romp or to go to drive or row. He was glad to have us go to church. His own attitude . . . was, that it was only a question for each person where the best church was,—in the solitary wood, the chamber, the talk with the serious friend, or in hearing the preacher. This was shown when a young woman working in his household, in answer to his inquiry whether she had been to the church, said brusquely, "No, she didn't trouble the church much." He said quietly, "Then you have somewhere a little chapel of your own," a courteous assumption which perhaps set her thinking. . . .

As our mother required us to learn a hymn on Sundays he would sometimes suggest one or two which he valued out of the rather unpromising church collection which we had, or put in our hands Herrick's White Island or Litany to the Holy Spirit, Herbert's Elixir or Pulley, or part of Milton's Hymn of the Nativity.

He liked to read and recite to us poems or prose passages a little above our heads, and on Sunday mornings often brought into the dining-room something rather old for us, and read aloud from Southey's Chronicle of the Cid, or Froissart's Chronicles, or Burke's speeches, or amusing passages from Sydney Smith or Charles Lamb or Lowell. One rainy Sunday when we could not go to walk we got permission from our mother to play Battledore and Shuttlecock for a little while, but no sooner did the sound of the shuttlecock on the parchment bathead ring through the house than we heard the study door open and our father's stride in the entry. He came in and said: "That sound was never heard in New England before on Sunday and must not be in my house. Put them away." . . .

On Sunday afternoons at four o'clock, when the children came from their Bible-reading in their mother's room he took them all to walk, more often towards Walden, or beyond to the Ledge ("My Garden"), the Cliffs, the old Baker Farm on Fairhaven, or Northward to Cæsar's Woods, Peter's Field, or to Copan (Oak Island) on the Great Meadows, or the old clearings, cellarholes and wild-apple orchards of the Estabrook country, and sometimes across the South Branch of the river to the tract named Conantum by Mr. Channing from the Conants, its proprietors.

He showed us his favorite plants, usually rather humble flowers such as the Lespideza . . . or the little blue Self-heal whose name recommended it. He led us to the vista in his woods beyond Walden that he found and improved with his hatchet; . . . and on the shores of frozen Walden on a dull winter's day hallooed for Echo in which he took great delight. . . .

Often as he walked he would recite fragments of ballads, old or modern; Svend Vonved, Battle of Harlaw, Scott's Dinas Emlinn, Alice Brand, and Childe Dyring, Wordsworth's Boy of Egremond, Byron's lines about Murat's Charge, and occasionally would try upon us lines of poems that he was composing, "The Boston Hymn," or the Romany Girl, "crooning" them to bring out their best melody.

He took the greatest interest in our recitation of poetry, and pleased himself that no one of us could sing, for he said he thought that he had observed that the two gifts of singing and oratory did not go together. Good declamation he highly prized, and used to imitate for us the recitation of certain demigods of the college in those days when all the undergraduates went with interest to hear the Seniors declaim.

On our return from school after "Speaking Afternoon" he always asked, "Did you do well?" "I don't know." "Did the boys study or play, or did they sit still and look at you?" "Several of them didn't attend." "But you must *oblige* them to. If the orator doesn't command his audience they will command him."

He cared much that we should do well in Latin and in Greek, liked to read our Virgil with us, and even *Viri Romæ*, and on days when I had stayed at home from school and congratulated myself that tasks were dodged, sent me to the study for "The thick little book on the fourth shelf," and spent an hour with me over *Erasmi Colloquia*. But with our dislike of mathematics he sympathized, said we came by it honestly, and would have let us drop the subject all too soon, but for the requirements of school and college curriculum. He was uneasy at seeing the multitude of books for young people that had begun to appear which prevented our reading the standard authors as children, as he and his brothers had done. He required [me] to read two pages of Plutarch's Lives every school day and ten pages on Saturdays and in vacation.

The modern languages he was careless about, for he said one could easily pick up French and German for himself.

He had the grace to leave to his children, after they began to grow up, the responsibility of deciding in more important questions concerning themselves, for which they cannot be too grateful to him; he did not command or forbid, but laid the principles and the facts before us and left the case in our hands.

Nothing could be better than his manner to children and young people, affectionate and with a marked respect for their personality, as if perhaps their inspiration or ideal might be better than his own, yet dignified and elevating by his expectations. He was at ease with them and questioned them kindly, but as if expecting from them something better than had yet appeared, so that he always inspired affection and awe, but never fear. The beauty, the sincerity, the hopefulness of young people charmed him.

He was hard at work in his study until his walking time, except for a half-hour spent in garden and orchard after breakfast, when he liked to have us with him and teach us the names of his pear- and apple-trees and their tenants, the birds. If we came into his study when little, we could stay so long as we would look at pictures quietly or draw. On week-days he walked alone, but on Sundays he showed us the shrines of the wood-gods and the home of Echo in the groves he loved.

When we were in bed my father would often come up and, sitting by us in the twilight, chant, to our great delight, a goodnight song . . . to the trees, the birds, the flowers, the members of the family, even the cow and the cat.

My father seldom romped with the children, and any silliness or giggling brought a stern look; the retailing any gossip or ill-natured personal allusions heard outside was instantly nipped in the bud. No flippant mention of love, in even the childish romances of school, could be made, and the subject of death was also sacred from any light speech or jest.

The annoyance which his own shyness and self-consciousness had cost him made him desire that young people should have whatever address and *aplomb* could be got by training, so he urged that they should dance and ride and engage in all out-of-door sports.

On in-door games he looked with a more jealous eye, remembering how he and his friends had amused themselves with good reading; only tolerated his children's acting in juvenile plays, and always disliked card-playing. On one occasion two of us had just learned some childish game of cards, and being dressed some time before breakfast, sat down to play. When he entered he exclaimed, "No! No! No! Put them away. . . . When the day's work is done, or you are sick, then perhaps they will do, but never in the daylight! No!" . . . [His] value of Nature and books as teachers made him grudge valuable time so spent.

He persistently kept meal-times pleasant—would allow no sour remnants of yesterday's wrong-doings to be served up again. Every day was to be fresh and new as a dewdrop from the hands of God. We may have failed yesterday, but we would never think of it again, and start right to-day.

We must be polite and kind to the servants, and his respect and courtesy toward them always made them love and honor him. . . .

When our young guests came he always made them at ease, found out what interested them, and talked of that, as if they were his equals, but in a way that set them thinking. One rule he held to faithfully—never to talk about himself. One's sicknesses and infirmities were never to be spoken of except in private. . . .

Boisterous laughing, any cheapness or vulgarity of speech or irreverence were firmly checked. We loved and stood in awe of him, but scolding was a weapon unknown in his armory, and trust was his greatest one. He never punished, seldom commanded or forbade. . . . He wished us to be brave . . . if it came in the line of duty.

The watchword which his Aunt Mary had given him and his brothers, "Always do what you are afraid to do," was prescribed to us and enforced as far as possible.

Fear was usually only ignorance, he said, of what to do in a given case, and one would soon learn. He wrote from England in 1847 to my mother:

"Bid Ellen and Edie thank God that they were born in New England, and bid them speak the truth and do the right forever and ever."

His written and spoken words reached young people, whom he loved because they were gay and brave, in far distant regions, helped them and often brought them to him for counsel, and it was this: "Be yourself; no base imitator of another, but your best self. There is something which you can do better than another. Listen to the inward voice and bravely obey that. Do the things at which you are great, not what you were never made for. Remember that we are

> 'Pipes through which the breath of God doth blow
> A momentary music.'

Hear what the morning says and believe that."

Edith Emerson Webster Gregg, "Emerson and His Children: Their Childhood Memories," *Harvard Library Bulletin*, 28 (October 1980): 407–14, 417, 419–23, 425–30.

From *Talks with Ralph Waldo Emerson* (1890)

CHARLES J. WOODBURY

Charles Johnson Woodbury, later a manufacturer and lecturer, met Emerson at Williams College in 1865. Emerson arrived to deliver one lecture, but the response from the students was so positive that he remained for a week (7–15 November) and delivered six lectures: "Social Aims in America," "Resources," "Table Talk," "Success," "Culture," and "American Life." The twenty-one-year-old Woodbury took advantage of Emerson's stay by walking and talking with him for most of the visit, and he eventually collected his notes on the experience as *Talks with Ralph Waldo Emerson*, which is the longest such work about Emerson.

When I recall Mr. Emerson personally, I recognize that a man more impersonal one seldom meets. There was nothing pronounced about him. Presence (in one meaning) he had none, because he was without the consciousness, self-esteem, and self-assertion which go so far to constitute it. But there was that behind the withdrawn manner which took possession with an exclusiveness no personal fascinations or magnetism could equal or explain. To every comer he was a fact and experience, undissuadable, penetrating to the region of motive and source of volition; and from the first moment, his was the "morning light which shines more and more unto the perfect day."

At the time of our first meeting, Mr. Emerson was sixty-two. His tall, slender figure had made slight obeisance to age; but the earlier portraits of him I had been familiar with ill-prepared me for his changed expression. The aggressive physiognomy was still there; the delicate, severe lips and piercing eyes. But they rarely flashed now, wearing instead an introspective grey; and the lips were rather those of a seer than a poet. The hair alone had kept its native colour, like dark wine. Both Rowse's and Wyatt Eaton's rather than Griswold's portraits revive him faithfully as he was at this time, and during the few later years that I saw him. Rowse especially has reproduced the large featuring of his face, with that wise, determined nose (called straight, like the Damascus road) which other Emersons have, and the tender, shrewd eyes, that until the very end kept so much sunshine in them. And what eyes they were! Whatever they looked at, they looked into, and that effortlessly. Such are not ordinary eyes; they are divining rods. I have noticed that most men successful in values, business men of the first order, have the same inquisitive peer. Under excitement his look was illuminated, and betrayed by turns the sagacity of the man of affairs and the "vision" of the clairvoyant. His more tranquil regard continually revealed yourself to yourself like the limpidity of a clear pool.

But the regnant feature of Mr. Emerson's personal contact was his voice: in converse agreeable, kindly, incisive, it was only to be heard when everything was congruous and still. But who that ever listened to it in public has forgotten the healthful experience? Not resonant like Phillips', and presenting fewer contrasts with itself than Beecher's, it seemed as neither of these to carry, as some rivers carry gold, the speaker's soul in it. And the voice, like the soul, knew no falling inflections. Calm and equable, the monologist went on, the voice always raised, suspense after suspense, still inconclusive when the auditor looked for rest, the theme growing clear until the postponed emphasis of the final pause, and that still an upward pitch; the lesson of which made me puzzle and ponder, and finally appeared to be ethical rather than rhetorical—that on all subjects we discourse inadequately, and can never come to a period. As if he should say: It is time to stop, but not to finish. There is more to be added to complete the presentation, but it cannot be spoken now on account of something else which must follow.

So he always stood on the rostrum, having cast away all the tricks that orators hold dear, gestureless, save now and then a slight movement of the hand, repelling as from the cold pole of a magnet; his eyes searching his manuscript, or raised over all of us and gazing forward into space, sometimes in the presence of a luminous expression, glowing like the lenses of some great light-gatherer; uttering sentence after sentence, with the accent of a man who insists on this present statement, but who believes that we cannot here come to the whole truth of the thing, and shall never quite find the end of it.

For the rest, so lifted and extraordinary was the elevation from which he approached the subjects he discussed; so clear his medium, and removed from lower currents and "occasions"; such was his insight, mastery, and moderation,—that he soon created in his audience a fine surprise, and, without delay, his own nerve and spirit. Then, such was his fairness and solicitation, so liberated was the manner of his address from dogmatism and self-assertiveness, that his audience was fain to project him free of the local circumstance, and to identify his presence as representative in this busy and material age of that solitary and timeless group of natures, the choice of all ages.

But the completed benediction was after he descended from the enforced dignity of the platform, and apart from the exacting restraints of the study. His bearing and contact had the exquisite power of a moral nature which has never been impaired by a wilful transgression. Nobility characterized his deportment.

Elevating is a weak word with which to describe the influence of his gentle serenity upon men; for even quite above themselves were they lifted by his presence, and found their highest moments his common ones.

The cause of this was that all his thoughts and life were abreast of the Holy Spirit and tried by it, so that every phenomenon assumed its natural place, demanding attention, but at no moment throwing the soul out of its relation with the Unseen. Even in those days when he was disturbing the movement of all the intelligent forces around him, and the entire atmosphere was in commotion because of him, there was one point of absolute calm, the centre of the cyclone.

. . . [H]is presence was a continual solicitation and reward. Although quiet almost to reserve (I never heard him laugh), his social bearing was distinguished by an old-school politeness, with just enough polish to divert the suspicion that his retirement had made him rustic; and his slight, half foreign etiquette was so uplifted by the presence of the moral sense, that his manners were celestial.

His conversation was always in the low tone of one accustomed to being listened to, and presupposed a philologist's knowledge of words, so that the language was followed doubtingly at first, but soon companionably, and, anon, it was plain that he opened horizons and left on almost everything he touched a remnant of originality. Moreover, one had with him the perpetual delight of hearing a thing said in its best way. You listened now to a quaint anecdote or satire, and now to an epithet, comparison, or excerpt, touched gently or sharply with his own criticism, until you breathed the high atmosphere where your companion dwelt, not as a spectator but as familiar; and, after parting, you remembered, more even than his vivid talk, his simple ways, the home-like feeling he diffused, and the forgetfulness that you were in the presence of our foremost American.

He was an intent listener. One was quite sure of his appreciation if deserved. But there was always in his personality a certain resistance, "a familiar remoteness;" and even when his companionship was most gentle and encouraging, it was searching and pungent like the odour and flavour of certain flowers and herbs. His books are aromal with the same quality. . . .

He was a most salutary companion. . . . To him, there was but one foundation of genuine courtesy as of genuine character, and that was the moral sense, so that though he never preached against bad physical habits and morals, his presence did not permit them. The sobriety, directness, honesty, and conscientiousness which he infused into a man were antiseptic, and eliminated slovenly and unfortunate habits of mind and body.[1]

It was taken for granted as a basis of companionship with him that one was living in constant obedience to the demands of his highest nature. He believed that the intellect and the moral sentiment should not be separated. Crass instincts he could forgive, and he had an almost divine patience with weakness and even indolence, but none with dishonesty. He anticipated the disclosures of Rémusat as he did the discoveries of Darwin, and despised the first Bonaparte because he cheated at cards. "It is one of those acts," he said to me, "which only men of a certain kind can commit. It cannot be extenuated."

So his bearing had a certain translucency, and begat it. . . .

A word about the nest and its good lares! Mr. Emerson rarely spoke of himself, but he had the passion for home which is characteristic of all manly natures, and told me that he believed in large families. His mother had twelve brothers and sisters . . . and his father and mother had eight children.

I asked him once about his boyhood, but the brief answer gave small glimpse of boyish spirits and joys; and reading in the meeting-house was probably his nearest to a boy's sins. Perhaps he was a man who never had a boyhood; I think it must have been always aged. And so not least among the marvels he awakened, was the pleasant query how one who never was a boy

---

1. Mr. Emerson said he smoked very (and we all know how he spared that overworn word) rarely, and never until he was fifty. He was a punctual man. I remember one afternoon we were going to drive. As I came into his room, prompt to the moment, I saw that he was already waiting. Every book and manuscript were put out of reach, not even the newspaper before him; but there he sat on the edge of the lounge, his coat on his arm, his hat in his hand. I never knew him a minute late at any appointment. The example of course caught me—at a cost, I suppose, of years. (Woodbury's note)

himself could cherish so subtle a sympathy with a boy's weakness and work and gladness and troubles.

But, notably from the mother, there was an atmosphere of charm and peace in the home that no jollity could substitute. All through the child life, the sweetness of living for one another was exemplified. Through youth into manhood, it was still the gentle order of the family. William taught school to help Waldo through college; Waldo taught school to help Edward; and Edward taught school to help Charles—all graduating from Cambridge between 1818 and 1828. Simplicity and mutual deference and love were the law of the household.

From *Talks with Ralph Waldo Emerson* (New York: Baker and Taylor, 1890), pp. 121–33.

From *Literary Recollections and Sketches* (1893)

FRANCIS ESPINASSE

Journalist and biographer Francis Espinasse was a friend of Jane Welsh and Thomas Carlyle and a frequent visitor to their house in London. In 1847 he was a newspaper writer in Manchester, where he met Emerson during his British lecture tour. His comments on Emerson's *Mind and Manners of the Nineteenth Century* and *Representative Men* lecture series show not only his reaction but also that of Thomas Carlyle. Also, it is interesting to compare Espinasse's summary of the Carlyles' comments on Emerson with their own words, printed earlier.† Anyone doubting Emerson's devotion to Neo-Platonic thought should pay attention to Espinasse's comments on Emerson's visit to Walworth ("the only literary pilgrimage which I knew him to make in London") in search of "memorials" of Thomas Taylor, the English classical scholar and Neo-Platonist, many of whose works were in the books Bronson Alcott brought back with him from England in 1842.

A letter warmly inviting Emerson to proceed to Chelsea immediately on arriving in England, had been sent by Carlyle to Manchester. I went with it to Liverpool to place it in Emerson's hands as soon as he should touch the soil of England. But the packet-ship which had borne him across the Atlantic did not arrive until two days after it was due, so I returned with the letter to Manchester. It was posted to Emerson at Liverpool, and reached him when he landed. On receiving it he came to Manchester only for an hour or two, and then went straight to the Carlyles at Chelsea. It was just after that visit, and on his return to Manchester, that I saw him in private for the first time. His commune with Carlyle at this their second meeting had not been quite so satisfactory as at their first one some fourteen years before, when Emerson made that well-remembered pilgrimage to Craigenputtock. To say nothing of other differences, Carlyle, still full of Cromwell, resented with needless heat Emerson's refusal to fall down and worship the Puritan hero. There was just a trace of irritation, the only one which I ever perceived in Emerson, in his first references to his Chelsea visit; but it soon disappeared, never to reappear. Sorrowing admiration was expressed in the remark made to one of us early during his stay in Manchester: 'Carlyle's heart is as large as the world, but he is growing morbid.' Emerson was lost in wonder at the vividness of Carlyle's conversation, which he compared to 'sculpture,' and pronounced to be even more marvellous than his books.

Emerson made Manchester his headquarters for several months, not only lecturing there, but returning to it every now and then from his lecturing tours in the manufacturing districts, and as far north as Edinburgh. He delivered two courses of lectures in Manchester, one of them at the Athenæum, the other, intended to be of a homelier kind, at the Mechanics' Institution. Those at the Athenæum belonged mainly to the series so well known afterwards under the title of 'Representative Men.' Emerson's manner in the lecture-room, like that which distinguished him in private, was one of perfect serenity. For any emotion that he displayed, there might have been no audience before him. He always read his lectures, and in a grave monotone for the most part, with rarely any emphasis. Much in them must have been 'caviare to the general,' but ever and anon some striking thought, strikingly expressed, produced a ripple of response from the audience, and the close of his finely discriminating lecture on Napoleon was followed by several rounds of applause, all this confirming what he once said to me, that such lecturing triumphs as fell to him were achieved by 'hits.' To the public success or failure of his lectures he appeared to be profoundly indifferent, a mood to which his experiences in American lecture-rooms had habituated him. He told me, with perfect equanimity, that at home he was accustomed to see hearers, after listening to him a little, walk out of the room, as much as to say that they had had enough of him. At his Manchester lectures the audiences were numerous and attentive. Whatever they might fail to understand, they evidently felt that this was a man of genius and of high and pure mind.

Out of the lecture-room Emerson's only public appearance in Manchester was at the annual soirée of the Manchester Athenæum, the late Sir Archibald (then plain Mr.) Alison in the chair. Emerson delivered on the occasion an effective little speech, unusually complimentary for him, since he made in it laudatory references to the Tory chairman's History of Europe, to Dickens, who had sent a letter of apology for non-attendance, and even to *Punch*. Better than this, it contained a noble passage on the greatness of the English character, afterwards expanded and minutely illustrated in the *English Traits*, of all Emerson's books the most interesting to English readers. . . .

Emerson's associates in Manchester were chiefly members of the little circle which had welcomed Carlyle to the cotton city some weeks before. He honoured my domicile with several visits. Coming on one occasion to breakfast, he brought with him photographs of his wife and children, saying *à propos* of that of Mrs. Emerson, 'If any of our family are saved, it will be through her merits.' On the same occasion he took up *The Christian Year*, which was lying about, and I was a little surprised to find so ethnic a philosopher point admiringly to the opening stanza, 'Hues of the rich unfolding morn,' etc. As an evening guest, among a circle of his juniors not given to silence, Emerson was very reticent but very amiable, listening patiently, with a benignant smile, to the argumentation and other talk going on. If he did broach a comment or an opinion it was generally . . . to cite something said by a thoughtful friend at home. In private conversation he told me that Carlyle had advised him to try some historical subject, his reply being that he had no genius for history. Referring to Carlyle's vehement denunciations of authorship, he said, 'If Mr. Carlyle can show me any better employment than literature, I shall be happy to betake myself to it.' Before finally quitting Manchester, Emerson gave a dinner-party to his Manchester friends and others from the northern and midland counties, with some of whom he had corresponded from Concord on high or deep spiritual matters. The guests were a strange collection of mystics, poets, prose-rhapsodists, editors, schoolmasters, ex-Unitarian ministers, and cultivated manufacturers, the only bond of union among them being a common regard and respect for Emerson. One of the guests . . . was a vegetarian, for whom a dinner of herbs had been considerately prepared. He was then a young man and had written a mystical book, which Emerson admired and which made him hopeful of its writer's future. It is a little characteristic of the difference between the Sage of Concord and the Sage of Chelsea,—that Carlyle's only comment on this and another mystical book by the same writer, was a contemptuous expression of wonder that 'a lad in a provincial town' should have presumed to handle such themes as he had dealt with. After the prandial and post-prandial babblement, to which our host as usual contributed nothing, he gave a serene close to the evening by reading to us his lecture on Plato. He had omitted it, probably as above the heads of an ordinary audience, from his series of lectures at the Manchester Athenæum on Representative Men. . . .

Soon afterwards I pitched my tent in London again, and saw something of Emerson there, at the Carlyles' and elsewhere. 'The seraphic man,' as Carlyle called him, was, like most other visitors at Chelsea, silent when Carlyle held forth. However, it was at the Carlyles' that I listened to the most copious utterance which in private I ever heard come from Emerson's lips—and it was not very copious. I can give only a very imperfect report of it. It may have been a deliverance of Emerson's own, but, as was not uncommon with him, he professed to be only repeating what had been said to him by a friend who complained of the far too general and exclusive domination of 'the alphabet.' In the course of his European travels this friend had been struck with the much that had been said and was known about men who had had to do with 'the alphabet,' that is, who had written anything, compared with the obscurity which had been left to enshroud great workers and doers from the first architect of Cologne Cathedral, Erwin of Steinbach onwards. A catalogue of illustrative contrasts followed. This apparent depreciation of literature from one who prized it so highly as Emerson did seem to me singular, but was, of course, echoed sympathetically by Carlyle. On another evening the conversation turning on lectures and lecturing, Carlyle good-humouredly bantered Emerson on the easiness of his platform-tasks, reading 'from a paper before him,' and its contrast with his own difficulties, those of 'a poor fellow, set up to hold forth without any paper' to help him. Emerson said nothing. In such very little private conversation as I had with him in London he laid great stress on the scholarship of England, especially its Oriental scholarship. Really the Englishman in whom Emerson seemed to me as much interested as in any other was that strange being Thomas Taylor, the Platonist and Neo-pagan whom some visitor once found in an attitude of worship before a silver shrine of Mercury! Taylor lived in Walworth, whither Emerson told me that he made a pilgrimage—the only literary pilgrimage which I knew him make in London—in search of memorials of this reviver of the worship of the gods of antiquity.

Between Carlyle and Bancroft, the historian of the United States and then American minister in London, Emerson was introduced everywhere, his reputation as a thinker of course powerfully aiding, and both in the aristocratic and intellectual circles of London society he saw everybody whom he could have cared to see, Carlyle reporting (what ought to have pleased that great apostle of silence) the complaint of 'the high people' that (unlike himself) Emerson had little to say to them. One of the effects on Emerson of the brilliancy of the society in which he found himself lionised for the first time was to make him very reluctant to lecture in London. To overcome this reluctance, resort was had to a device of which I heard no whisper at the time, and which, either through modesty or pride, Emerson seems never to have mentioned even in his letters to relatives and friends at home. It came to my knowledge only recently, when exploring the paper-masses left behind him by the late John Forster. Among them is the original, with the signatories' autographs attached, of a memorial addressed to Emerson, respectfully requesting him to deliver a course of lectures in London, signed by Bulwer Lytton, Carlyle, Procter (Barry Cornwall), Charles Dickens, and the inevitable Forster himself. Two courses of lectures by Emerson in London did come off, the earlier of them (on the 'Mind and Manners of the Nineteenth Century') being delivered to a guinea-paying audience in a hall in Edward Street, Portman Square. . . . I had a long talk with Carlyle about one of these Edward Street lectures. When I spoke of the high ethical ideal which Emerson held up to us, Carlyle replied that Emerson's ethics consisted chiefly of 'prohibitions.' In a striking passage of the lecture, Emerson, whom again I report very imperfectly, had compared man's life on earth to a bird alighting on a rock, resting for a while, and then flying away into infinite space. I made some reference to this similitude, and Carlyle rejoined 'Merchant! you figure well.' On asking for some explanation of this enigmatic deliverance, Carlyle told me the story of an impecunious Dumfriesshire man, to whom, on entering a shop, a tradesman . . . had tendered an account. The debtor had no money with which to settle the bill, but after carefully inspecting its caligraphy and arithmetic he said to his creditor in a mournfully complimentary tone: 'Merchant! you figure well.' The bearing of this anecdote on Emerson's similitude, I leave it to the reader to discover. Mrs. Carlyle was more dissatisfied than her husband with Emerson's ethics. Dilating in his high-flown optimistic way on the ultimate triumph of good over evil, the lecturer went the length of saying that even when in a certain haunt of sensual vice, unmentionable to ears polite (though Emerson called it by its plain English name), man is still tending upwards. . . . Mrs. Carlyle's moral indignation at this statement knew no bounds, and for some time she could scarcely speak of Emerson with patience. I now and then fancied that after Emerson had been banqueted and welcomed by so many great and distinguished people in London, she viewed him, with a certain wife-like jealousy, as a sort of rival of her husband. Emerson's admiration for her abated visibly, till at last he was heard to say that the society of 'the lady' (Mrs. Carlyle made no pretension to profundity) was worth cultivating, mainly because she was the person who could tell you most about the husband. Very soon after the delivery of the first lecture I accompanied Carlyle to Emerson's domicile, a visit apparently intended to be one of congratulation on his lecturing success. Emerson was at home, and Carlyle seemed to find the process of congratulation rather embarrassing. . . . Elsewhere than in Emerson's presence, 'Moonshine' pithily expressed Carlyle's opinion of his London lectures. . . .

From *Literary Recollections and Sketches* (London: Hodder and Stoughton, 1893), pp. 156–64.

"Random Reminiscences of Emerson" (1893)

WILLIAM HENRY FURNESS

Born in Boston, the Unitarian minister, theologian, reformer, and prolific author William Henry Furness was, along with Samuel Bradford, one of Emerson's truest lifelong friends. After graduating from the Harvard Divinity School
in 1823, Furness became the pastor of the Unitarian Church in Philadelphia,
where he remained for the next seventy years. An early supporter of the Transcendentalist movement and member of the Transcendental Club, Furness
preached a humanized Christ and a belief in Christianity based on natural, not
supernatural, evidence, and in his *Remarks on the Four Gospels*, published in
1836, he announced himself squarely in the liberal camp of Unitarianism led by
Emerson and Theodore Parker. Over the years Furness and Emerson maintained a regular correspondence, and Furness helped to arrange lecture en-
gagements for Emerson in Philadelphia which, as he indicates in his reminiscences, were very profitable for his friend.

   In Furness's copy of James Elliot Cabot's *A Memoir of Ralph Waldo Emerson*,
his daughter wrote an account of her father's relationship with Emerson as dic-
tated to her by him. Much is contained in the reminiscences that follow, but
one paragraph that is not deserves notice here. On the subject of Emerson's
character, Furness said:

> I cannot analyze his character, and tell you what manner of person he was. One trait
> was very conspicuous, the perfect serenity of his temper to all who had any acquain-
> tance with him. He had the closest affinity with all that is good and true. I asked him
> once, when we were walking together . . . in Philadelphia, if he did not see something
> good in the physiognomy of the people he met in the streets. "O yes," he exclaimed,
> "the angel Gabriel is ever coming round the corner." It was this disposition that led
> him to magnify everyone who said anything that struck him and into which he himself
> probably put a significance that the speaker had not thought of. "Many of his geese
> were swans." (Quoted in *Records of a Lifelong Friendship 1807–1882: Ralph Waldo Emer-
> son and William Henry Furness*, ed. H[orace]. H[enry]. F[urness]. [Boston and New York:
> Houghton Mifflin, (1910)], p. xvi.)

I cannot remember the time when Ralph Waldo Emerson and myself were not acquainted. Our earliest acquaintance must have neighbored to our babyhood. I recollect playing with him and the late Samuel Bradford . . . under my mother's eye, on the floor in the old house where I was born, in Federal Street, Boston, when our ages ranged between six and eight. I was the eldest, Ralph the youngest.

For our A B C we went to a Dame's school in Summer Street, opposite to Trinity Church, a homely wooden building then, with neither steeple nor tower. The rector was Dr. Gardiner, of whom it was told that, when a parishioner of his, the Hon. Mr. Lloyd, for a long time Massachusetts Senator, complained to him that he had made a wounding allusion to himself in his sermon, the doctor replied that he had not written a sermon for twenty years.

Although Emerson's memory failed towards the last, he never forgot, I believe, a pocket handkerchief of mine which I brought to the school, emblazoned with prints illustrative of one of Mother Goose's immortal stories. He referred to it more than once, in his old age.

What beautiful picture-books children have now! Not so was it in our young days. One of the books from which we learned the alphabet had in it a picture of "the rude boy who got up into a man's apple-tree." So coarsely engraved was it that it was almost impossible to distinguish the boy's head from the apples. The print, however, gave that play to the imagination which children love.

Emerson and I next went to a writing-school, to learn that art. We sat along-side each other; and I can see him now, working hard, with his tongue out, moving in accord with his pen. Years after, when I received the first letter from him, I marveled at the flowing hand he had achieved.

Even in those early days he wrote verses, chiefly patriotic, I remember, on the naval victories of the day,—the battle of The Constitution and The Guerriere, for example.

We were very proud of the stars and stripes, which puts me in mind: our national motto, "E pluribus unum," does not mean, as I imagine it is generally understood, one made up of many, but one *out* of many. My friend, the late Edward Law, a Harvard man of the class of 1819, once suggested a finer motto for this nation, "Inseparabilis, Insuperabilis," which requires no knowledge of Latin to be understood.

[185]

My outspoken admiration for these early verses of Ralph was great, and I was repaid by his praises of my drawings. I was rather distinguished in those days for my artistic productions, which were chiefly horses. The Boston Hussars, who had at that time adopted a splendid new uniform, the delight of all the children, were my favorite models. The horses I drew could draw me, I suspect, far better than I them. . . .

Emerson was all genius, of miraculous insight. But he could not draw, nor sing, nor play, not even on a Jew's-harp, a musical instrument popular among boys in those days. If, by some sleight of hand, or sleight of talent,— which is it?—one did any of such like things that he could not do, Emerson extolled him to the skies. This is the reason, I imagine,—so fond was he of praising,—why his swans turned out to be—not swans. In fact, he had no talent; only pure genius. He could not use our beautiful literary paper money. He had to coin his own language in the fire of his own genius. It was all bullion, without a particle of alloy; solid gold. I once said in print, somewhere, that since Shakespeare no one had used words so grandly as Emerson. An English admirer of his, Mr. Ireland, quoted this remark, evidently regarding it as a bit of extravagant eulogy. When I first read that exquisite little poem of Emerson's, The Titmouse, in which he tells of being lost in the woods in a New England snow-storm that raged around him so fiercely that he feared he should not get safely out of it, and a titmouse came, hopping from twig to twig, chirping as merrily as if he were overflowing with the enjoyment of a balmy midsummer's day, and the wee bird is described as

"this atom in full breath
Hurling defiance at *vast death*,"

I turned, without a moment's delay, to my Shakespeare Concordance, to discover whether or not Emerson had borrowed from Shakespeare that epithet "vast" as applied to death, so true to the situation, to the all-surrounding storm, threatening death everywhere. The phrase was not in the Concordance. Thoroughly and genuinely Shakespearean as it is, it is Emerson's own.

When we were in college,—Emerson was a year after me,—Rhetoric was all the rage. No one was more completely under the spell than he. A finely turned sentence, a happy figure of speech, threw us into a spasm of enthusiasm. Edward Everett was a master in that line. As Emerson said in one of his lectures here in Philadelphia, the boys of those college days got by heart passages of Everett's sermons and addresses. Here is an instance in point, which I quote from my boyish memory. Everett was hardly more than a boy himself when he was ordained pastor of Brattle Street Church,—only nineteen years of age. He preached once in the college chapel. One of the things he said, apropos I do not recollect of what, ran thus: "In the Capuchin church in Vienna sixty-six emperors are sleeping; none of your mushroom emperors, but men whose fathers and grandfathers were kings." I do not think Emerson ever became insensible to the charm of the Everetts. There was a younger brother of Edward, John, a brilliant, promising youth, remarkably like Edward in person, voice, and mind. He died young. Emerson told me that his own elder brother, William, once had a quarrel with John Everett (the two were classmates), which was made up, after exchanging notes. Emerson quoted with great admiration a passage in one of John Everett's notes in which the writer referred to "trifles that children resent, and boys magnify." . . .

Emerson was a right loyal friend. I preached my first sermons in Boston in 1823, being then twenty-one years of age. Emerson once came to hear me. The next day I got a letter from him that tore my preaching all to shreds,— not a whole piece left. I dare say he was not really so hard on me as it seemed then. Self-love is so tender, so thin-skinned, that it cannot for the moment distinguish the prick of a pin from the stab of a dagger. There was no coating of sugar on the pill, no credit given me for anything. I found it hard to keep in mind that "Faithful are the wounds of a friend." . . .

In his latter days he was troubled with aphasia, which manifested itself in a strikingly characteristic way. His insight was so keen that he could never abide mere names. Most of us, when we are ill, find something to comfort us when the doctors give names to our sicknesses. Not so with Emerson. He penetrated beyond names, and dealt only with realities. Accordingly, when this infirmity of memory came upon him, he forgot the names of the most familiar things, but he could describe them so that one instantly knew what he meant. Once he was telling me about a friend of his in Concord, who, he said, was employed in—here he hesitated—in one of those places where you get money. "A bank?" "Oh, yes," he replied, "in the bank." Speaking of another friend, he said, in like manner, that he was "interested in those things that go to and fro." "Railroads?" I asked. "Ah, yes, railroads," was his answer. This decay of memory grew upon him so rapidly that to his nearest and dearest there was somewhat of reconciliation to his leaving them when he did. Had his life been prolonged, the time might have come when he would not have known his own kindred. Had that ever been the case, I am inclined to think that Samuel Bradford and I, associated as we were with his very earliest childhood, would have been the last that he would have failed to recognize. . . .

I doubt that Emerson was ever better paid for his lectures than in Philadelphia. When I handed him a check for twelve hundred dollars for . . . six lectures, "What a swindle!" was his exclamation. . . .

Emerson's habit was . . . to jot down on scraps of paper the thoughts that came to him, and stow them away in pigeon-holes. When he was in want of a lecture, he culled it from these notes. But he had great trouble in finding titles for the essays, lectures, poems, that he wrote. . . .

There are more things than one that Emerson has written that I do not comprehend. I do not know what he means when he says "the soul knows not persons." I am inclined to think the soul knows nothing else. I cannot reconcile this saying with his affirmation that "the principle of veneration never dies." But I must submit to Coleridge's rule,—"When you cannot understand a man's ignorance, account yourself ignorant of his understanding." Emerson was not bound to be consistent. "Consistency," he says,—"it is a fool's word. Say what you think to-day in cannon-balls, even though it contradicts what you said yesterday."

Atlantic Monthly Magazine, 71 (March 1893): 344–48.

"The Philosophers' Camp. Emerson, Agassiz, Lowell, and Others in the Adirondacks" (1893)

W. J. STILLMAN

In August 1858, Emerson joined James Russell Lowell, Louis Agassiz, Ebenezer Rockwood Hoar, John Holmes, Horatio Woodman, and others on an excursion to the Adirondack wilderness in upstate New York. The American artist, art critic for the *New York Evening Post*, and avid outdoorsman William James Stillman made the party's arrangements, and his account of the excursion and of Emerson's behavior while on it presents us with a very different Ralph Waldo Emerson from the one most often portrayed in the reminiscences collected in this volume. For in "The Philosophers' Camp"—for the first and virtually only time in his life—the philosopher of nature puts his idealized character and reputation on the line by purchasing a hunting rifle and heading out into the wilds of nature.

Although Emerson memorialized the excursion in his poem "The Adirondacs," Stillman's record of the trip is by far the more realistic of the two. This is not to say that Stillman was not himself susceptible to Emerson's charm or even to Emerson's disposition to idealize his own and others' character and experience; indeed, in a summary account of the excursion which he included in his "Autobiography," Stillman defines the value of his days in the Adirondacks as the opportunity they provided him to associate with an Emerson who, while under the "undiluted influence of the great mother, Nature," was liberated from social conventions and gained a degree of manly "self-sufficiency":

> Of all the mental experiences of my past life, nothing else survives with the vividness of my summers in the Adirondacks with Emerson. The crystalline limpidity of his character, free from all conventions, prejudices, or personal color, gave a facility for the study of the man, limited only by the range of vision of the student. How far my vision was competent for this study is not for me to decide; so far as it went I profited, and so far as my experience of men goes he is unique, not so much because of intellectual power, but because of this absolute transparency of intellect, perfect receptivity, and pure devotion to the truth. In the days of persecution and martyrdom, Emerson would have gone to the stake smiling and undismayed. . . . ("Autobiography of W. J. Stillman," *Atlantic Monthly Magazine*, 85 [May 1900]: 622.)

In the days when the great wilderness in northern New-York, now generally known as the Adirondack region, was still little known, its only visitors being a few landscape-painters and sportsmen, I, then being of the former, became so deeply attracted to this almost undisturbed primeval forest that every summer drew me back to it; and during a short residence in Cambridge, my reports, and perhaps my enthusiasm, so impressed those with whom I was thrown into contact that on one of my returns I led back a company from the circle which had its center under the shadow of old Harvard. The first expedition included Lowell and several common friends, and was rather an exploration and verification of my reports than a serious undertaking, but was important, as it led to the formation of a club whose purpose was the recurrence of its members' for a short time each summer, to the undiluted influence of the great mother, Nature. . . . I was requested to take the direction of a more important expedition the year following; and the company included Lowell, Emerson, Agassiz, Dr. Jeffries Wyman . . . Dr. Estes Howe, John Holmes . . . Judge Hoar, Horatio Woodman, Amos Binney, and myself. . . . I went some days ahead of the company, and located the camp at Follansbee Pond, a lake of the Raquette chain, out of the track of hunters or chance tourists, but where game was still plentiful and good fishing not far away; for our main sustenance was to be what nature sent us. . . .

Emerson, as I read him, had no self-sufficiency. He lived and felt with the minimum of personal color, reflecting nature and man; and the study of the guide, the savage man thrown out of society like a chip from a log under the ax of the chopper, returning to the status of pure individuality,—men such as our guides were,—aroused in the philosopher the enthusiasm of a new fact. He often spoke of it, and watched the men as a naturalist does the animals he classifies. I remember Longfellow's once saying of Emerson that he used his friends as he did lemons—when he could squeeze nothing more from them, he threw them away; but this, while in one sense true, does Emerson a radical injustice. He had no vanity, no self-importance; truth and philosophy were so supreme in their hold on him that neither himself nor any other self was worth so much as the solution of a problem in life. To get this solution he was willing to squeeze himself like a lemon, if need were; and why should he be otherwise disposed to his neighbor? There are others who knew Emerson better than I did or could, and possibly Longfellow did, though that observation makes me doubt that there was any real sympathy between them. But what seems to me the truth is that Emerson instinctively divided men into two classes, with one of which he formed personal attachments which, though tranquil and undemonstrative as was his nature, were lasting; in the other he simply found his objects of study, problems to be solved and their solutions recorded. There was the least conceivable self-assertion in him; he was the best listener, a genuine thinker, or one whom he thought to be such, ever had; and always seemed to prefer to listen rather than to talk, to observe and study rather than to discourse. So he did not say much before Nature; he took in her influences as the earth takes the rain. He was minutely interested in seeing how the old guides reversed the tendencies of civilization: how when they went to sleep on the ground they put on their coats, but took them off when they got up; wore their hats in camp, but went on the lake bareheaded.

The entire absorption of his personality in the subject-matter of study was childlike; he left no cranny of novelty unsearched. I remember that one Sunday morning when the state of the larder made it necessary for the guides to get a deer, Emerson was more disposed for quiet meditation, having at that time no interest in the hunt; so I took him in my boat, and while those of the company whose habits did not interfere with the enjoyment of the chase on Sunday went to the watching-posts with the guides, we sought the remotest nook of the lake-shore. It was a magnificent morning, and in the silence of the forest the baying of the hounds, as they took the scent on the hills above us and followed the deer in his doublings and evasions, filled the air, and the echoes redoubled the music. When the deer are in good condition, as in August, they generally take a long run before they come to water, and we heard the dogs sweeping round over the hills at the further end of the lake, and coming back, ranging to and fro, till the expectancy and the new sensation grew in effect on Emerson, and he could resist no longer. "Let us go after the deer!" he exclaimed, and though, having come out for meditation, we had no gun with us, we were soon flying down the lake from our remotest corner to where the baying led to the shore. But we were too late: Lowell had already killed the deer before we got there.

It was interesting to see how Emerson grew into the camp life. As at first he had refused to carry a rifle, and decided to take one only for uniformity, so in the early days of our forest residence he declined to take any part in the hunting or fishing: but we had not been long in camp before he caught the temper of the occasion, and began to desire to kill his deer. Luck failed him in the drives in which he took part, the deer always coming in to some other watcher, and we decided to try night-hunting; i. e., stealing up to the deer as they browse in the pads along the shallow water, carrying in the bow of the boat a light which blinds the animal, the lantern throwing all its light forward and the hunter sitting invisible in the shadow. This manner of hunting is possible only on very dark nights, and was resorted to only when venison was needed and the drive had failed. If the man who paddles the boat is dexterous, the deer can be approached to within a few yards without being alarmed; but in the darkness it is very difficult for those not accustomed to the appearance of the animal to distinguish him from the rocks or shrubs around, for in the intent examination of the strange phenomenon of the light he remains motionless, except that now and then he will beat the water with his hoofs to drive away the flies. We took the best guide at the paddle, Emerson taking the firing-seat behind the lamp, and I in the middle with my rifle, ready in case he missed his shot.

We went down the lake to the large bay at the left of the outlet, now noted on the map of the State survey as "Agassiz Bay," which is a mistake, for we named this "Osprey Bay," from the osprey nest in one of its tall pines, the bay opposite the camp at the south end of the lake being named in honor of Agassiz. The shore is an alternation of stretches of sandy beach where the white pond-lily thrives, and offers food for the deer, and rocky points separate the beaches as if by screens, so that any movement in one of the little bays is not visible in another. There is something weird in silently gliding along a spectral diorama of irrecognizable landscape, with rocks and trees slipping by like phantasms; for the motion of the boat is not distinguishable, and the only sound is the occasional grating of the rushes on the bottom of the boat. It is, in fact, the most exciting form of deer-hunting for certain temperaments, and the poet was strongly impressed. The practised ear of the guide soon caught the sound of the footfall of a deer making his way down to the shore, and he turned the glare of the lamp on the beach, moving directly on him till he was within twenty yards. The signal to fire was given and repeated, but Emerson could distinguish nothing. "Shoot!" finally whispered the guide in the faintest breath. "Shoot!" I repeated nearer. But the deer was invisible to him, and we drifted to a boat's length from him before the animal took fright, and bolted for the woods, undisturbed by a hasty shot I sent after him, and we heard his triumphant whistle and gallop dying away in the forest depths. Emerson was stupefied. We rounded the next point, and found a deer already on the feeding-ground, to repeat the experience. The deer stood broadside to him, in full view, in the shallow water; but straining his vision to the utmost, he could distinguish nothing like a deer, and when we had got so near that the same result was imminent, I fired, and the buck fell dead. "Well," said Emerson, "if that was a deer, I shall fire at the first square thing I see"; but we saw no more that night. . . .

Each disappointment, however, plunged him more deeply into the excitement of the chase, and he was most anxious to kill his deer before he went home, unable to resist the contagion of the passion for it. He said to me one day, "I must kill a deer before we go home, even if the guide has to hold him by the tail." At that season of the year, when the deer are in their short coat, the body sinks at once if shot in the deep water; and on overtaking the quarry in the lake, if the deerslayer was not sure of his shot, the guide used to run the boat alongside of it, and catch it by the tail, when the shot became a sure one. As we hunted only when we needed the meat, we did not risk the loss of the deer, and when a poor shot held the gun, the quarry was caught by the tail and killed in this unsportsmanlike way. That survival of the earliest passion of the primitive man, the passion of the chase, overcame even the philosophic mind of Emerson, once exposed to the original influences, and he recognized his ancestral bent. Few of us who live an active life fail to be attracted by this first of all occupations of the yet uncivilized man. Emerson never had the gratification of his desire; the deer never came to him on the drive, and his repetition of the night-hunt was no more successful.

The starry magnificence of those nights, with their pure mountain air, was another source of delight hardly to be imagined by those who have not known it by experience. There seemed to be more stars visible than anywhere else I had ever been. . . . The tall white pines, which when full grown rise from one hundred and fifty to two hundred feet, towering nearly half their height above the mass of deciduous trees . . . seemed to be gigantic human beings moving in procession to the east. I had, the year before, painted a picture of the subject, and Emerson had been struck by it at the Athenæum . . . and when we were established in camp, almost the first thing he asked to see was the "procession of the pines"; and our last evening on the lake was spent together watching the glow dying out behind a noble line of the marching pines on the shore of Follansbee Water.

In memory of that summer, and the intimacy of camp life which strips the man of all disguises, Emerson seems to me to be magnified with the lapse of time, as Mont Blanc towers above his fellows with distance.

Century Magazine, 46 (August 1893): 598, 601–603.

"My First Visit to New England" (1894)

WILLIAM DEAN HOWELLS

As a young staffer on the *Ohio State Journal*, William Dean Howells made a literary tour of New York and New England in 1860. He visited Walt Whitman in New York and became acquainted with the bohemian crowd at Pfaff's restaurant on Bleeker Street; in New England he visited Nathaniel Hawthorne, Henry Thoreau, and Emerson in Concord. Following an appointment from 1861 to 1865 as the American consul in Venice, Howells returned to the United States, where for the next twenty-five years he held important editorial positions at the *Atlantic Monthly, Harper's Magazine*, and *Cosmopolitan Magazine*, and he settled into a distinguished career as a novelist and as a major critical spokesman for the realistic school of American fiction.

Howells's visits to Thoreau and Emerson in 1860 were the only real exceptions to a generally positive tour. In contrast to reports by other aspiring young people collected in this volume, Howells's report of his visit to Emerson—written in 1894, more than thirty years after the fact—stands out as one of the very few instances in which a writer did not leave the meeting impressed by Emerson's openness and encouragement of, in this case, his ambition to be a poet. Perhaps Howells was merely being a bit too sensitive, or perhaps he inadvertently provoked Emerson when, in response to his question about whether he knew Ellery Channing's poems, Howells replied that he knew them only through Poe's negative critiques. In any case, when he published his "Impressions of Emerson" as his contribution to the centenary celebration of Emerson's birth, Howells borrowed liberally from the report that follows, but he also added to it several complimentary remarks about Emerson's appearance as he remembered it and his enduring appeal as a lecturer. On the subject of Emerson's image as it was typically reproduced in photographs during the centenary, he wrote: "I found the likenesses all very like; no photograph could well err as to the beautiful Greek serenity of Emerson's looks; and yet they all seemed to me a shade, or several shades, severer than he seemed; they lacked that certain wise sweetness, remotely touched with humor, which was the first and last characteristic of his face." But perhaps Howells's warmest praise of Emerson occurs in his description of attending one of his lectures during his later years. Instead of criticizing Emerson for fumbling with his manuscript and

---

(*continued*)

seeming to forget his place, Howells transforms these lapses into illustrations of Emerson's charm on the platform:

> He was already beginning to forget, to achieve an identity independent of the memory which constitutes the unsevered consciousness of other men. This gift of purely spiritual continuity evinced itself publicly as well as privately, and it was the singular pleasure of hearing him lecture, to see him lose his place in his manuscript, turn the leaves over with inaudible sighs, and then go smiling on. Once I remember how, when some pages fell to the floor and were picked up for him and put before him, he patiently waited the result with an unconcern as great as that of any in his audience. He was, in fact, the least anxious of those present, for by that time it had come about that the old popular . . . doubt of him had turned into a love and reverence so deep and true that his listeners all cared more than he to have the distractions of the accident end in his triumph. (*Harper's Weekly Magazine*, 47 [16 May 1903]: 784.)

I rather wonder that I had the courage, after [my visit to Thoreau], to present the card Hawthorne had given me to Emerson. I must have gone to him at once, however, for I cannot make out any interval of time between my visit to the disciple and my visit to the master. I think it was Emerson himself who opened his door to me, for I have a vision of the fine old man standing tall on his threshold, with the card in his hand, and looking from it to me with a vague serenity, while I waited a moment on the door-step below him. He would have been about sixty, but I remember nothing of age in his aspect, though I have called him an old man. His hair, I am sure, was still entirely dark, and his face had a kind of marble youthfulness, chiselled to a delicate intelligence by the highest and noblest thinking that any man has done. There was a strange charm in Emerson's eyes, which I felt then and always, something like that I saw in Lincoln's, but shyer, but sweeter and less sad. His smile was the very sweetest I have ever beheld, and the contour of the mask and the line of the profile were in keeping with this incomparable sweetness of the mouth, at once grave and quaint, though quaint is not quite the word for it either, but subtly, not unkindly arch, which again is not the word.

It was his great fortune to have been mostly misunderstood, and to have reached the dense intelligence of his fellow-men after a whole lifetime of perfectly simple and lucid appeal, and his countenance expressed the patience and forbearance of a wise man content to bide his time. It would be hard to persuade people now that Emerson once represented to the popular mind all that was most hopelessly impossible, and that in a certain sort he was a national joke, the type of the incomprehensible, the byword of the poor paragrapher. He had perhaps disabused the community somewhat by presenting himself here and there as a lecturer, and talking face to face with men in terms which they could not refuse to find as clear as they were wise; he was more and more read, by certain persons, here and there; but we are still so far behind him in the reach of his far-thinking that it need not be matter of wonder that twenty years before his death he was the most misunderstood man in America. Yet in that twilight where he dwelt he loomed large upon the imagination; the minds that could not conceive him were still aware of his greatness. I myself had not read much of him, but I knew the essays he was printing in the Atlantic, and I knew certain of his poems, though by no means many; yet I had this sense of him, that he was . . . a presence of force and beauty and wisdom, uncompanioned in our literature. . . .

I do not know in just what sort he made me welcome, but I am aware of sitting with him in his study or library, and of his presently speaking of Hawthorne, whom I probably celebrated as I best could, and whom he praised for his personal excellence, and for his fine qualities as a neighbor. "But his last book," he added, reflectively, "is a mere mush," and I perceived that this great man was no better equipped to judge an artistic fiction than the groundlings who were then crying out upon the indefinite close of the Marble Faun. Apparently he had read it, as they had, for the story, but it seems to me now . . . that as far as the problem of evil was involved, the book must leave it where it found it. . . . Emerson had, in fact, a defective sense as to specific pieces of literature; he praised extravagantly, and in the wrong place, especially among the new things, and he failed to see the worth of much that was fine and precious beside the line of his fancy.

He began to talk to me about the West. . . . I did not find what Emerson had to say of my section very accurate or important, though it was kindly enough, and just enough as to what the West ought to do in literature. He thought it a pity that a literary periodical which had lately been started in Cincinnati should be appealing to the East for contributions, instead of relying upon writers nearer home; and he listened with what patience he could to my modest opinion that we had not the writers nearer home. I never was one of those Westerners who believed that the West was kept out of literature by the jealousy of the East, and I tried to explain why we had not the men to write that magazine full in Ohio. . . .

I felt rather guilty in my ignorance, and I had a notion that it did not commend me, but happily at this moment Mr. Emerson was called to dinner, and he asked me to come with him. After dinner we walked about in his "pleached garden" a little, and then we came again into his library, where I meant to linger only till I could fitly get away. He questioned me about what I had seen of Concord, and whom besides Hawthorne I had met, and when I told him only Thoreau, he asked me if I knew the poems of . . . Channing. I have known them since, and felt their quality, which I have gladly owned a genuine and original poetry; but I answered then truly that I knew them only from Poe's criticisms: cruel and spiteful things which I should be ashamed of enjoying as I once did.

"Whose criticisms?" asked Emerson.

"Poe's," I said again.

"Oh," he cried out . . . as if he had returned from a far search for my meaning, "*you mean the jingle-man!*"

I do not know why this should have put me to such confusion, but if I had written the criticisms myself I do not think I could have been more abashed. Perhaps I felt an edge of reproof, of admonition, in a characterization of Poe which the world will hardly agree with; though I do not agree with the world about him, myself, in its admiration. At any rate, it made an end of me . . . and I remained as if already absent, while Emerson questioned me as to what I had written in the Atlantic Monthly. He had evidently read none of my contributions, for he looked at them, in the bound volume of the magazine which he got down, with the effect of being wholly strange to them, and then gravely affixed my initials to each. He followed me to the door, still speaking of poetry, and as he took a kindly enough leave of me, he said one might very well give a pleasant hour to it now and then.

A pleasant hour to poetry! I was meaning to give all time and all eternity to poetry, and I should by no means have wished to find pleasure in it; I should have thought that a proof of inferior quality in the work; I should preferred anxiety, anguish even, to pleasure. But if Emerson thought from the glance he gave my verses that I had better not lavish myself upon that kind of thing, unless there was a great deal more of me than I could have made apparent in our meeting, no doubt he was right. I was only too painfully aware of my shortcoming, but I felt that it was shorter-coming than it need have been. I had somehow not prospered in my visit to Emerson . . . and I came away wondering in what sort I had gone wrong. . . . [As] I must needs blame myself for something, I fell upon the fact that in my confused retreat from Emerson's presence I had failed in a certain slight point of ceremony, and I magnified this into an offence of capital importance. I went home to my hotel, and passed the afternoon in pure misery.

"My First Visit to New England. Fourth Part," *Harper's New Monthly Magazine*, 89 (August 1894): 448–50.

From *Sketches from Concord and Appledore* (1895)

FRANK PRESTON STEARNS

> Frank Preston Stearns was the son of George Luther Stearns, a reformer who
> aided John Brown in Kansas and who advocated the enlistment of blacks in the
> army during the Civil War. The son took a different direction in life. Frank was
> educated at F. B. Sanborn's school in Concord and Harvard University, and
> later became an authority on Italian art. The extended comments printed here,
> drawn from the chapter "Emerson Himself," treat Emerson's personality, daily
> habits and manners, effectiveness as a lecturer, involvement with the political
> issues of the day (although Stearns confuses Alcott with Thoreau in an apocry-
> phal story about paying poll taxes and being in jail), and international fame. As
> Margaret Fuller does earlier, Stearns notes that Emerson "avoided controver-
> sies and often showed great tact in escaping from arguments." He is one of the
> few early writers on Emerson to raise the issue of how the inheritance Emerson
> received from the estate of his first wife, Ellen Tucker Emerson, might have in-
> fluenced his later career.

Emerson might be seen on his way to the post-office at precisely half-past
five every afternoon, after the crowd there had dispersed. His step was delib-
erate and dignified, and though his tall lean figure was not a symmetrical
one, nor were his movements graceful, yet there was something very pleasant
in the aspect of him even at a distance. . . . He knew all the people old and
young in the village, and had a kindly word or a smile for every one of them.
His smile was better than anything he said. There is no word in the language
that describes it. It was neither sweet nor saintly, but more like what a German poet called the mild radiance of a hidden sun. No picture, photograph
or bust of Emerson has ever done him justice for this reason; only such a
master as Giorgione could have painted his portrait.

Every morning after reading the "Boston Advertiser" he would go to his
study, to take up the work of the day previous and cross out every word in it
that could possibly be spared. This procedure and his taste for unusual
words is what gives the peculiar style to his writing. It was characteristic of
him physically and mentally. He had a spare figure; was sparing of speech,

sparing of praise, and sparing of time; in all things temperate and stoical. He had an aquiline face, made up of powerful features without an inch of spare territory. . . . His eyes were sometimes exceedingly brilliant; his nose was strong and aquiline; and the lower part of his face, especially the mouth, was notably like the busts of Julius Cæsar. His voice was a baritone of rapid inflections, and when he was very much in earnest it changed to a deep bass. He once said, "Whenever I look in the glass I feel a depression of spirits"; but his friends did not feel so. He was always an agreeable object to them, even in his last years when he looked in his study like an old eagle in his eyrie. . . .

He was a modern Stoic, and carried that kind of life to a high degree of perfection. He sometimes smoked a cigar, and sometimes drank a glass of wine, but the only real luxury he indulged in was dining with the Atlantic Club once a month in Boston. During his lecturing tours he was the recipient of a great deal of hospitality, and became the objective centre of many a social gathering; but how much he enjoyed this it would be difficult to tell. He was too modest and genuine to like being lionized. He had neither pride, vanity, nor self-conceit; and his great celebrity never weighed heavily upon him, or discovered itself in his manners. In this respect he carried his stoicism a little too far, for he never would permit any one to talk with him about himself, and enthusiastic admirers of his genius commonly met with a rather cold reception. He repelled everything in the shape of a compliment. . . . You could not call Emerson an epicure, but he knew how to appreciate a fine dinner. Several witnesses have given their testimony in regard to his partiality for what he called "pie." He was also fond of pears; knew the best varieties and the order in which they ripened. He used to say that there is only ten minutes in which a pear is fairly ripe: before that it is too hard and afterwards too soft. His friend Dr. F. H. Hedge once made a similar remark concerning ripe scholars.

Perhaps the most remarkable trait in his character was his absolute self-poise. He had a balanced mind if there ever was one. Carlyle considered the "Conduct of Life" to be Emerson's best book, and there was reason why it should be. It was the subject of all others which he knew most about. Conduct had been the study of his life. Behavior was a fine art with him, cultivated partly from motives of prudence but more for its own sake. From early morning till bed-time he was always the same, always self-possessed. There was no relaxation of it; he was like an athlete in full training. It was difficult to place him in a position where he did not appear to advantage. But he expected nearly as much from others, and had small patience with those who from ignorance or carelessness infringed the rules of etiquette. One of his expressions was, that death or mutilation was the only excuse for being late to dinner. The notion that poets are an unpractical class of people is pure illusion. . . . Emerson [was] in all things eminently practical. He would sometimes say, "I allow myself to be cheated by one Irishman"; but I do not think he was cheated very much.

In fair weather he always left his books half an hour or so before dinner and walked out, to get fresh-air and see what was going forward on his little place. . . . He says in the "Conduct of Life": "The scholar goes into his garden to obtain a juster statement of his thought. He puts down his hand to pull up a weed. Behind that is a second; behind the second is a third; behind the third a fourth; and beyond that a thousand and four." Who can doubt that this was a personal experience with him, as it has been with some others?

There are many anecdotes of his good sense and sagacity, and the following is perhaps equal to any of them. One summer there was a camp-meeting of spiritualists at Walden Pond, and every evening they held an entertainment of speeches, singing and music, to which a small admittance-fee was charged. It happened, however, that the picnic pavilion was situated close to Mr. Emerson's land, and numbers of Concord people went out of curiosity and leaning against his fence heard and saw everything that went on. A committee of spiritualists consequently called on Mr. Emerson and requested permission to collect fees from those who stole their entertainment in this manner. At first thought this might not seem to be unreasonable; but Emerson replied, "No, I have always enjoyed the privilege of walking upon my neighbors' fields, and I cannot now refuse the same right to them." Could a chief justice have decided the case better?

Emerson's *no* was always decisive, and if one person could not induce him to change his mind I do not believe twenty millions would have succeeded in doing so. When he was involved in a lawsuit regarding some property, and the suggestion was made that he should compromise it, he said: "By no means. If it is mine I want the whole of it: if it is not mine I do not want any of it."

He avoided controversies and often showed great tact in escaping from an argument. What he had once published was of no consequence to him, and he cared little whether others liked it or not. If people advanced opinions or judgments with which he disagreed he made a plain statement of the fact and then changed the subject of conversation. Opponents who wished to corner him, and had perhaps set snares for him to fall into, found themselves outwitted by his unfailing desire for peace and harmony.

He went to the polls and voted; he attended town-meetings and political caucuses, but never took an active share in them. The prohibition of liquor, the tariff question, the woman suffrage movement, and other like vexatious matters he left severely alone. I doubt if any one discovered from first to last what his real opinions were on these subjects. At the Boston Radical Club in 1868 he was asked to give an opinion on woman suffrage, and he replied that he had no doubt that when all women had agreed as to what they wanted, what was in fact best for them, they could easily obtain it through the home influence. These he would say are questions of judgment. The slavery question was a matter of principle; and on that point he gave forth no uncertain sound. He did not, however, engage actively in the controversy till the passage of the fugitive-slave bill warned him how seriously the republic was in danger. . . .

The popular legend that during the Mexican war Mr. Alcott refused to pay taxes that supported an unjust invasion, and was imprisoned for this, is so far true; but it can not be true that when Emerson came to visit him in jail to pay the tax-bill he said, "Bronson, why are you here?" and that Alcott answered, "Waldo, why are you not here?"; for they never called each other anything but Mr. Emerson and Mr. Alcott. . . .

Goethe says in his analysis of manners that the man of noble manners may sometimes give way to his emotions, the man of well-bred manners never. Emerson's manners were half way between these two; a fortunate union of natural courtesy and dignified reserve. It was not possible to be familiar with him. They were better than fine manners, or even well-bred manners, for they were so natural and simple as scarcely to attract attention. Yet he was not a man of noble manners, for he never fully acted out himself. Carlyle had noble manners, but was lacking in courtesy.

Emerson's house stands about twenty-five yards from the street, and there is a smooth white-marble walk from his gate to the front-door. This, together with the pine trees he planted for protection against the north wind, had a cool refreshing effect in midsummer, but at other seasons gave the visitor rather a chilly reception. There was something in Emerson himself that reminded one of this white-marble walk; not that he was cold-hearted, far from it, nor was he lacking tenderness; but warmth of color he had not. He was too purely moral to be altogether human. He never could have written a tragedy, or made a speech like that of John Adams on the question of separation. How could it be otherwise? Can the descendant of five generations of New England clergymen have the same blood in his veins that warmed the hearts of Marshal Ney and Mirabeau? . . .

. . . His friends were like himself, cool-headed and scrupulous; but they were not the persons who cared most for him and appreciated him the best. Such men as Theodore Parker, M. D. Conway, David A. Wasson and Wendell Phillips did more for Emerson almost than his own writings, in spreading his reputation and celebrating his genius. Wherever Phillips and Parker lectured in the west and were asked, as often happened, who were the best of the New England lecturers, they always placed Emerson at the head of the list. They served as mediators between him and the large class of persons who could not readily understand him.

If he was an exacting moralist, he was never a narrow or pettifogging one. It is true he laid down the rule that a young lady had always the right to break off an engagement, but not so a gentleman, for he has the opportunity, which she has not, of making his own choice,—what no man would have said who was aware of the arts and stratagems which women often practise to obtain the man they desire; but he was not generally a censorious man.

He believed firmly in the old saying of every man to his trade. He never preached sermons on week-days; or discoursed on public and private duties; or lectured about self-sacrifice and the necessity of living for others. He believed that such talk did quite as much harm as good. "Do not try to be good," he would say, "but true to yourself." Wisdom was the best of all virtues because it included all. . . .

If Emerson had not inherited a good property early in life, his career would hardly have been possible. He never was able to publish more than a third of what he wrote, and his books were not a source of large profit to him. He was obliged to make up the deficiency by lecturing. With what fortitude he did this, considering his slender physique, travelling long distances in the coldest weather over such railroads as then were, with a dismal hotel and bad food at the end of every journey, will always be remembered of him. No wonder that he consoled himself with such maxims as, "No man has ever estimated his own troubles too lightly." . . . Truly it was severe discipline. At Niagara Falls in 1863 the hotel caught fire and Emerson rushed forth at midnight, manuscripts in hand.... The compensation for it was that in this way he made the acquaintance of many interesting and distinguished persons. It also added to his celebrity.

He was the same under all circumstances. It has been said that in his poems we feel the essayist; but perhaps even more we recognize the poet in his essays. So too in his conversation at table and in the parlor, there was something that reminded one of the lecturer: when he appeared on the platform before his audience he was always the plain country gentleman. He affected no graces of oratory, and shunned everything like rhetorical flourish. He was the first of our public speakers to introduce this improvement which has since found its way into the court-room and the theatre. His manner was direct, terse and earnest, with an habitual pause or hesitation to select just the right verb or adjective that would convey the idea he wished to express. His delivery was suited to his thought. His hearers were not commonly pleased with it at first, but if they continued to listen most of them came to have a great liking for it. He had a habit of pausing now and then and turning over the pages before him, as if he had lost his place or was looking for a passage which he could not find; but he never made any explanation for it, and his own family did not know the reason. It may have been done to rest himself; or perhaps to give time for his ideas to settle in the minds of his audience. Some people were foolishly annoyed by it; but not those who understood him. He used to say that either a speaker commands his audience, or his audience commands him.

He was the best lecturer of his time: the one who wore the best. Between 1860 and 1870 he gave four courses of lectures in Boston which were well and profitably attended. No one else could have done this, except perhaps Agassiz. There were others who drew larger houses, but, the quality was not so good. Very rarely have such cultivated and intellectual audiences been brought together. A few of his most ardent admirers used to carry operaglasses with them in order to watch the expression of his face....

... He had the most telling way of saying a thing, and knew how to give their full force to his wonderfully brilliant sentences. These would sometimes electrify his hearers, as people are roused on the announcement of some great and fortunate event.

He liked the society of statesmen, scientists, business men, railroad managers, of all who could tell him about what was going on in the world—

something, he complained, that the newspapers would not do for him. He preferred their society to that of other poets and scholars. Though an unlimited reader of books he was not properly a scholar himself, and perhaps he felt his own limitation too much in their company.

He studied little at college and it is doubtful if he afterwards made a thorough and systematic investigation of any subject. He was called a philosopher, but he knew little more than the outlines of metaphysics. He could read French fairly, but Latin was the only language with which he was well acquainted. Carlyle tried to persuade him to study German. He did not believe in study, but in the inspiration of nature. This did well enough for him, but he made a mistake in applying the same principle to others.

He was wont to excuse Alcott's rambling rhapsodical conversations on the ground that it was the only talent the man had, that he must do that, or nothing; but many people considered that Emerson was more to blame in the matter than Alcott himself. A person who makes a profession of philosophy, as Alcott certainly did, ought to be well acquainted with the writings of other philosophers of his own time; and it surely would have done no harm for Emerson to have suggested this to him. When the Boston Radical Club was formed Emerson thought it would be a good opportunity for Alcott to place his ideas before the public, but Alcott found himself at a disadvantage among the scholarly minds he encountered there.

. . . [We] may suspect that he read books not so much for what was in them as for ideas which they suggested to him, and which he might make use of in his essays and lectures. Alcott said that he carried slips of paper with him on which to jot down these considerations by the way. Thus he came to value books too much from a single point of view, and his friends were sometimes surprised at what he recommended them to read. . . .

He was a frequent visitor at the Boston Athenæum, and seized upon every new book of value as soon as it appeared: was the first to read translations of the Zendavesta and Confucius. He read almost every readable book in the English language as well as translations from all languages. He said he would as soon think of swimming across Charles River when he might make use of a bridge as to read a foreign book in the original if he could obtain a good translation. . . .

Emerson's real fault, if he may be said to have had one, was his optimism. Because he had been born with genius and was otherwise fortunate he thought every one else might succeed as easily as he had. In this way he often did people great injustice. If they were unfortunate he concluded that it must be their own fault. . . . If he heard of anyone who could not obtain work he would say there is always plenty to do for willing hands. Those who were incapacitated by nature from earning their own living fared no better. He thought there was something which every one could do better than anybody else—which might possibly be true if there were as many professions as individuals. When some one spoke of a young German poet, whom it was thought but for his untimely death might have been the rival of Schiller, he said, "Yes, but he died; that was against him."

This line of thought logically resulted also in a kind of pessimism. He seemed at times to despise human nature. Somewhere about 1860 he wrote to a friend, "There is not one man in twenty that is worth the ground he stands on"; and speaking of Napoleon he affirms that, in the well-nigh universal negligence and inefficiency of mankind, we cannot be too thankful for this prompt and ready actor. No one who realizes the hard and bitter struggle for daily bread with which three-fourths of the human race are constantly occupied, would have written such a sentence. . . .

He had one trait of character which his biographers have not mentioned, and which might pass by the name of incredulity. He was the most difficult of men to persuade of any strange and remarkable event. Neither did he take the least pains to conceal his disbelief; and when you were telling him the living truth this was rather difficult to bear. When we said that a woodpecker had been seen in Walden woods nearly as large as a crow and quite as black, he shook his head and looked up at the pine trees. That was not according to his idea of a woodpecker. Neither did he like to hear anything which tended to prove the depravity of human nature. . . . He liked to tell the truth better than he did to hear it. . . .

He was the most famous American of his time; not so celebrated perhaps in his own country as President Lincoln, but in foreign countries he surpassed all others,—such is the deep impression which a great writer makes on the minds of men. In Europe he was looked upon as the best representative of our Western Hemisphere. . . .

He had no public receptions in foreign cities, but everywhere the finest people united to honor him. On his second visit to England he complained that his time was almost consumed in answering letters of invitation. An English guest at the Harvard Phi Beta Kappa dinner said that when he returned home he would be asked two questions,—if he had seen Niagara

Falls, and if he had met Emerson. He was a particular favorite with the English nobility, and whenever we saw a glittering carriage rolling down Concord turn-pike we felt sure it contained some earl or viscount who was paying his compliments to the poet of the pines. Emerson liked to entertain these distinguished visitors in his modest little parlor, but he never slighted his old friends for them; for he lived the wisdom that he taught, and the final virtue of this man was the religious humility of his nature.

From *Sketches from Concord and Appledore* (New York: Putnam's, 1895), pp. 89–107, 109–16.

"A Little Gossip" (1900)

REBECCA HARDING DAVIS

In this reminiscence of her first journey to New England, Rebecca Harding Davis describes her early desire to become a writer and her first meetings with the Hawthornes, Bronson and Louisa May Alcott, Elizabeth Palmer Peabody, Oliver Wendell Holmes, and Emerson, among others. The year was 1862, and since she hailed from Virginia, Davis's experience of the Civil War was a topic of interest wherever she went. In Concord, which she visited at Nathaniel Hawthorne's invitation, Davis was impressed with the character, integrity, and friendliness of some of her new acquaintances; she was especially fond of Hawthorne and Louisa May Alcott, but she had no patience with the "seers"—Bronson Alcott and Emerson. She is quite severe with Emerson, criticizing him for his aloofness and egotism and for his tendency to use people, including his friends, as objects of study; indeed, nearly forty years after first meeting him, Davis remained completely resistant to Emerson as a person and to his philosophy.

I remember listening during one long summer morning to Louisa Alcott's father as he chanted pæans to the war, the "armed angel which was wakening the nation to a lofty life unknown before."

We were in the little parlor of the Wayside, Mr. Hawthorne's house. . . . Mr. Alcott stood in front of the fireplace, . . . his pale eyes turning quickly from one listener to another to hold them quiet, his hands waving to keep time with the orotund sentences which had a stale, familiar ring. . . . Mr. Emerson stood listening, his head sunk on his breast, with profound submissive attention, but Hawthorne sat astride of a chair, his arms folded on the back, . . . and his laughing, sagacious eyes watching us, full of mockery.

I had just come up from a border State where I had seen the actual war; the filthy spewings of it; the political jobbery in Union and Confederate camps; the malignant personal hatreds wearing patriotic masks, and glutted by burning homes and outraged women. . . . War may be an armed angel with a mission, but she has the personal habits of the slums. This would-be

Seer who was talking of it, and the real Seer who listened, knew no more of war as it was than I had done . . . when I dreamed of bannered legions of crusaders *debouching* in misty fields. . . .

Of the group of famous people in Concord in 1862 Mr. Emerson was best known to the country at large. He was the typical Yankee in appearance. The tall, gaunt man with the watchful, patient face and slightly dazed eyes, his hands clasped behind his back, that came slowly down the shady village street toward the Wayside that summer day was Uncle Sam himself in ill-fitting brown clothes. I often have wondered that none of his biographers have noticed the likeness. Voice and look and manner were full of the most exquisite courtesy, yet I doubt whether he was conscious of his courtesy or meant to be deferential. Emerson, first of all, was a student of man, an explorer into the dim, obscure regions of human intelligence. He studied souls as a philologist does words or an entomologist beetles. He approached each man with bent head and eager eyes. "What new thing shall I find here?" they said.

I went to Concord, a young woman from the backwoods, firm in the belief that Emerson was the first of living men. He was the modern Moses who had talked with God apart and could interpret Him to us.

When I heard him coming into the parlor at the Wayside my body literally grew stiff and my tongue dry with awe. And in ten minutes I was telling him all that I had seen of the war, the words tumbling over each other, so convinced was I of his eagerness to hear. He was eager. If Edison had been there he would have been just as eager to wrench out of him the secret of electricity, or if it had been a freed slave he would have compelled him to show the scars on his back and lay bare his rejoicing, ignorant, half-animal soul, and an hour later he would have forgotten that Edison or the negro or I were in the World—having taken from each what he wanted.

Naturally Mr. Emerson valued the abnormal freaks among human souls most highly, just as the unclassable word or the mongrel beetle are dearest to the grammarian or the naturalist. The only man to whose authority he bowed was Alcott, the vague, would-be prophet, whose ravings he did not pretend to fathom. He apparently shared in the popular belief that eccentricity was a sign of genius.

He said to me suddenly once, "I wish Thoreau had not died before you came. He was an interesting study."

"Why?" I asked.

"Why? Thoreau?" He hesitated, thinking, going apparently to the bottom of the matter, and said, presently: "Henry often reminded me of an animal in human form. He had the eye of a bird, the scent of a dog, the most acute, delicate intelligence. But no soul. No," he repeated, shaking his head with decision, "Henry could not have had a human soul."

His own perception of character was an intuition. He felt a fine trait as he would a fine strain of music. Coming once to Philadelphia he said, almost as soon as he entered the house, "So Philip Randolph has gone! That man had the sweetest moral nature I ever knew. There never was a man so lacking in self-consciousness. The other day I saw in the London *Times* that 'the American, Randolph, one of the three greatest chess players in the world was dead.' I knew Philip intimately since he was a boy, and I never heard him mention the game. I did not even know that he played it. How fine that was!" he said, walking up and down the room. . . .

Emerson himself was as little likely to parade his merits as Randolph, but not from any lack of self-appreciation. On the contrary, his interest in his Ego was so dominant that it probably never occurred to him to ask what others thought of him. He took from each man his drop of stored honey, and after that the man counted for no more to him than any other robbed bee. I do not think that even the worship which his disciples gave him interested him enough to either amuse or annoy him.

It was worship. No such homage has ever been paid to any American. His teaching influenced at once the trend of thought here and in England; the strongest men then living became promptly his disciples or his active antagonists.

. . . [T]here were vast outlying provinces of intelligence where he reigned absolutely as does the unseen Grand Llama over his adoring votaries. . . . To them came this new prophet with his discovery of the God within themselves. They hailed it with acclamation. . . . Up to the old gray house among the pines in Concord they went—hordes of wild-eyed Harvard undergraduates and lean, underpaid working women, each with a disease of the soul to be cured by the new Healer. . . .

Outside of these circles of disciples there was then throughout the country a certain vague pride in Emerson as an American prophet. We were in the first flush of our triumph in the beginnings of a national literature. . . . In the West and South there was no definite idea as to what truth this Concord man had brought into the world. But in any case it was American truth and not English. Emerson's popularity, therefore, . . . was wide, but vague and impersonal.

Scribner's Magazine, 28 (November 1900): 563, 565–66.

[Emerson in the Yosemite Valley] (1901)

JOHN MUIR

Between 11 April and 30 May 1871, Emerson traveled overland to California and then back to Concord at the invitation of John Murray Forbes, his close friend and father-in-law of his daughter Edith. The company, which included, in addition to Emerson and Forbes, Colonel William Hathaway and Mrs. Edith Emerson Forbes, and James Bradley Thayer, gathered in Chicago, where they settled into the private Pullman that Forbes had arranged for the journey. The elder Forbes had arranged the trip to the West as a recuperative journey for Emerson. Less than a week before he went to Chicago, Emerson had completed the second of his *Natural History of the Intellect* philosophy courses at Harvard, and over the seven weeks of the course, family and friends became alarmed at how increasingly exhausted and frail he appeared.

Emerson called on Brigham Young in Salt Lake City on his way to California—an unsatisfactory visit, Emerson thought—and once in San Francisco he took on the gait of a tourist, riding through Chinatown and visiting the local sites; he also lectured on "Immortality" and "Resources" at Horatio Stebbins's Unitarian Church. But the high point of his journey was the thirteen-day excursion he took with his party to the Sierras and the Yosemite Valley. There he measured a 210-foot sugar pine with Wilkie James; visited Crystal Lake and Mirror Lake; spent a few days in the company of John Muir; toured Mariposa Grove with Galen Clark, the park superintendent, and, following the tradition of visiting dignitaries, named a sequoia "Samoset"; and stayed overnight at a ferry hotel on the Tuolumne River. Returning to San Francisco, he delivered two more lectures, one on "Chivalry" at Stebbins's church and the other on "Homes, and How to Make Them Happy" at Brayton Hall in Oakland.

The standard account of Emerson's trip to California is Thayer's *A Western Journey with Mr. Emerson* (Boston: Little, Brown, 1884). The account by Muir that follows, which is much less known, first appeared as "The Forests of Yosemite Park," *Atlantic Monthly Magazine*, 85 (April 1900): 493–507.

[The] noble oaks and . . . rock-shading, stream-embowering trees are as nothing amid the vast abounding billowy forests of conifers. During my first years in the Sierra I was ever calling on everybody within reach to admire them, but I found no one half warm enough until Emerson came. I had read his essays, and felt sure that of all men he would best interpret the sayings of these noble mountains and trees. Nor was my faith weakened when I met him in Yosemite. He seemed as serene as a sequoia, his head in the empyrean; and forgetting his age, plans, duties, ties of every sort, I proposed an immeasurable camping trip back in the heart of the mountains. He seemed anxious to go, but considerately mentioned his party. I said: "Never mind. The mountains are calling; run away, and let plans and parties and dragging lowland duties all 'gang tapsal-teerie.' We'll go up a cañon singing your own song, 'Good-by, proud world! I'm going home,' in divine earnest. Up there lies a new heaven and a new earth; let us go to the show." But alas, it was too late,—too near the sundown of his life. The shadows were growing long, and he leaned on his friends. His party, full of indoor philosophy, failed to see the natural beauty and fullness of promise of my wild plan, and laughed at it in good-natured ignorance, as if it were necessarily amusing to imagine that Boston people might be led to accept Sierra manifestations of God at the price of rough camping. Anyhow, they would have none of it, and held Mr. Emerson to the hotels and trails.

After spending only five tourist days in Yosemite he was led away, but I saw him two days more; for I was kindly invited to go with the party as far as the Mariposa big trees. I told Mr. Emerson that I would gladly go to the sequoias with him, if he would camp in the grove. He consented heartily, and I felt sure that we would have at least one good wild memorable night around a sequoia camp-fire. Next day we rode through the magnificent forests of the Merced basin, and I kept calling his attention to the sugar pines, quoting his wood-notes, "Come listen what the pine tree saith," etc., pointing out the noblest as kings and high priests, the most eloquent and commanding preachers of all the mountain forests, stretching forth their century-old arms in benediction over the worshiping congregations crowded about them. He gazed in devout admiration, saying but little, while his fine smile faded away.

Early in the afternoon, when we reached Clark's Station, I was surprised to see the party dismount. And when I asked if we were not going up into the grove to camp they said: "No; it would never do to lie out in the night air. Mr. Emerson might take cold; and you know, Mr. Muir, that would be a dreadful thing." In vain I urged, that only in homes and hotels were colds caught, that nobody ever was known to take cold camping in these woods, that there was not a single cough or sneeze in all the Sierra. Then I pictured the big climate-changing, inspiring fire I would make, praised the beauty and fragrance of sequoia flame, told how the great trees would stand about us transfigured in the purple light, while the stars looked down between the great domes; ending by urging them to come on and make an immortal Emerson night of it. But the house habit was not to be overcome nor the strange dread of pure night air, though it is only cooled day air with a little dew in it. So the carpet dust and unknowable reeks were preferred. And to think of this being a Boston choice! Sad commentary on culture and the glorious transcendentalism.

Accustomed to reach whatever place I started for, I was going up the mountain alone to camp, and wait the coming of the party next day. But since Emerson was so soon to vanish, I concluded to stop with him. He hardly spoke a word all the evening, yet it was a great pleasure simply to be near him, warming in the light of his face as at a fire. In the morning we rode up the trail through a noble forest of pine and fir into the famous Mariposa Grove, and stayed an hour or two, mostly in ordinary tourist fashion,—looking at the biggest giants, measuring them with a tape line, riding through prostrate fire-bored trunks, etc., though Mr. Emerson was alone occasionally, sauntering about as if under a spell. As we walked through a fine group, he quoted, "There were giants in those days," recognizing the antiquity of the race. To commemorate his visit, Mr. Galen Clark, the guardian of the grove, selected the finest of the unnamed trees and requested him to give it a name. He named it Samoset, after the New England sachem, as the best that occurred to him.

The poor bit of measured time was soon spent, and while the saddles were being adjusted I again urged Emerson to stay. "You are yourself a sequoia," I said. "Stop and get acquainted with your big brethren." But he was past his prime, and was now as a child in the hands of his affectionate but sadly civilized friends, who seemed as full of old-fashioned conformity as of bold intellectual independence. It was the afternoon of the day and the afternoon of his life, and his course was now westward down all the mountains into the sunset. The party mounted and rode away in wondrous contentment, apparently, tracing the trail through ceanothus and dogwood bushes, around the bases of the big trees, up the slope of the sequoia basin, and over the divide. I followed to the edge of the grove. Emerson lingered in the rear of the train, and when he reached the top of the ridge, after all the rest of the party were over and out of sight, he turned his horse, took off his hat and waved me a last good-by. I felt lonely, so sure had I been that Emerson of all men would be the quickest to see the mountains and sing them. Gazing awhile on the spot where he vanished, I sauntered back into the heart of the grove, made a bed of sequoia plumes and ferns by the side of a stream, gathered a store of firewood, and then walked about until sundown. The birds, robins, thrushes, warblers, etc., that had kept out of sight, came about me, now that all was quiet, and made cheer. After sundown I built a great fire, and as usual had it all to myself. And though lonesome for the first time in these forests, I quickly took heart again,—the trees had not gone to Boston, nor the birds; and as I sat by the fire, Emerson was still with me in spirit, though I never again saw him in the flesh. He sent books and wrote, cheering me on; advised me not to stay too long in solitude. Soon he hoped that my guardian angel would intimate that my probation was at a close. Then I was to roll up my herbariums, sketches, and poems (though I never knew I had any poems), and come to his house; and when I tired of him and his humble surroundings, he would show me to better people.

But there remained many a forest to wander through, many a mountain and glacier to cross, before I was to see his Wachusett and Monadnock, Boston and Concord. It was seventeen years after our parting on the Wawona ridge that I stood beside his grave under a pine tree on the hill above Sleepy Hollow. He had gone to higher Sierras, and, as I fancied, was again waving his hand in friendly recognition.

From *Our National Parks* (Boston and New York: Houghton, Mifflin, 1901), pp. 131–36.

From *The Centenary of the Birth of Ralph Waldo Emerson* (1903)

WILLIAM JAMES AND CAROLINE HAZARD

One of the most important of the many events that celebrated the centenary in 1903 of Emerson's birth was the program arranged in Concord by the Social Circle, later published as a book. This group, which admitted (male) members by invitation only, was Concord's most distinguished discussion club, and boasted members from every range of life, from farmers and blacksmiths to Emerson himself (and later, his son). Indeed, Emerson often thought that his being offered membership in the Concord Social Circle was a greater honor than his admission to any other club to which he belonged.

Throughout the day and evening of 25 May (Emerson's birthday), a series of speakers, including Charles Eliot Norton, Thomas Wentworth Higginson, George Frisbie Hoar, John Shepard Keyes, and Edward Waldo Emerson, addressed virtually all aspects of Emerson's reputation and connection with Concord. Of those whose remarks are printed here, William James was the brother of the novelist Henry James and is credited with being the father of the philosophical systems of pragmatism and pluralism. In works such as *Principles of Psychology* (1890), *Varieties of Religious Experience* (1902), and *Pragmatism* (1907), James displayed a shared interest with Emerson about the primacy of the intuition, the importance of comparative religion, and the need for our minds and souls to be in harmony. James's address, in which he gives his impressions of "an artist whose medium was verbal and who wrought in spiritual material," is one of the few earlier works to treat Emerson's philosophical inclinations seriously. Caroline Hazard, an educator, novelist, poet, and president of Wellesley College, discusses the appeal that Emerson's words and own family life have to the women of her day.

"Address of William James"

The pathos of death is this, that when the days of one's life are ended, those days that were so crowded with business and felt so heavy in their passing, what remains of one in memory should usually be so slight a thing. The phantom of an attitude, the echo of a certain mode of thought, a few pages of print, some invention, or some victory we gained in a brief critical hour, are all that can survive the best of us. It is as if the whole of a man's significance had now shrunk into the phantom of an attitude, into a mere musical note or phrase, suggestive of his singularity—happy are those whose singularity gives a note so clear as to be victorious over the inevitable pity of such a diminution and abridgment.

An ideal wraith like this, of Emerson's singularity, hovers over all Concord to-day, taking in the minds of those of you who were his neighbors and intimates a somewhat fuller shape, . . . bringing home to all of us the notion of a spirit indescribably precious. The form that so lately moved upon these streets and country roads, or awaited in these fields and woods the beloved Muse's visits, is now dust; but the soul's note, the spiritual voice, rises strong and clear above the uproar of the times, and seems securely destined to exert an ennobling influence over future generations.

What gave a flavor so matchless to Emerson's individuality was, even more than his rich mental gifts, their combination. Rarely has a man so known the limits of his genius or so unfailingly kept within them. "Stand by your order," he used to say to youthful students; and perhaps the paramount impression one gets of his life is of his loyalty to his own type and mission. The type was that of what he liked to call the scholar, the perceiver of pure truth, and the mission was that of the reporter in worthy form of each perception. The day is good, he said, in which we have the most perceptions. There are times when the cawing of a crow, a weed, a snow-flake, or a farmer planting in his field, become symbols to the intellect of truths equal to those which the most majestic phenomena can open. Let me mind my own charge, then, walk alone, consult the sky, the field and forest, sedulously waiting every morning for the news concerning the structure of the universe which the good Spirit will give me.

This was the first half of Emerson, but only half; for his genius was insatiate for expression, and his truth had to be clad in the right verbal garment. The form of the garment was so vital with Emerson that it is impossible to separate it from the matter. They form a chemical combination,—thoughts which would be trivial expressed otherwise are important through the nouns and verbs to which he married them. The style is the man, it has been said: the man Emerson's mission culminated in his style, and if we must define him in one word, we have to call him Artist. He was an artist whose medium was verbal and who wrought in spiritual material.

This duty of spiritual seeing and reporting determined the whole tenor of his life. It was to shield it from invasion and distraction that he dwelt in the country, and that he consistently declined to entangle himself with associations or to encumber himself with functions which, however he might believe in them, he felt were duties for other men and not for him. Even the care of his garden, "with its stoopings and fingerings in a few yards of space," he found "narrowing and poisoning," and took to long free walks and saunterings instead, without apology. "Causes" innumerable sought to enlist him as their "worker"—all got his smile and word of sympathy, but none entrapped him into service. The struggle against slavery itself, deeply as it appealed to him, found him firm: "God must govern his own world, and knows his way out of this pit without my desertion of my post, which has none to guard it but me. I have quite other slaves to face than those Negroes, to wit, imprisoned thoughts far back in the brain of man, and which have no watchman or lover or defender but me." This in reply to the possible questions of his conscience. To hot-blooded moralists with more objective ideas of duty, such a fidelity to the limits of his genius must often have made him seem provokingly remote and unavailable; but we who can see things in more liberal perspective must unqualifiedly approve the results. . . .

The insight and creed from which Emerson's life followed can be best summed up in his own verse:—

> "So nigh is grandeur to our dust,
> So near is God to man!"

Through the individual fact there ever shone for him the effulgence of the Universal Reason. The great Cosmic Intellect terminates and houses itself in mortal men and passing hours. Each of us is an angle of its eternal vision, and the only way to be true to our Maker is to be loyal to ourselves. . . .

If the individual open thus directly into the Absolute, it follows that there is something in each and all of us, even the lowliest, that ought not to consent to borrowing traditions and living at second hand. "If John was perfect, why are you and I alive?" writes Emerson. "As long as any man exists there is some need of him; let him fight for his own." This faith that in a life at first hand there is something sacred is perhaps the most characteristic note in

Emerson's writings. The hottest side of him is this non-conformist persuasion, and if his temper could ever verge on common irascibility, it would be by reason of the passionate character of his feelings on this point. The world is still new and untried. In seeing freshly, and not in hearing of what others saw, shall a man find what truth is. "Each one of us can bask in the great morning which rises out of the Eastern Sea, and be himself one of the children of the light." . . .

The matchless eloquence with which Emerson proclaimed the sovereignty of the living individual electrified and emancipated his generation, and this bugle-blast will doubtless be regarded by future critics as the soul of his message. The present man is the aboriginal reality, the Institution is derivative, and the past man is irrelevant and obliterate for present issues. . . .

Emerson's belief that the individual must in reason be adequate to the vocation for which the Spirit of the world has called him into being is the source of those sublime pages, hearteners and sustainers of our youth, in which he urges his hearers to be incorruptibly true to their own private conscience. Nothing can harm the man who rests in his appointed place and character. Such a man is invulnerable; he balances the universe, balances it as much by keeping small when he is small as by being great and spreading when he is great. . . .

. . . "[The] deep to-day which all men scorn" receive[s] from Emerson superb revindication. "Other world! there is no other world." All God's life opens into the individual particular, and here and now, or nowhere, is reality. "The present hour is the decisive hour, and every day is doomsday."

Such a conviction that Divinity is everywhere may easily make of one an optimist of the sentimental type that refuses to speak ill of anything. Emerson's drastic perception of differences kept him at the opposite pole from this weakness. After you have seen men a few times, he could say, you find most of them as alike as their barns and pantries, and soon as musty and as dreary. Never was such a fastidious lover of significance and distinction, and never an eye so keen for their discovery. His optimism had nothing in common with that indiscriminate hurrahing for the Universe with which Walt Whitman has made us familiar. For Emerson, the individual fact and moment were indeed suffused with absolute radiance, but it was upon a condition that saved the situation—they must be worthy specimens,—sincere, authentic, archetypal; they must have made connection with what he calls the Moral Sentiment, they must in some way act as symbolic mouthpieces of

[220]

the Universe's meaning. To know just which thing does act in this way, and which thing fails to make the true connection, is the secret . . . of seership, and doubtless we must not expect of the seer too rigorous a consistency. Emerson himself was a real seer. He could perceive the full squalor of the individual fact, but he could also see the transfiguration. He might easily have found himself saying of some present-day agitator against our Philippine conquest what he said of this or that reformer of his own time. He might have called him, as a private person, a tedious bore and canter. But he would infallibly have added what he then added: "It is strange and horrible to say this, for I feel that under him and his partiality . . . is the earth and the sea, and all that in them is, and the axis round which the Universe revolves passes through his body." . . .

. . . [This] is Emerson's revelation:—The point of any pen can be an epitome of reality; the commonest person's act, if genuinely actuated, can lay hold on eternity. This vision is the head-spring of all his outpourings; and it is for this truth, given to no previous literary artist to express in such penetratingly persuasive tones, that posterity will reckon him a prophet, and, perhaps neglecting other pages, piously turn to those that convey this message. His life was one long conversation with the invisible divine, expressing itself through individuals and particulars:—"So nigh is grandeur to our dust, so near is God to man!"

I spoke of how shrunken the wraith, how thin the echo, of men is after they are departed. Emerson's wraith comes to me now as if it were but the very voice of this victorious argument. His words to this effect are certain to be quoted and extracted more and more as time goes on, and to take their place among the Scriptures of humanity.

"Speech of Caroline Hazard"

I am sure it is a great honor to be accounted a member of this Social Circle for this one evening, an honor which I prize very highly. I must say, when your Chairman of the day asked me to come here and say a word, I feared that I should be what Mr. Emerson would call "an unauthorized talker." But I have the authority, not only of the kind invitation of your Chairman, but what Mr. Emerson would recognize as the true authority—the authority of the affection and gratitude which I have—which all women must have—for the work which Mr. Emerson did for women as well as for men. It seems to me that that splendid message of the dignity of the person and of the worth of personality which he preached and was the preëminent example of—that message which he spoke to all young men and young women—comes with an especial force to the young women of to-day. When we think what New England was one hundred years ago, how it was truly a provincial New England,—a New England connected with the mother country by the closest ties, but still connected only with the mother country and not with the great world currents,—we also think of what Mr. Emerson did in widening that connection, in making the connection with the whole of German literature, with the revival of the study of Dante, and with all of those other currents of literature which have enriched our lives, and flow from his preaching and his awakening.

The dignity which he gave to the individual with his call to awake and arise—this splendid call to personality—sounded not only for men but for women. "The whole realm of history and biography," he says, "is to increase my self-respect. Then I venture; then I will also essay to be." And it was to what has been called the misrepresented and neglected sex that this call came with perhaps especial emphasis. It was a call to service. There were many women who were content with their daily round of duty, who found in it certainly all the room they could ask for self-denial; but the call to awaken to their own personality, to a conception of the worth of their own souls and the right that they had to live their own lives,—this call came with an especial force, as it seems to me, to the women of his day. We hope we have learned the lesson. There were some who carried the lesson farther than he ever intended, perhaps, but that call was a call which has aroused all that is best in the women of our land. Mr. Emerson himself, in his own beautiful and gracious life, in his association with women, recognized what the place of women could be in society and in the world. They had been too long merely pretty playthings. The young girl who ruled with an arbitrary authority for a brief hour, and then was consigned to household cares, too often as a housekeeper rather than as a companion of her husband—all that Mr. Emerson saw, and in his own life showed how it need not be. The value of his women friends, the value of the women of his own household, he cherished and in every way increased by his own gracious and loving deference and the dignity of his own character. And so his splendid message of the value of personality, is a gift for us women to be especially grateful for. . . .

It was here in these Concord meadows that he taught us that man may have fellowship with God,—"that man in the bush with God may meet."

This was the source of his joy; this was the strength of his personality; this was the message which he preached to the men and women of his day. . . .

From *The Centenary of the Birth of Ralph Waldo Emerson* (Cambridge, Mass.: Riverside Press, 1903), pp. 67–72, 75–77, 99–103.

"Personal Glimpses of Emerson" (1903)

Julian Hawthorne

Julian Hawthorne, Nathaniel and Sophia Hawthorne's son, wrote extensively about the relationship between his father and Emerson. For several years between 1842 and 1864 the Hawthornes and the Emersons were neighbors in Concord, first when the Hawthornes rented the Old Manse, the Emerson family's ancestral home, and then when they lived at Wayside.

The exact nature of the relationship between Emerson and Hawthorne has been the subject of many—often conflicting—interpretations. While they do not settle the matter once and for all, Julian Hawthorne's accounts of the relationship have the advantage of his own long view of the history between these two very different men. In *Nathaniel Hawthorne and His Wife: A Biography* (1884), he draws on his parents' letters to show his father's early admiration of Emerson and his mother's sense of Emerson's delight with Hawthorne. In *Hawthorne and His Circle* (New York and London: Harper & Brothers, 1903), he reports many anecdotes of his own and his father's relations with Emerson, providing this succinct estimate of the differences between his father and Emerson and how those differences were manifested in their relationship:

> My father read Emerson with enjoyment; though more and more, as he advanced in life, he was disposed to question the expediency of stating truth in a disembodied form; he preferred it incarnate, as it appears in life and in story. But he could not talk to Emerson; his pleasure in his society did not express itself in that form. Emerson, on the other hand, assiduously cultivated my father's company, and, contrary to his general habit, talked to him continuously; but he could not read his romances; he admitted that he had never been able to finish one of them. He loved to observe him; to watch his silence, which was full of a kind of speech which he was able to appreciate; "Hawthorne rides well his horse of the night!" My father was Gothic; Emerson was Roman and Greek. But each was profoundly original and independent. My father was the shyer and more solitary of the two, and yet persons in need of human sympathy were able to reach a more interior region in him than they could in Emerson. For the latter's thought was concerned with types and classes, while the former had the individual touch. He distrusted rules, but had faith in exceptions and idiosyncrasies. Emerson was nobly and magnanimously public; my father, exquisitely and inevitably private; together they met the needs of nearly all that is worthy in human nature. (p. 68)

In the spring of 1853, when I was going on seven years old, my father took me down Concord highway, from the Wayside westward, to a square white house which stood a little drawn back from the road, and veiled somewhat by dark pine trees. On the left, as we faced it, was a fenced area of several acres partly devoted to a vegetable garden, and partly in lawn—though not such a well-kept lawn as one sees in Concord nowadays. Here, too, were other trees, and in the boughs of one of them was a great, rude harp, fashioned of boughs; which, as I afterwards learned, could be played upon by the invisible fingers of storm winds, and would then send forth mighty strains of wild music, to mingle with the shrieks and howls of the blast, as though to symbolize that, in the midst of the outward stress and disorderly wrath of nature, there was an inner harmony and reason. This was the Æolian harp built by Bronson Alcott for his friend Emerson. For many years it held its place and gave its music. There was likewise, in the same neighborhood, a rustic summer-house, constructed by the same architect, and even then falling into decay. The only other thing that attracted my attention in connection with the home of Emerson was the pathway of white limestone flags which led up from the gate to the porch of entrance. It was the only pavement of the kind I had ever seen, and it is to this day, I believe, the only marble-paved path in Concord.

Meanwhile, Mr. Emerson himself had no doubt responded to my father's knock or ring, and they were conversing together; but I have no recollection of him until some little while later, when, the conference over, he accompanied us down to the gate, and out into the road. Here, a minor road branched off at an acute angle from the main highway, down which the British had marched and retreated in 1776; and in the angle formed by the junction there was a thick and dark grove of pines, not fenced off; it was carpeted with a dense stratum of reddish-brown pine needles. On the borders of this grove it was that I first became consciously aware of our famous philosopher and poet. The soft, warm, spring sunshine shone upon him; he wore a black felt hat and a black frock coat, unbuttoned; his face was clipper-built, and the expression extraordinarily bright, keen, and cordial. He looked down at me, and smiled, and took my hand in his, which was large, firm, and massive,—the hand of a farmer, though it was not rough or horny. He spoke in a pleasant voice, slowly, and with noticeable intonations; the sentences were brief, but they seemed to be significant. There was a nice-looking boy there, about two years my senior; he had big, blue eyes and a friendly aspect;

Emerson made us known to each other, and it was understood that we were to be friends. At this point, the door of memory closes, and Emerson is not again revealed to me until seven years later, after we had been in Europe, and had returned to dwell in Concord.

During the following seven years I saw him constantly, and in many circumstances. Often, on my way to Sanborn's school and back, I would meet him, walking with his head bowed forward, but keeping a bright lookout ahead of him (unlike Channing, whose eyes ever sought the ground), and as we drew near, the unique Emersonian smile would glimmer in his face; he would sometimes stop to speak a few words, generally in the form of a question; but as a rule he would simply say "Good-bye," or "Good-night" (as the case might be), and pass on with his long, measured steps. "How do you do?" was a form of greeting that I seldom, if ever, heard from Emerson's lips; it is perhaps a foolish form, and I used to think that Emerson proved the thoroughness of his philosophy by guarding his speech even in a thing so trifling.

At other times I would see him, transiently, in his study, where the walls were all made of books in sober bindings, and there was a table strewn with papers and writings; but here I never lingered long, but went forward through an alcove which led into the parlor and dining room. These study-glimpses of Emerson showed him mild and absorbed, and always, in the midst of his absorption, with a lovely expression of kindly welcome. Once in a while, when, at his son's invitation, I came in to lunch, he would sit at the head of the table, but with a manner as if he were the least considerable person there; and he would address many questions to the visitor, and listen closely to his replies, as if he looked for some wisdom, or at least information, from the unripe boy. His bearing towards his wife and daughters was of the most loving courtesy, and withal of deference, as though he would take his orders from them. Surely there was never greater personal humility than in this man, who was one of the proudest and boldest avouchers of the inalienable dignity of human nature that ever lived.

Again, I would see him at friends' houses, in conversation with other famous dignitaries of New England—Alcott, Wendell Phillips, Channing, Thoreau, Hoar, and many others. He was inevitably the centre of the group, and when he spoke, all listened, though he never spoke to all, but addressed himself to some single interlocutor, and seemed to wish that words so unimportant as his should not be magnified. But his friends were a unit against this modesty; there was freshness, reason, and beauty in all he said. Society, in the high sense, was always created where he was, and took on a dignity and value that prophesied of a Golden Age.

Finally, I was always on a bench in the Concord Town Hall when Emerson was advertised to speak. In the winter Lyceum course at Concord, all the great orators of the time appeared in their turn; but none of the lectures, with the exception of those of Phillips and of Beecher, were so fully attended as his. His topics were commonly of perennial interest, though they could not be termed popular; they touched the deeps of thought, but they were full of that inimitable Emersonian quality which attracts the man in the street almost as much as the thinker and philosopher. Sentences leaped out, every now and then, which went straight to the heart and sense of the whole audience. . . .

He was dressed, on these evenings, in black broadcloth; either a very ill-cut dress coat, or a buttoned-up frock coat almost as ill-fitting; with a high, uncomfortable stock and an upright collar. Emerson's figure was naturally awkward; he had narrow and sloping shoulders, large arms and hands and feet, and he had a habit of projecting forward his head, precisely as an eagle on the perch does, and with the same piercing look from the eyes. As he stood before the audience, behind the desk, he let his hands hang folded before him, or used them to turn the leaves of his manuscript; his gestures were very few; the one most often used was a clenching of the right fist, the fingers upward, and bringing down the forearm with a motion of power till it was at right angles with the upper arm; in its mingling of reserve with force, a very characteristic movement. He could hardly be said to read his manuscript; he probably knew it by heart; he would merely keep in touch with it as he went along. But I have seldom heard him speak with no notes whatever, though I know he was well able to do so when occasion demanded. Frequently, after finishing a passage, he would turn over leaf after leaf, sometimes to the number of a dozen or more, and begin again after the leap; making his hearers feel as if they were losing invaluable things. But what he gave was always so satisfying to the mind that it seemed ungenerous to demand more; and Emerson, of course, was only thinking of the time limit which the Lyceum course had fixed.

Like Beecher, he stood square upon both feet; but there was nevertheless a slight shifting movement from one foot to the other, not ordinarily noticeable; though, one evening, Emerson happened to have on a pair of creaking boots, and this creaking permeated the eloquence of the lecture in a manner most discomfortable to the audience, and doubtless to Emerson himself;

though he, recognizing that it was incurable in the circumstances, unless he should pull his boots off, heroically disregarded it, and gave his lecture with tranquillity to the end. I do not recall the subject of that lecture, but I can never forget the boots.

After leaving Harvard, I went to Europe, and returned only after an absence of many years, in 1882. During part of this time, Emerson had been gradually lapsing into silence; the quality of his mind seemed not impaired, but certain external faculties had ceased to fulfil their entire functions. In the inner recesses of his consciousness he was aware of these deficiencies, and with an innocent wisdom retired from active productiveness; he dwelt in a semi-spiritual retreat, communing, doubtless, with the Source of intelligence, but estranged from mortal preoccupations. The memory of names and all manner of arbitrary phrases left him, and faces were forgotten; though the essence of things still seemed to be accessible to his apprehension. . . . The light of the passing day was as a mirage to him; but the sun shone clearly upon the regions of the past, and he probably lived in them and felt the ground there solid beneath his feet. His face, in these times, was quiescent, as of one who dreams awake; but ever and anon that keen, investigating look would gleam out from it, as in old days, and he would lift his head as if about to speak in his old way. He resigned himself to the care of his daughter Ellen, and was led about by her, and tended affectionately by her, like an angel half asleep. It was a touching and in no respect a painful spectacle. I visited him once in his study, with the old books still thronging the shelves; and he discoursed to me about Carlyle, as if his visit to him had been of but a few days since; once in a while he would break off to ask his daughter the name of the person to whom he was talking. It was like conversing through a veil, or with a man in another planet, with the communication imperfectly established. But what he said of Carlyle was with all his original force and pith.

I saw him no more; but on the day of his funeral I walked with the rest of Concord, and with many men of eminence from all parts of the country, to the grave in Sleepy Hollow. It seemed to me that all of the old Concord was left in that grave. The crowd returned to their homes; but these streets and houses were no longer Concord in the deeper sense. The last of the great magicians had departed, and taken with him the spirit that is the life.

Booklovers Magazine, 1 (February 1903): 149, 151, 153, 157, 161, 164.

"Emerson: The Teacher and the Man" (1903)

MONCURE D. CONWAY

The Unitarian and freethought minister, biographer, historian, and abolitionist Moncure Daniel Conway was a frequent commentator on Emerson's life and thought. He wrote generally appreciative reviews of Emerson's lectures, essays, and poems, interpreted his position in the evolution of Transcendentalism for both American and English readers, and published two book-length studies of Emerson in the year following his death: *Emerson at Home and Abroad* (1882) and *Emerson and His Views of Nature* (1883). Conway's discussions of Emerson's relationship with Hawthorne and Thoreau, his remarks on Emerson's involvement with the antislavery movement and his anticipation of theories of evolution, and his informative treatment of Emerson's three trips to England make *Emerson at Home and Abroad* the more valuable of the two books. In "Emerson: The Teacher and the Man," written on the occasion of the centenary of Emerson's birth, Conway reconstructs his relationship with Emerson from their first meeting in 1853 to Emerson's death, and he acknowledges his early debt to Emerson for introducing him to Thoreau, Elizabeth Hoar, Elizabeth Palmer Peabody, and the Ripleys as well as to Eastern philosophy and poetry. As suggested in the introduction to this volume, because Conway had a tendency to rewrite personal history to his own advantage, this essay—as with many of Conway's writings on Emerson—has to be read with a certain degree of critical detachment.

May 3, 1853, is a date under which I wrote a couplet from Emerson's "Woodnotes":

> 'T was one of the charmèd days
> When the genius of God doth flow.

On that day I first met Emerson. Carrying a letter from Dr. Palfrey, I sent it in from the door, and the children came to say he was out but would return to dinner at one, and their mother wished me to remain. The three children entertained me pleasantly in the garden, and I was soon sent for. He met me at the door with a welcome that relieved my trepidation, and invited me into

[229]

his library. He said that he remembered receiving a letter from one of my name a year or two before. On learning that I was now studying in Cambridge Divinity School and had come to Concord simply to see him, he called from his library door, "Queeny!" Mrs. Emerson came, and I was invited to remain some days. I had to return, however, to college that evening, and though I expressed a wish that his day should not be long interfered with he insisted on my passing the afternoon with him, and took me on a walk. He inquired about the influences by which my changes had been effected, saying with a smile: "The gods generally provide the young thinker with friends." When I told him of the effect of the brief extract from his "Essay on History" found in *Blackwood* when I was eighteen, he said that when the mind had reached a certain stage it might sometimes be crystallized by a slight touch. I told him that I had found several sympathetic friends among the Hicksite Quakers in Maryland, to whom I had loaned his book. It had cost me sore trials to leave my people, but it was a great relief to be no longer under constraint to accommodate myself to dogmas. Emerson said that the denials of dogma were also liable to harden into dogmatic form, and added something about the comparative unimportance of the anti-trinitarian polemic. What mattered arithmetical tripersonality or monopersonality? "I have good grounds for being unitarian and trinitarian too; I need not nibble at one loaf forever, but eat it and go on to earn another." I realized that the mere academic question had been costing me some needless headaches, yet my real trouble had not been with the label but with false and low ideas of God and man. "It is indeed deplorable," he said, "that there should be creeds that tend to take man back to the chimpanzee."

I was too recently free from my bonds, and the wounds from them still smarted too much, to rise at once into the pure ether. But on our walk my prophet, bountifully giving his hours to my need, led me by gentlest hints to the day then shining for me. He remarked that the voices of some boatmen out on the water (Walden) were intoned by distance into music; and that the curves made by their oars became under the sunlight a succession of beautiful bows. This may have started a train of thought related to the abhorrence I had expressed of the old dogmas, to which I had added something about the repugnance with which I had witnessed some Catholic ceremonies. "Yet," he said, "they possess beauty in the distance. When one sees them on the stage—processions of priests in their vestments chanting their hymns— they are in their place and offend no sentiment."

As we were moving among bushes Emerson suddenly exclaimed: "Ah! there is one of the gods of the wood!" I looked and saw nothing; then turned to him and followed his glance, but still beheld nothing unusual. He was looking with a beaming eye along the path that lay before us through a thicket. "Where?" I asked. "Did you see it?" he said, now moving on. "No, I saw nothing—what was it?" "No matter," said he gently. I repeated my question, but he still said smilingly: "Never mind if you did not see it."

I had my riddle to think of. What god of the wood was that which I did not see? I kept my eyes wide open after that, and had no more to say about eschatology, the absolute, etc. My instruction in the supremacy of the present hour began not so much in Emerson's words as in himself. Standing there beside the ruin of the shanty where Thoreau lived a year on $28, Emerson appeared to me an incarnation of the wondrous day. Once when I spoke of eschatology he had said: "An actually existent fly is more important than a possibly existent angel." Herein perhaps was the secret of that sylvan god I had missed seeing. The actual squirrel or pretty snake lost by my translunary speculation was a note in the symphony of organic nature. . . .

Of that day I always think as one that never ended. The summer of 1853 I passed at Concord. I found a pleasant home with the Misses Hunt on Ponkatasset Hill. I often had walks with Thoreau, who told me that the greatness of Emerson was that he beheld the invisible facts of the moral and intellectual worlds with the exactness of a naturalist observing and classifying objects of the visible world; he enabled us also to see them, and in their relations.

Emerson gave me advice about reading and loaned me books from his library. When he first took me for introduction to Thoreau, the latter asked what we were studying at Divinity College. I answered, "the Scriptures." "Which?" he asked. So crude was I yet that I was puzzled until Emerson said: "You will find Thoreau a sad pagan." Thoreau's remark had especially interested me, and Emerson told me he would be glad to have me use his collection of Oriental books. It was before the time of the Buddhist cult in America, and Emerson's collection included chiefly translations of the great Hindu works, and still more the Persian. He told me that he considered the Persian religion and writings to be intellectually superior to all others. The other scriptures were important and interesting, especially the "Bhagavat Gita," admirable in Wilkins's translation, but from the Persians one may get actual additions to thought and knowledge. He loaned me some translations from the "Avesta," and the entire "Desatir" and . . . introduced me to the never-fading "Rose Garden" of Saadi.

Emerson had as quick eyes in his heart as in his head. He appreciated, without need of any suggestion, the situation of a youth bereft of home and relatives for the sake of new beliefs, of which in turn he must also be bereft. He used to give me advice about my health; he took care that I should know the best women—the Ripleys, Elizabeth Hoar, and others,—and I was invited to all the picnics. He and his wife gave me, indeed, a home, and the delight I found in comradeship with their children healed the hurts suffered by past alienations.

Beautiful, indeed, was Emerson in his home. Mrs. Emerson, along with her interest in emancipation and other reforms, held a mystical kind of religion which she had thought out for herself, and though unorthodox spoke at times with favor of the miracles. Emerson's comment in such matters was always careful. "But where," he said once, "can you find a greater miracle than by looking into the eyes of your child?" Once when we were calling at the house of a neighbor where Miss Elizabeth Peabody was staying, some point she raised about Christ led me to cite a criticism that troubled her. When we went out Emerson said it was a question of importance to what extent one must be tender with cherished superstitions. "At a theatre where children were enjoying a spectacle one would hardly tell them that the fairy is an ordinary woman and her gold spangles bits of paper." I told him penitently that it had not occurred to me as a possibility that grown people who had so long been in the rationalistic atmosphere of Concord might yet preserve the beliefs of childhood in certain things; but I took the lesson to heart.

Critic, 42 (May 1903): 406–408.

"A Sculptor's Reminiscences of Emerson" (1916)

DANIEL CHESTER FRENCH

> One of America's finest monumental sculptors, Daniel Chester French received
> his first art training in Concord from Louisa May Alcott's sister, May. He stud-
> ied in Boston and New York before his big break, the commission in 1875 for a
> statue of the Minute Man in Concord, now an iconographic American figure
> (which has Emerson's "Concord Hymn" inscribed on its base). The success of
> this statue allowed him to study in Italy for a year, after which he spent a decade
> in Washington, D.C. A neoclassical sculptor, French often traveled to Europe
> for inspiration, but he is best known for his very American productions, includ-
> ing a bust (1879) and a full-length seated statue of Emerson (1914), both of
> which are in the Concord Free Public Library, "Mourning Victory" (1908) at the
> Melvin Memorial in Sleepy Hollow Cemetery at Concord, and the seated statue
> of Abraham Lincoln (1920) at the Lincoln Memorial in Washington, D.C. His
> account of Emerson, while containing both a valuable portrait of him in Con-
> cord and Emerson's comments on Nathaniel Hawthorne, is most interesting
> for being the only extended account we have of someone who captured Emer-
> son's image, be it a sculptor or a photographer. Emerson appreciated the bust,
> commenting to French, as reported by Robert Underwood Johnson in *Remem-
> bered Yesterdays,*† "That's the face I shave every morning."

[My] impressions of Emerson [carry] me back to the days of my youth, in
the quiet little New England town that ever since the April morning when its
"embattled farmers" confronted the British at the old North Bridge, has
been famous for the performances of her sons. None of them has so impressed his character and personality upon it or upon the world as did this
divinely inspired teacher. Of his effect upon the world at large I have no need
to speak, but in Concord he stood for what amounted to a sort of community conscience, his high ideals of life creating a standard that made
people ashamed to act, or even to think, ignobly. . . .

My own acquaintance with Mr. Emerson began when my father took up
his abode in Concord in 1867. Already he was an elderly man. The most
vivid impression of him that I have brought away from that time was of a tall

figure, walking the village streets enveloped in a long black cloak or shawl, and looking as I imagined Dante must have looked as he walked the streets of Florence.

Young as I was, I was impressed, as every one was, with his dignified, serene presence. We have all had the common experience of disappointment in meeting some celebrity whose works we have long known and esteemed, because the man himself did not realize our ideal of him, but Emerson seemed as great as he really was—this very tall, spare, loosely hung figure with small head and rather large hands and feet, with clothes worn for use and without thought of them. It was none of these things that made all who approached him aware that they were in the presence of a demigod. Perhaps it was the soul that shone out upon you from his face; or the deep, full, beautiful voice with its matchless enunciation and perfect diction; or the clear, piercing eyes; or the courtesy towards man or child, high or lowly, which was unfailing; or a combination of all these and much besides that went to make up the indefinable atmosphere that invested this man, whose presence was a benediction.

I have spoken of the influence of Emerson's personality upon the community. It was one of the evidences of his symmetrically rounded nature that the respect and admiration in which he was held by the outside world were shared by his townsmen, who were, one and all, as proud of him as if he had been their own kin. He was a good citizen and neighbor, exemplary in the common, every-day relations of life, reasonable and just, so that the idle gossip of the village passed him by—a tribute that those may not appreciate who have not lived in a small town.

The unaffected simplicity as well as the kindliness of the man may be illustrated by his attitude toward me, a youth of twenty. When spending an evening at his house soon after his return from abroad, he seated me comfortably in a chair before a big magnifying glass and, himself standing, placed in position for me to see a collection of photographs of pictures and statues and places in which he knew I would be interested. Had I been of his own age and importance he could not have treated me with more deference or taken more pains for my entertainment and enlightment.

A few years later a friend asked me to secure Mr. Emerson's autograph for her collection. As he turned the pages of her autograph-book, he said: "I ought to write something besides my name" and going to his note-book he selected the following lines:

> "This fleeting moment is an edifice
> that the Omnipotent cannot rebuild."

The preciousness of the present moment is reiterated in many forms in Emerson's writings—as in that masterly crystallization of the idea, his "Days."

It was in the spring of 1879 that Mr. Emerson granted my request that he would sit to me for a bust. My improvised studio was, for his convenience, a room on the lower floor of his house, and here, almost daily for a month, patiently and uncomplainingly, this good man sat to me, more from the wish to do me a favor than from any great interest in the work itself.

A newspaper critic has spoken of this bust as "French's topographical survey of Emerson's face" and this it certainly was, if nothing more; for at that time I used a system of triangulation with almost countless measurements that I had learned in the studios of Hiram Powers and Thomas Ball in Florence. To be sure I tried, as they did, to add to my cold facts and attempted to catch somewhat of the glorified expression—the "lighting up" that people noted in Emerson's face, but probably the head is chiefly valuable for being as close a record of his features as my conscientious endeavors could attain.

The comments of my distinguished sitter during the progress of the work, as was to be expected, were interesting or amusing. Thus during the first session when I expressed regret at putting him to so much trouble he responded: "This is as easy as sleeping." Later, when he looked at the result of several days' work he said: "The trouble is that the more it resembles me the worse it looks." Of another bust that had been made of him it is recalled that he said: "It looks as harmless as a parsnip." Could any simile be more apt to describe a characterless portrait?

He talked to me of poetry and spoke of having received a poem from a man in Washington which he considered unusual and which he had sent with his commendation to the Editor of the *Atlantic Monthly*, who thought it not good enough to publish. Mr. Emerson remarked: "Old age can hardly have deprived me of my power to judge poetry."

He referred affectionately to Thoreau, who was among his closest friends in Concord and said he was his own worst enemy; that he regarded all men with contempt—except the farmer and the workingman, whom he pitied.

As illustrating his want of appreciation of music he recounted his first experience in singing. He attended a singing-school and the teacher told him to "chord." He said he didn't know what that meant, but supposed it was to produce a sound, which he did, whereupon the teacher suggested that he might go and need not return.

Of special interest was his account of his only interview with Ruskin. He was at Oxford and heard Ruskin lecture and then called upon him at his rooms. Ruskin became excited and talked so about humanity in general that Mr. Emerson could not bear it and told him he would have to go, and he and his daughter Ellen departed. He said that "Ruskin seemed to think that all mankind was going to the devil.". . .

He told me of the coming of Hawthorne to dwell in the old Manse in Concord, and of his own failure to gain intimacy with the newcomer through the medium of the conventional exchange of calls. He said he felt that something must be done to break down the barrier which Hawthorne's natural shyness probably augmented, and he went to him and proposed that they should take a walk together—twenty miles—over to the little town of Harvard, spend the night at the Shaker Village and walk back to Concord the next day. Hawthorne accepted the invitation and the program was carried out. "Now" said Mr. Emerson "while two men might travel forty miles together in the steam-cars, or even ride in a chaise as far as that, without becoming acquainted, it is hardly possible for two men to *walk* forty miles in each other's company without feeling that they know each other pretty well. Mr. Hawthorne and I had no further difficulty."

My statue of Emerson, which is in marble and stands in the Concord Free Public Library, was made two years ago from such materials in the way of photographs and daguerrotypes as could be collected, together with my study of his head as a foundation. It seemed proper to represent him in his prime, and again I endeavored to fix the elusive, illuminated expression of which I have spoken; also, to perpetuate the peculiar sidewise thrust of the head on the neck that was characteristic of him, conveying an impression of mental searching. The gown which was used as drapery was one that he wore in his study in the winter and took the name by which it was known in the household, "the Gaberlunzie," from the character of Eddie Ochiltree in Scott's "Antiquary." It is still in existence and in the possession of his daughter. It is a heavy, wadded and quilted, dark blue garment, and one can easily believe that its voluminous folds were very grateful to the poet and essayist of a winter's morning in his study in the northwest corner of the house.

No statue or picture, however true it might be to a passing phase, could be an adequate representation of his face, the expression of which changed with his thoughts and mirrored them. Henry James has spoken of "the over-modeled American face." Whether he intended this as a tribute to the intelligence of the Americans or not, it seems to be true that the higher the development of intellect in a race, the more complicated become the forms of the face, and, in less marked degree, those of the body. Emerson's face bore out this theory and, in spite of the boldness of the general plan, had an infinity of detail, the delicacy of which evinced the refinement of the soul that evolved it.

Art World, 1 (October 1916): 44, 47.

From *Remembered Yesterdays* (1923)

ROBERT UNDERWOOD JOHNSON

Robert Underwood Johnson, poet and translator, edited the *Century Magazine* from 1873 to 1909. His affinity for the Romantic poets led him to cofound in 1903 the Keats-Shelley Memorial Association and establish the library at the house in Rome where Keats had died. Johnson heard Emerson lecture on "Art and Nature" on 27 November 1871 in Chicago and offer brief remarks in 1875 in Concord (a complement to the lines from his "Concord Hymn" about "the shot heard round the world" that Johnson quotes, first published in *Proceedings at the Centennial Celebration of Concord Fight* [1875]). Johnson's account, which contains a number of unique anecdotes about Emerson and his admirers, also promotes Emerson as a link to the security of the past, presenting him as one whose "sane mind and pure spirit will do much to save America from the destructive mania . . . threatening the stability of the world" in the aftermath of World War I.

Among the great figures whom I saw in my youth and of whom, to my deep regret, I saw little, when I might have seen more, was Ralph Waldo Emerson, in my mature opinion our greatest man of letters, our foremost poet and one of the most imaginative in English literature.

My first sight of him was in Chicago in the winter of 1871–72, after the big fire, when he came to lecture in a church on the South Side. There was a large audience, for the people were trying to recover from their calamity by cultivating intellectual and musical activities. I have forgotten the subject, but I have a vivid remembrance of the speaker's rapt and gentle attitude, as though he were in a trance, turning his head from side to side and looking up at the ceiling as he delivered his weighty sentences. The effect was as if an apocalyptic angel had passed that way.

The only other time I saw him was at the Concord Centennial 1875. My trip from New York to Concord was my first visit to New England. It was in the company of my friend William Fayal Clarke, of *St. Nicholas*. To us young fellows, who had spent our boyhood in the West,—we were for four years together in Indiana at Earlham College,—it was a memorable experience. We were in high spirits and everything was a source of jollity. The sight of the stone walls of New England was a surprise. . . . They seemed to us characteristic of the solidity and, if I may say so, the rigidity of Puritan Massachusetts.

There was an immense throng at Concord and it was only by having been at the Boston station betimes that we got places in the train, in which respect we were more fortunate than Howells and Mark Twain, who by reason of the crowd missed the occasion altogether.

The celebration was inspiring. There were two sets of exercise, one at the Dinner tent and one at the Oration tent, where we were. President Grant was there and George William Curtis gave the oration. Mr. Emerson made an address of which I remember this sentence: "The thunderbolt falls on an inch of ground, but the light of it fills the horizon." It expressed with cogency the idea of "the shot heard round the world." . . .

That afternoon, as lovers of Emerson, Clarke and I walked up and down in front of his white house and his woodpile, longing to go in. Alas! in those days I was too timid to make an advance to so great a man. But we felt the spell of the historic little town and looking up at French's inspiring "Minute Man" we recited the "Concord Bridge." . . . Then we visited Walden Pond to see the hut of the hermit naturalist Thoreau. But all our romantic feeling was reserved for the Old Manse and Hawthorne's grave in the forest cemetery, where Emerson's resting place now is, marked by a great boulder. And how I regret that we could not have had a personal touch with that beautiful spirit!

Here are some anecdotes of Emerson that I believe have never been in print.

Late in life, when he was supposed to be failing in mind, it was said that he went out walking in the twilight on the Lexington Road with his daughter Ellen. Looking up at the stars he said to his companion, "Those things above us, are they not the creation of will?"—from which it might be inferred that he was meditating on the deepest problem of the universe, the fact being that what he desired to know was whether the telephone lines that stretched from pole to pole had been constructed by his son-in-law, "Will" Forbes, who (the story goes) at that time was one of the officers of the telephone company of that region.

This sounds *ben trovato*, but the following incident certainly is not invented, for it was told me by the young man to whom it occurred, Frank Dempster Sherman, who at his death was a professor in Columbia University and at the time of the incident was a writer of *vers de société* and other poetry. At the height of his admiration for Emerson Sherman went to Concord on a pilgrimage and, like Clarke and myself and Howells, walked up and down in front of Emerson's woodpile, longing but hesitating to go in and see the great man. At last he plucked up his courage, opened the gate, and went on to the house and knocked, even then having to resist the impulse to run away. The door was opened by Mr. Emerson himself in dressing gown and slippers, and the poet cordially invited his visitor to come in, and he gave Sherman a delightful half-hour. At the close of the interview the young man took from his pocket a copy of Emerson's Poems and made bold to ask the author to write his name in it. Emerson affably complied and then, turning to Sherman, he asked him to be good enough to write *his* name for *him*. Sherman told me that he was so "flabbergasted" by this request that, as he afterward recalled, he succeeded in writing only the first two thirds of his name—*Frank Dempster!*

One of the precious records of Emerson is the beautiful bust of him made by Daniel Chester French soon after the sculptor's return to Concord from his foreign studies. French told me that while he was at work Emerson said nothing about the bust, but when it finished and French asked, "Well, Mr. Emerson, what do you think of it?" the Sage replied, "That's the face I shave every morning."... The simplicity of this appreciation was on a par with his quizzical compliment to a man of whom his opinion was desired, "I believe him capable of virtue." This bust shows him in old age,—the compact, round head, the strong aquiline profile and the ineffable and spiritual smile. In the town library of Concord is a sitting figure of him by French showing him in his mature middle age—one of the best pieces by that distinguished sculptor.... I never look upon these portraits of the gentle philosopher and poet, who by teaching the teachers has had so great influence upon American life, without thinking of Father Taylor's retort to some unco' orthodox who asserted that Emerson go to hell: "Well, if he does, he will change the climate and the emigration will turn in that direction." Again that eloquent Methodist missionary said of his Unitarian colleague: "I have watched him and find in him no fault. I have laid my ear close to his heart and I cannot detect any jar in the machinery."

[240]

The influence of Emerson's sane mind and pure spirit will do much to save America from the destructive mania that is threatening the stability of the world.

From *Remembered Yesterdays* (Boston: Little, Brown, 1923), pp. 325–29.

From *My Garden of Memory: An Autobiography* (1923)

KATE DOUGLAS WIGGIN

Kate Douglas (Smith) Wiggin was an early pioneer of the kindergarten move-ment in America. The author of travel books for adults and stories for children, her most famous work was *Rebecca of Sunnybrook Farm* (1903). In the summer of 1880, she was brought to Concord by Elizabeth Palmer Peabody—another founder of the kindergarten in America—to attend the meetings of the Concord School of Philosophy, and while there, she also made the circuit of Concord so-ciety under Peabody's direction. In the selection that follows, which was drawn from her "Personal Recollections of Emerson" published just after Emerson's death, Wiggin—who in 1882 wrote as Kate D. Smith—shows the continued at-traction of Emerson as an inspirational figure for philosophers, reformers, and educators, even after his mental capacities had been diminished by age.

After my brief journey from Boston, as I neared the celebrated village of Concord, I roused myself from my preparatory metaphysical studies to look at my traveling companions. Some of them were evidently to be my fellow-students, for once in a while I caught gentle murmurs of egos and non-egos, participations and self-determination. A fat, loquacious man walked up to me as I stood on the platform and offered to take me up into town for fifteen cents.

I told him where I desired to be driven, and, after treating me to a search-ing stare for a second, he asked, with sincere curiosity:

"Be you one of them Phy-loss-er-fers? The woods is chuck full of 'em now. I went in the hall the other day just a-purpose to hear 'em charnt with their eyes shet. I'd jest like to see one of 'em grubbin' stumps out of an old timber patch."

Nothing daunted, I reached Miss Peabody's house at seven o'clock, and received a warm greeting.

"Now, my child, you shall go to your room and have a good sleep, so that you may be fresh for to-morrow," said my friend.

"I shall not sleep at all while I am here," I said disdainfully. "Please let me tuck your hand under my arm, and we will walk slowly together toward the chapel to hear about the 'Psychic and the Material Body of Man.'"

Next morning we were early in our places. On one side of the lecture room was the platform occupied by the Faculty. Behind it were four windows, and on this lovely August morning they were wide open, and the willow and elm branches hung into the room. Without, there was a concert of bees and birds and crickets, united in chirps and hum and song. On that day there sat upon the platform the venerable Mr. Alcott, Dean of the Faculty; Dr. William T. Harris, celebrated both in education and speculative philosophy; the Chinese Professor of Harvard College; Mr. Sanborn, the energetic Secretary; and Mrs. Julia Ward Howe, who was to lecture on Modern Society—for this was Woman's Day at Concord. By the east window sat a lovely creature with a matchless crown of red-gold hair. I knew her at a glance, for Mrs. Rose Hawthorne Lathrop had the beautiful Hawthorne hair, and a face, too, as perfect as sculptured marble.

Emerson frequently came to the School and listened closely to the lectures, with a pensive, quiet expression, and eyes cast down. His face, so well known to all in its kindly simplicity, was full of sweetness, strength, and common sense.

He looked a thorough New Englander, and his bearing was full of dignity and reserve. Indeed, he was absolutely a law unto himself, and yet his personality was always kept in the background, so far as self-assertion or egotism was concerned. Yes, I thought, he is just what Mr. Alcott calls him, "a student of the landscape, of mankind, of rugged strength, wherever found. He likes plain people, plain ways, plain clothes, prefers earnest persons, shuns publicity, loves solitude and knows its uses"; and when I came to have the honor of knowing him, though ever so slightly, he was the identical man of his books, the essence of refinement in thought, full of serenity and cheerful faith, united with a simple plainness of speech.

As the days passed, I began to grow into Concord. The atmosphere was contagious. Before one knew exactly what transcendentalism was, one "caught" it—and for that matter it was impossible to resist the prevailing dreaminess. . . .

Every morning I went to the nine o'clock lecture, which lasted until eleven or a little after, when the conversation began and went on until twelve.

After the lecture was ended, the subject was thrown open to discussion and there was an opportunity to ask questions. Usually there would be a silence of several minutes, and then Mr. Alcott would announce in his solemn, musical tones, "I have a thought," and, after a weighty pause, proceed to some Orphic utterance. Alcott, indeed, was what might be called the leader on the floor. He was ably seconded by Miss Elizabeth Peabody, . . . [who] was well known as one of the very first persons who had brought the German kindergarten ideal to America, and for her lifelong zeal in behalf of all kinds of philanthropies and educational reforms. Henry James was accused of having caricatured her in his novel "The Bostonians," in the figure of the dear, visionary, benevolent old lady who is perpetually engaged in promoting "causes," attending conventions, carrying on correspondence, forming committees, drawing up resolutions, and the like, but, as a matter of fact, Mr. James never met her and denied the "soft impeachment."

After the morning sessions I usually walked along the homeward path with Mr. Alcott, and with Dr. Harris, of St. Louis, whom I had known previously in educational matters, and their kindly and helpful conversation always served as a sort of textbook to the often profound and metaphysical lectures. I visited Mr. Emerson's house on many different occasions; a plain, square wooden one, standing behind a grove of pine trees, concealing it from the passer-by. At the rear was a large garden, which had been famous for years for its roses and rare collection of hollyhocks—the flowers that Wordsworth loved.

There are spacious rooms on both sides of the house, divided by a long hall. On the right was the study, lined on one side with plain shelves of books. A large writing-table occupied the center of the room, which had on one side a huge fireplace over which hung a fine copy of Michelangelo's Fates. Here were many little curiosities in letters and books—reminiscences of Landor, Coleridge, Wordsworth, Carlyle, Thoreau, and the patriot John Brown; a photograph, too, of chatty little Frederika Bremer, who came there from Sweden in 1849, and whose dress-buttons, it is recorded, never were on terms of intimacy with their buttonholes.

I remember well a most beautiful portrait of his wife. Mrs. Emerson (always called "Queenie" by her husband) was as dainty and spirituelle a woman as one could imagine. Her complexion was as delicate as a rose-leaf, her eyes a vivid dark blue, and her snow-white hair was ornamented with an indescribable little tulle cap, tied under her soft chin with pale blue ribbons. It was such a lovely adjunct to a lovely personality that more than one "sonnet" or "ode" to "Mrs. Emerson's cap" was written during my visit to Concord. Her gown used always to be of plain black silk, and her exquisite appearance, in conjunction with her sweet, quiet manner, made her the center of admiration in that little circle. The eldest daughter, Miss Ellen Emerson, the last member of the home trio, was, indeed, "the angel of the house." Her daughterly devotion was unparalleled; she was her father's strength and comfort, and, when his memory began to fail, his best interpreter.

The house was rich in reminiscences, for almost every person of note who visited this country partook of its genial hospitality.

On one occasion, a voluble lady who was passing the Sabbath in Concord, went up to Mr. Emerson, saying, in rather a loud voice: "Don't you remember me, Mr. Emerson? I met you ten years ago at Dr. B.'s house."

I can see now the painful struggle of memory in the eyes, the patient look about the mouth, and hear the intensely pathetic ring in the voice as he answered brokenly, "I am a very old man, madam; I cannot remember many things."

He was still erect in his carriage, however, and seemed generally to be in good health, his only distressing symptom being his failing memory. He seemed to be always a glad and attentive listener, and, if he sometimes kept aloof from general conversation where there were many people present, he was always studiously thoughtful of the comfort and pleasure of his guests.

On the summer afternoons I often strolled through Sleepy Hollow burying-ground in company with Mr. Emerson, Mr. Alcott, Mr. Channing, and Miss Elizabeth Peabody. I can recall it as if it were yesterday: the walk in quiet mood from the hillside chapel, through fragrant orchards, to the ridge overlooking historic fields. The air was vocal with perpetual melody of birds and bees, the sun shone warm and bright, the air was sweet and balmy, and the whole landscape as tenderly serene as if death had never entered the world.—Now, to that little coterie of dear, old friends neither summer nor winter, bird nor blossom nor bee, can ever be the same again; for they have all drifted into the Great Silence.

We wandered slowly among the graves of the illustrious dead, while each of the honored living related happy anecdotes of the comrades passed over and yonder.

We lingered a moment by the resting-place of a certain Miss Abigail Dudley, for they have epitaphs in Concord burying-ground; and even quaint hollyhocks, dandelions, hardhack, whiteweed, goldenrod, and other flowers of Puritan stock, are allowed to grow peacefully about the fences and in the sunny places between the trees.

I was tired, I remember, for had I not just been precipitated into the full doctrine of Platonic philosophy and psychology, cosmologic and theologic outlines, and the Dæmon of Socrates, that morning? I sank on the grassy turf beside the marble stone designed

By its durability
To perpetuate the memory,
And by its color
to signify the moral character
of
Abigail Dudley.

I looked up. The day was warm, and they had all bared their heads to the breeze. Mr. Channing had helped Miss Peabody to a seat, while Mr. Emerson and Mr. Alcott rested at the foot of a great, leafy oak tree.

I never shall forget it: the sight of the four aged, benignant heads (three of them white with the snows of almost eighty winters) on which the mellow August sunshine poured its flood of light. There was no thought of time in the minds of these geniuses. They paused in their leisurely gait, sat down on a flat gravestone to discuss high themes, moved to another, always forgetting their hats or sticks or portfolios, which I gathered up in safety and retained until the proper moment when they might remember their next engagement. I shall never forget "Abigail Dudley's" stone, for there it was that Miss Peabody passed her hand over my ruffled curly front locks and said, on the last of these homeward journeys through the graveyard:

"Our young guest has developed much during this week! Another year she must be a real student, and I hope that her hair will be drawn back smoothly from her fine forehead."

My one task in life was to conceal the height of my Websterian brow, but my head was bowed with shame over this criticism by my dear old friend, when to my amazement Mr. Emerson said absent-mindedly from an adjacent tombstone: "I have seen smoother heads with less in them."

Needless to say, I think I had never spoken in his hearing, save perhaps to ask a question of Mr. Alcott, who only remembered my presence when he needed his hat or cane or wished to be guided to the gate nearest his house. (None of them knew where they lived if a metaphysical point were under discussion.)

I sank under the glory of this unexpected tribute and silently concluded that the great man was thinking of some one or somebody else, but in any case he had said it in the presence of witnesses!

From *My Garden of Memory: An Autobiography* (Boston: Houghton Mifflin, 1923), pp. 148–54.

"Recollections of Emerson, His Household and Friends" (1924)

Elizabeth Oakes Smith

Lecturer, reformer, novelist, poet, and for a brief time the pastor of the Independent Church in Canastota, New York, Elizabeth Oakes Smith was something of a nineteenth-century "Renaissance woman." The wife of Seba Smith, editor of the *Eastern Argus*, Oakes Smith (as she was known) published widely in the *Ladies' Companion*, the *Southern Literary Messenger*, *Godey's Lady's Book*, and *Graham's American Monthly Magazine*; brought public attention to women's rights and abolitionism when she took to the lecture circuit in the 1850s; and wrote novels that touched upon spiritualism, sentiment, and the plight of the urban poor. Oakes Smith launched her career as a lecturer in 1851, and on 31 December of that year she delivered a lecture on "Womanhood" in Concord before an audience that included Lidian Emerson and Mary Moody Emerson. She had come to Concord at Waldo's and Lidian's invitation, and while there she made the acquaintance of Bronson Alcott, Elizabeth Hoar, Henry Thoreau, and others of the cast of Transcendentalists who gathered around Emerson. The recollections that follow are based on Oakes Smith's personal observation of the Emerson household and Emerson's interactions with his friends during the several weeks in 1851 and 1852 that she lived at "Bush" as the Emersons' guest.

I had already spoken in Boston, my way made easy by that eloquent Greek and sincere man, Wendell Phillips, and had been well received there. Notwithstanding this, I certainly felt many misgivings when invited to speak to an audience made up of Mr. Emerson's admirers, acolytes and townspeople. When, therefore, Mr. and Mrs. Emerson came in from Concord to Boston, calling upon me, and inviting me to their hospitable home, I was not only gratified but made more comfortable in mind.

The evening I spoke before the lyceum of Concord was not only a night of sleet and rain, but the ground, also, was one mass of what Down-East people call slush. Yet I am sure my lady friends will be glad to know I had a full house and an approving auditory. I must own, however, that Mr. Emerson did not hear me; he was to speak the same evening before the Lyceum of Marblehead.

Before I went into the hall where I was to speak, I was confronted by Aunt Mary Emerson; now Aunt Mary was a character held in some awe. She was a small, quick-moving woman, with eyes sharp and penetrating[;] ... she not only looked at you but through you.

We were all cloaked and ready to leave when Mrs. Emerson had the precaution to take me aside and whisper in my ear what might have seemed necessary.

"Now possibly," she said, "Aunt Mary may not stay to hear your lecture out; she has a way, when not quite pleased with a speaker, of getting up and going out, scattering shawl and gloves or hood all along the aisle; you need not mind it."

My subject was "Womanhood," and I am happy to say Aunt Mary heard me through and gave me her hand at the close.

I passed some weeks in the family of Mr. Emerson and was much interested in Mrs. Emerson, with her weird, grey eyes, and faultless repartee. She was always appropriately dressed as the wife of a philosopher should be: plain black, long folds of drapery, and a delicate white coif over her silver turning hair. She was stately in manner, justifying the term "Queeny," by which her husband always addressed her. In return there was a simple grace in the tender respect of this model wife.

I saw sometimes the sister-in-law of Mr. Emerson, always dressed in widow's weeds, living upon the sweet memory of Charles Chauncy Emerson, who died young. She was treated with something like worship in the family. Mr. Emerson used to say of her, "Angels must do as they will," and she certainly carried with her a heavenly presence. The mother of Mr. Emerson, gone into the winter of life, was surrounded by all that the despairing Macbeth declared—

"should accompany old age,
As honour, love, obedience, troops of friends."

She found all lavished upon her by reverent children and grandchildren.

It was, indeed, a model household, everything fresh as a rose and nice as the most exacting Brownie could wish. There was the wholesome and tempting breakfast, and the long talks over the coffee, Mr. Emerson so quietly breathing out his precious aphorisms.

If a man is head of a household, as he ought to be, a pretty fair estimate may be formed of the quality of the man, by the quality of the household; and here Mr. Emerson may be fairly regarded as a model man, a sort of family Socrates without a Xantippe.

Mr. Emerson was not a man to laugh any more than Edgar A. Poe. The nearest I saw him come to a laugh was at a trifle at the breakfast table. Mrs. Emerson was on the point of pouring out the coffee, when a cat gave out a piteous mew.

"There, I have forgotten her breakfast," cried Mrs. Emerson, leaving the table in haste. She was gone but a moment, and, turning to her husband, she said with a smile, "Now, don't tell me that somewhere off in Africa is a fly with a broken wing, that I ought to look after."

"Is that the way he treats you? Is that the way he turns your sensibilities into contempt?" I exclaimed.

"Yes, that is the way, and in just the very words."

"Well, that is all right; what is a wife for but to sharpen up the wits of her husband?" To this Mr. Emerson cordially assented with something more than a smile. . . .

While I was with Mr. Emerson I had a feeling that we did not talk a great deal; there were certainly long pauses, a word—something not quite complete, and then a saying—fresh, unexpected. He was fond of these fragments, as it were, of ideas. I can see now that a fluent converser would have been intolerable to him. He would have admired Macaulay but in those "splendid flashes of silence," about which Sidney Smith speaks.

Mr. Emerson's library impressed me with a sense of dim solitude: a large room with shelves for books and a plain, round table in the centre. It seemed to have no outlook, to be isolated; and there was an aspect of solitude, an almost monastic simplicity fit for some austere anchorite. But when I saw Mr. Emerson softly move about the room, his arms not merely folded but hugged upon his breast, his head slightly inclined, leaving the introversive eyes under the brow, I understood that no outlook was needed. . . .

On the table was an old scrap book—with paragraphs written on odds and ends of paper—Sibylline leaves to be collected and arranged at some future time. I think the library did not impress me pleasantly; it had something ghostly about it, an aloofness, a concentrated mono-mannishness, the result of the genius that lived and breathed there.

The days passed with Emerson, Alcott, Thoreau, and other Transcendentalists, were the breathings of ambrosia; the aroma lingers on life like remembered music. True, I sometimes felt these oracular sayings were far-fetched, and had a flavor of affectation about them, but they were full of suggestion, and were doubtless the language of those who lived more with books than with men. I certainly was not disposed to cavil at what told sometimes in my favor.

For instance, Mr. Alcott went to Concord with me on the occasion of my lecture. At the close he said, "You have given us a lyric."

Mr. Thoreau, also, that gentle Arcadian of the nineteenth century, gave me his hand gravely, and said with solemn emphasis, "You have spoken!" which good Mr. Alcott interpreted to mean, "You have brought an oracle."

There was a harmless bagatelle current in Concord which was amusing for its sly humor. It seems Mr. Emerson had been passing an evening with Mrs. Thoreau, the lady who so shocked Aunt Mary by wearing a pink ribband upon her grey hair. After he left, Mrs. Thoreau was heard to say with sweet naivete, "How much Mr. Emerson does talk like my Henry."

The tenderest friendship existed between Mr. Emerson and Mr. Alcott. Mr. Alcott, whom Boston people call the modern Plato, is a creation so unique, so unlike anything to be expected in Yankee land, that he seems a waif from some outstanding star, or Plato himself undergoing a Pythagorean metempsychosis. Seeing the two men together it seemed perfectly natural that each should dwell largely in the heart of the other; for each possessed a certain geniality, entirely removed from vulgar receptiveness or complacency, an enlarged humanity, and a generous hospitality to the new and untried, with that unexplainable something which sets a man apart from all other men. Each characterized by the utmost purity of life and integrity of purpose, they could not fail to be friends.

There was always a force and pithiness in the conversation of Mr. Emerson, which was that of a full man, with no idle words; and sometimes they stick to the memory. I think I was less awed than enthused by it, and went on and said my says without hesitation, dead to all self-consciousness, oblivious to either praise or blame. Once while I was talking in this way, Mr. Emerson suddenly arrested me by saying, "You must come and live in Concord, and we shall have an oracle."

Alas! it is not Concord; the inspiring god must be Mr. Emerson himself.

He had a way, startling to the uninitiated, of suddenly asking a question, often quite foreign to the subject in hand, which caused me to say to him once, "You are oracular, Mr. Emerson, and seek oracles." . . .

One evening Mr. Emerson said to me, "How do you think Boston compares with New York society?" to which I am afraid I answered almost impertinently.

"I must say I think New York far superior to Boston. If society represent humanitarian and progressive ideas, they are about equal; but it seems to me that society for genial, social purposes is almost lacking in Boston. They meet together to discuss; they utilize each other; they sound you, teach you, never enjoy you."

"You think them more utilitarian than aesthetic?"

"Perhaps that is the impression made upon me. The women seem all propagandists, and the men leaders in something or other. They all seem to have a specialty and go out to promote it. New Yorkers study at home and go into society to please and be pleased."

"Perhaps for that reason society in New York is more shallow and the knowledge more superficial."

"I have not thought so; New Yorkers have not the intense admiration for each other that Bostonians have; they are not cliquish; they are not so pedantic. Their culture is rather to be inferred than defined, as seen in a pervading taste and elegance of manner."

"I have thought there might be something in their manner that at once puts a stranger at his ease," he replied.

"New York men and women dress better, look better, and stand better. The women have a pleased, elegant air; they are handsome and carry about them a harmless consciousness of the fact, which plain Margaret Fuller could never quite pardon."

Mr. Emerson bowed acquiescence, and I went on, airing my vocabulary perhaps too much. . . .

When Mr. Emerson gave . . . his great lecture, entitled Power, I went with Mrs. Emerson and Mr. Alcott into Boston to hear it, and there I saw were brought into use these odds and ends of paper I had seen upon the library table. Nothing could be more simple and unpretending than Mr. Emerson's manner in the lecture room. His voice seemed scarcely, if any, raised above his ordinary colloquial tone; his gestures were few, and he certainly looked like no other man I ever heard speak. Indeed, he did not, as we so often hear it said of others, remind you of somebody else. He was himself only. A sphinx if you will, a prophet, a something aloof, creating a solitude.

Mr. Emerson was by no means indifferent to the impression which his ideas might make upon an audience. I sat in breathless expectation of every word uttered. His manner was so simple, so undemonstrative, so in harmony with the uttered thought, so superior to any attempts at oratory, which . . . is the expression of a ruder age when feeling must hold the intellect in abeyance.

As Mr. Emerson, closing, came down the aisle, he was warmly greeted right and left; as he approached the bright minded Mrs. C.—I noticed he uttered the one word,

"Well?" interrogatively, and with an almost childish simplicity, to which she replied:

"Oh, Mr. Emerson, you made me feel so powerless, as if I could do nothing."

Mr. Emerson looked grave and turning to me, repeated the enigmatical monosyllable, "Well?" in the same manner, to which I replied, "In listening to you, Mr. Emerson, no achievement seemed impossible; it was as though I might remove mountains."

"Ah, that is well," he answered cordially. . . .

Mr. Emerson was tall and slender, with long legs, which he had a way of twisting into knots when interested. The bones of the head must have been very thin, for it looked compact, rising mostly above the crest of the ears. His temperament was delicate and refined. One would speak and think of him as of a piece of statuary.

Persons of culture retain the look of youth longer than the ignorant; but I found Mr. Emerson looking much younger than I had expected, and remarked to him that he and Mr. Ripley of Brook Farm memory were among the youngest looking men, who were supposed to have passed the dew of youth, that I had ever seen.

"Nevertheless, I must be growing old," he said, "for people begin to tell me I look like my relations, which is a sure sign." . . .

I do not think Mr. Emerson's face was an expressive one; he was too self-sustained. It was a sphinx which one might study in vain to read.

His voice was winning and pleasing, never loud, but with the rare quality of distinctness. It sounded always as if coming from a distance. . . .

Emerson fully illustrated all we are seeking to learn about heredity. He was the product of a long line: eight generations of ancestors, whose pursuits had been pulpit-wise; whose proclivities were grooved in the high moralities.

I ventured to say to Mr. Emerson in this connection:

"Perhaps in the great evolution of thought, old dogmas of vicarious suffering, and the remission of sin by the shedding of blood, may resolve themselves into this transmission of blood by heredity which is to be the ultimate Redeemer." He gave me a silent reply with his calm, mystic eyes—nothing more. . . .

In seeing a man so entirely himself and no other, one felt as Montaigne has said, that " 'Tis an absolute, and as it were, a divine perfection, for a man to know how loyally to enjoy his being." This Mr. Emerson truly realized.

"Recollections of Emerson, His Household and Friends," from *Selections from the Autobiography of Elizabeth Oakes Smith*, ed. Mary Alice Wyman (Lewiston, Maine: Lewiston Journal Company, 1924), pp. 134–37, 139–41, 143–47.

Index